Collins

Your Life

The whole-school solution for PSHE and Citizenship

John Foster

William Collins' dream of knowledge for all began with the publication of his first book in 1819. A self-educated mill worker, he not only enriched millions of lives, but also founded a flourishing publishing house. Today, staying true to this spirit, Collins books are packed with inspiration, innovation and practical expertise. They place you at the centre of a world of possibility and give you exactly what you need to explore it.

Collins. Freedom to teach

Published by Collins
An imprint of HarperCollins*Publishers*
77–85 Fulham Palace Road
Hammersmith
London
W6 8JB

Browse the complete Collins catalogue at
www.collins.co.uk

© HarperCollins*Publishers* Limited 2014

10 9 8 7 6 5 4

ISBN 978-0-00-759272-2

John Foster asserts his moral right to be identified as the author of this work.

British Library Cataloguing in Publication Data
A Catalogue record for this publication is available from the British Library

Commissioned by Letitia Luff
Managed by Caroline Green
Edited by Vicky Leech
Designed by Jordan Publishing Design Limited
Typeset by Ken Vail Graphic Design
Copy-edited by Donna Cole
Proofread by Karen Williams
Cover design by Angela English
Production by Rachel Weaver
Cover photographs © Shariff Che Lah/Dreamstime (t), Dudarev Mikhail/Shutterstock (c), Yanlev/Dreamstime (b)
Printed and bound by CPI Group (UK) Ltd, Croydon, CR0 4YY

Contents

Introduction

How to use these resources

These teacher resources are designed to provide materials that the PSHE and Citizenship Key Stage 3 co-ordinator and their Year 7, 8 and 9 team leaders can give to individual teachers to help them use the *Your Life Student Books* to deliver effective personal, social, health and economic education and citizenship lessons. The bulk of the resources, therefore, consists of ideas for lesson plans – between two and four for each of the units in the course, depending on the length of the unit.

This introduction illustrates how the three *Your Life Student Books* meet the requirements of the Key Stage 3 National Curriculum programme of study for Citizenship presented in the statutory guidance. How the books provide a course in Personal Social and Health Education can be seen in the table on pages 4 and 5 of each of the Student Books.

The section on 'Planning and delivering PSHE and Citizenship lessons' explains how the lesson plans are structured to enable them to be adapted to fit a school's own timetable, depending on how PSHE and Citizenship are delivered within a particular school.

The Introduction also contains advice on developing group discussions and on keeping a PSHE and citizenship file. There are also sections on how continuous assessment can be carried out and a section offering suggestions for helping students with special educational needs.

Each lesson plan is presented on a single sheet, so that it can be duplicated and given to individual members of the Year team. The lesson plans indicate clearly which part of either the Key Stage 3 Citizenship contents or PSHE course are being covered and state the objective of the lesson. Each one begins with a Starter and contains suggestions for a range of activities and for a Plenary session. There are also suggestions for extension activities, many of which involve the use of ICT.

Co-ordinators can use the lesson plans in two ways: either they can be circulated at a planning meeting with the appropriate Year team members present and, after discussion, adapted to suit the needs of their particular classes. Alternatively, they can be distributed to individual teachers. In the latter case, the teacher is offered a quick and easy guide to planning their PSHE or Citizenship lesson, albeit without the opportunity for joint planning.

The teacher resources also provide the co-ordinator with the means to ensure that there is assessment of the Citizenship strand of the course, by providing an assessment copymaster for each of the Citizenship units of the course. Further opportunities for assessment, of both the Citizenship and PSHE strands of the course, are indicated in the lesson plans.

The enclosed CD-ROM contains Word and PDF files of all the lesson plans and copymasters, so you can either tailor and edit them, print them or photocopy them – whichever is easier. In order to use the PDF files you must have Acrobat Reader installed.

How the *Your Life* course meets the requirements of the National Curriculum programme of study for Citizenship at Key Stage 3

The statutory guidance for Citizenship stresses the importance of effective citizenship education in developing political awareness and in preparing pupils to take their place in society as responsible citizens. The particular units of *Your Life Student Books 1–3* that meet the aims of the Citizenship curriculum and the subject content specified in the programme of study are detailed below.

Aims

- To develop a sound knowledge and understanding of how the United Kingdom is governed, its political system and how citizens participate actively in its system of government

Your Life 1	Unit 19	You as a citizen – how Britain is governed
Your Life 2	Unit 18	You as a citizen – Britain's government
Your Life 3	Unit 16	You and your opinions – which political party do you support?

- To develop a sound knowledge and understanding of the role of law and the justice system in our society and how laws are shaped and enforced

Your Life 1	Unit 8	You and the law – why we have laws
Your Life 1	Unit 12	You and the law – children's rights
Your Life 2	Unit 8	You and the law – the police
Your Life 3	Unit 15	You and the law – youth justice
Your Life 3	Unit 9	You and the law – crimes and punishments

- To develop an interest in, and commitment to, participation in volunteering as well as other forms of responsible activity that they will take with them into adulthood

Your Life 1	Unit 15	You and the community – being a good neighbour
Your Life 1	Unit 21	You and the community – taking action: raising money for charity
Your Life 2	Unit 15	You and the community – the school as a community
Your Life 2	Unit 20	You and the community – taking action
Your Life 3	Unit 20	You and the community – pressure groups and campaigning

- To equip pupils with the skills to think critically and debate political questions, to enable them to manage their money on a day-to-day basis, and plan for future financial needs

Your Life 1	Unit 17	You and your opinions – how to express your ideas
Your Life 2	Unit 16	You and your opinions – speaking your mind
Your Life 1	Unit 11	You and your money – pocket money, budgeting and saving
Your Life 1	Unit 16	You and your money – you as a consumer
Your Life 2	Unit 4	You and your money – making the most of your money
Your Life 2	Unit 9	You and your money – gambling
Your Life 3	Unit 6	You and your money – banking and ways of saving
Your Life 3	Unit 18	You and your money – you as a consumer

Subject content

- Knowledge of the development of the political system of democratic government in the United Kingdom, including the roles of citizens, Parliament and the monarch

Your Life 1	Unit 19	You as a citizen – how Britain is governed
Your Life 2	Unit 18	You as a citizen – Britain's government
Your Life 3	Unit 16	You and your opinions – which political party do you support?

- Knowledge of the operation of Parliament, including voting and elections, and the role of political parties

Your Life 1	Unit 19	You as a citizen – how Britain is governed
Your Life 2	Unit 18	You as a citizen – Britain's government

- Knowledge of the precious liberties enjoyed by the citizens of the United Kingdom

Your Life 3	Unit 2	You and your responsibilities – racism, prejudice and discrimination
Your Life 3	Unit 5	You and your rights – civil liberties

■ Knowledge of the nature of rules and laws and the justice system, including the role of the police and the operation of courts and tribunals

Your Life 1	Unit 8	You and the law – why we have laws
Your Life 1	Unit 12	You and the law – children's rights
Your Life 2	Unit 8	You and the law – the police
Your Life 3	Unit 9	You and the law – crimes and punishments
Your Life 3	Unit 15	You and the law – youth justice

■ Knowledge of the roles played by public institutions and voluntary groups in society, and the ways in which citizens work together to improve their communities, including opportunities to participate in school-based activities

Your Life 1	Unit 15	You and the community – being a good neighbour
Your Life 2	Unit 15	You and the community – the school as a community
Your Life 2	Unit 20	You and the community – taking action
Your Life 3	Unit 20	You and the community – pressure groups and campaigning

■ Knowledge of the functions and uses of money, the importance of budgeting, and managing risk

Your Life 1	Unit 11	You and your money – pocket-money, budgeting and saving
Your Life 1	Unit 16	You and your money – you as a consumer
Your Life 2	Unit 4	You and your money – making the most of your money
Your Life 2	Unit 9	You and your money – gambling
Your Life 3	Unit 6	You and your money – banking and ways of saving
Your Life 3	Unit 18	You and your money – you as a consumer

Planning and delivering PSHE and Citizenship lessons

Planning the course

The three *Your Life Student Books* together provide a comprehensive course in PSHE and Citizenship for Key Stage 3. Using the *Your Life* books as the core of a course meets the requirements of the statutory guidance for citizenship and provides a coherent PSHE programme. Specific units in the 'Keeping Healthy' strand of the course also provide appropriate sex and relationships education that can be incorporated into a school's own sex education policy. Similarly, there are units in the 'Personal Development' strand designed to develop students' awareness of themselves and their aptitudes that can be used in conjunction with the school's careers and guidance programme.

As the units in each of the books are arranged in five strands ('Personal Development', 'Social Education', 'Keeping Healthy', 'Becoming an Active Citizen', 'Economic and Financial Capability') it is possible to plan the course strand by strand. This arrangement may suit schools in which the PSHE course is being delivered by a team of teachers with expertise in different areas. However, the units within each strand are freestanding and can, therefore, be delivered in any order. Schools can either plan to use the units in whatever sequence they choose or, alternatively, use them in the order in which they appear in the books. Whatever the school may decide, there is sufficient material in each book to provide the basis for a full year's course.

Planning a unit

Each of the units in *Your Life Student Book 1*, *2* and *3* covers a specific area of either the PSHE or Citizenship curriculum in two to four lessons. The lessons within a unit are planned so that there is a clear progression in the building of the student's knowledge and understanding of the topic. Thus in Unit 9 of *Your Life Student Book* 1, the first lesson explores what bullying is and who gets bullied, the second lesson explains why people bully and what it feels like to be bullied and the third lesson examines the different ways of reacting to bullying and discusses what to do if you are being bullied. Similarly, in Unit 14 of *Your Life Student Book 2*, the first lesson presents information on the effects of drinking alcohol, and on teenage drinking and the laws about alcohol, leading to an exploration in the second lesson of the problems that excessive drinking can cause.

It is important that the PSHE and Citizenship co-ordinator draws the attention of the teachers in their team to these links between lessons at the start of a unit. It is, therefore, suggested that the lesson plans are distributed to teachers unit-by-unit rather than lesson-by-lesson.

Using the lesson plans

Each lesson plan is presented on a separate sheet, so that it can easily be duplicated and distributed to teachers. The lesson plans all have the same structure so that they are easy to follow:

- The learning **objective** is stated, so that it can be made clear to the students. It can be written up on the board and explained at the beginning, and referred to during the lesson. If it is the second, third or fourth lesson of a unit, it can be explained how the learning objective links to and follows on from the previous lesson(s) and how it is related to any subsequent lesson(s).

- Details are given of any **resources** that are required for the activities. These are mainly optional. Often, the only resources that are needed are copies of the copymaster for that unit, and then only if the teacher decides to incorporate one of the suggested extension activities into the main lesson.

- A short **starter** activity is suggested as a way in to the topic. These take a variety of forms. In many instances, the starter activity involves asking the students to do a brainstorm (e.g. to suggest the reasons why people gamble), with the teacher listing their ideas on the board. A detailed exploration of the question follows during the main part of the lesson. Another type of starter activity asks the students to draw on their own experiences. For example, in the lesson on safety in the home, students are asked to share their experiences of accidents in the home, explaining what caused them and whether anyone was on hand who was able to give first aid. Other starter activities involve the explanation of key terms, such as 'stereotyping' and 'discrimination', and writing definitions of them on the board. Often, it is possible to incorporate the explanation of the learning objective as part of the starter activity. The length of time allocated to the starter activity will obviously vary, depending on the activity, but typically it is expected to last about five minutes.

- There are **suggested activities** for the main part of the lesson. Many of the activities involve the students studying an article prior to discussing it in pairs or groups, then sharing their ideas in a class discussion. Others present the students with test-yourself quizzes, e.g. about their homework habits, or ask them to consider different ways of behaving in a particular situation by performing role plays. There are also suggestions for writing activities, ranging from making lists and writing emails to designing leaflets.

  There are sufficient suggestions to fill an hour's lesson. However, the length of the PSHE and Citizenship lesson varies from school to school, and in many cases may be less than an hour. Therefore, when planning the lesson, teachers may have to select which of the suggested activities to include – the more activities that are completed, the more comprehensively a topic will be covered. But in the majority of the lessons it is not essential for all the activities to be done in order for the learning objective to be achieved.

- There is a **plenary** activity designed to round off the lesson by drawing attention to what has been learned. This is usually an oral activity, during which the teacher may summarise the main points of the lesson in some way, e.g. by asking the class to say what key messages they would try to put across as part of a campaign to warn about the risks of drugtaking, and writing their suggestions on the board. The aim of the plenary activity is to review and reinforce the learning that has taken place in the main body of the lesson.

- For each lesson, there are a number of **extension activities**. These provide activities that can be done either within the main lesson as additional activities or set as follow-up work. This section includes the activities that can be developed using the copymasters. It also contains suggestions for activities that require more time than a single lesson to complete, e.g. for the extended writing of a magazine article and the holding of a mock election. There are also research activities with details of websites that the students can visit in order to find more information on the topic.

- In one of the lesson plans for each of the Citizenship units of the course, there is an **assessment** section referring to the Assessment copymaster (e.g. 7A) that can be used as part of the lesson to assess the students' knowledge and understanding and/or skills.

Developing group discussions

Many of the activities in the *Your Life* course involve groups in discussing issues and sharing opinions, thus providing individuals with an opportunity to consider various viewpoints and develop their own ideas. It is important, therefore, not only to set out ground rules for discussion in order to ensure that students respect each other's feelings and views, but also to ensure that the discussion remains focused and is conducted in an orderly way.

A useful way of setting up the ground rules is to involve the students themselves in doing so as part of an introductory lesson at the beginning of the course, in which the teacher explains the aims and purpose of the course and the type of work they will be doing. The class can be split into groups and each group given a large sheet of paper. They can then be invited to suggest the kind of rules that are needed in order to make sure that a discussion in class is successful, so that everyone can say what they think without fear of being ridiculed or feeling embarrassed, so that people can listen to other people's points of view, and so that everyone can participate in the discussion. The groups can then be asked to report their suggestions to the rest of the class and the class can work together to agree a list of ground rules, which the teacher can write on the board. A member of the class can then type the ground rules on a word processor and print them out, so that each person has a copy of them in their PSHE and Citizenship file. An enlarged copy can be printed out and put on display in the classroom.

If groups are to conduct their discussions in an orderly fashion, someone must ensure that the ground rules are adhered to. One of the keys to successful group discussions is to make the class aware of the importance of appointing someone to chair the discussion, and of the key role of the chairperson. Explain that it is the responsibility of the chairperson to organise and control the discussion. The characteristics of a good chairperson are explained on page 76 of *Your Life Student Book* 1 and it is suggested that the lesson on group discussions on pages 76–77 is included early in the course. The lesson also includes guidelines for individuals on how to participate in group discussions and the points made in these guidelines can be compared to those in the class's ground rules.

One of the problems of group discussions is keeping the groups focused on the task. One way of doing this is to ask each group to appoint a secretary. The role of the secretary is to keep track of any decisions made by the group or of the main opinions expressed in the group. Many students will find this a difficult role to fill, as it requires the person not only to listen carefully to what is said and to pick out and summarise the main points, but also to write them down. However, requiring someone in the group to write something down, albeit in note form, is often an effective way of ensuring that the group remains on-task.

Alternatively, the group can appoint a reporter, whose role is to report the group's ideas at the start of a follow-up class discussion. While this requires the same listening and summarising skills as the secretary's role, it avoids the need for any writing. Formalising how a group report their ideas to the rest of the class by encouraging them to appoint a reporter is another way of helping to keep them on-task.

Keeping a PSHE and Citizenship file

It is recommended that the students are given a file at the beginning of the first year of the course and that they build up the file over the three years. The file could include:

- a copy of the course programme – this might be a copy of the appropriate Year 7, Year 8 or Year 9 table in the introductions to each of the student's books (e.g. pages 4–5 of *Your Life Student Book 1*) showing the five different strands of the course, or a copy of the school's own course programme. Having a copy of the course in their file means that students can understand how the lessons meet the requirements of the curriculum;

- reference sheets, such as the ground rules for group discussions (see above)

- written work completed during the course, including assessments

- information and advice leaflets, e.g. on drugs, first aid.

The file can thus provide a record of what has been covered and learned during the PSHE and Citizenship course for teachers, students and their parents.

Assessment

Continuous assessment forms an important and integral part of the *Your Life* course. To facilitate the assessment of the Citizenship strand, the file contains 24 Assessment copymasters – one for each of the Citizenship units in the course. These take a variety of forms, ranging from multiple-choice tests and true/false quizzes to crosswords and word puzzles, the writing of checklists and producing flowcharts or step-by-step guidelines.

The copymasters are designed to assess students' knowledge and understanding, and/or their skills, rather than their attitudes and values. While it is feasible to test the students' skills at expressing their views, a PSHE and Citizenship course can only have objectives to equip students with the information on which to base their opinions and to develop their skills of decision-making, rather than to make up their minds for them and to tell them what to think.

Introduction

Many of the activities, which are included in the PSHE strands of the course, provide opportunities for assessment. These are indicated, wherever they occur, within the lesson plans and there is at least one assessment opportunity per unit. The Citizenship units also contain a number of other opportunities for assessment, in addition to the assessment activities contained on the copymasters, and these too are noted in the lesson plans.

Often it is a writing activity, following the reading of an article and/or a group or class discussion of an issue, which provides the opportunity for assessment. This may be a straightforward test of knowledge, e.g. in Unit 7 of *Your Life Student Book 1* students are asked to design a leaflet on 'Ten Things You Should Know About Smoking' and in Unit 17 of *Your Life Student Book 3* they have to design an internet web page giving key information about HIV and AIDS. Alternatively, the writing activity may involve demonstrating understanding, e.g. of the causes and effects of global warming by writing an email to a newspaper expressing their concern about global warming and saying what they think the government should be doing about it (Unit 19 of *Your Life Student Book 3*) or of the causes of arguments between brothers and sisters and how to help family members get on better (Unit 4 of *Your Life Student Book 3*).

However, it is important that there should be oral assessments as well as written assessments, so that all students can be assessed whatever their literacy skills. Many of the writing activities could be adapted and done orally. For example, where students are asked to write an email, they could give a verbal explanation of what the email would contain.

Throughout the course, there are many suggestions for students to share what they have learned in class discussions. These, too, can be used for assessment. For example, in Unit 2 of *Your Life Student Book 3* there is the opportunity to assess their understanding of racial discrimination during a class discussion.

Role plays also offer the chance to assess students' understanding and skills, e.g. the role play at handling peer pressure to join in and do something they do not want to do in Unit 2 in *Your Life Student Book 2* can be used to assess their understanding of strategies for saying 'No'. Similarly, the role play in Unit 10 of *Your Life Student Book 3* can be used to assess their understanding of the difference between assertive, aggressive and passive behaviour.

Whenever an assessment is being made, it is suggested that the students are informed. The more a school shows that it values what students are learning in PSHE lessons by making students aware that their learning is being assessed, the more highly the students are likely to value the course.

Supporting students with special educational needs

Teaching methods and learning styles

Using varied teaching methods and learning styles helps to provide teachers with opportunities to address students' individual needs in the classroom and to support students with special educational needs more effectively.

This file suggests a variety of teaching methods and learning styles, and these methods, coupled with good SEN practice in the classroom, can provide effective support to include students of all abilities in Citizenship and PSHE lessons.

Other strategies to support needs

Differentiating resources

Some of the suggested writing activities in this file may need to be differentiated in order to cater for the different levels of need in the classroom. This can be done in a variety of ways by:

- breaking down writing tasks into more manageable chunks, allowing students to deal with writing tasks more easily, e.g. writing frames can be used to give structure to some of the tasks suggested, such as writing a story, letter, article, diary, making notes, fact sheet, articles and replies

- presenting complementary, adapted resources that cater for the different ability levels in the group

- pitching group activities at different levels to cater for the varying ability levels in the group

- providing more complex activities to stretch the more able students – there are a variety of extension activities that would provide appropriate work for some of the more able learners.

Using peer support

In the activities where pupils are required to read information individually prior to discussion, teachers can make use of peer support, e.g. a teacher can pair a good reader with a weaker reader. Using peer support in this way can also be extended to group work, with the teacher structuring the groups so that there is at least one good reader in each group. Group-reading activities require careful structuring to make sure that all students with lower reading ages do not go into one group.

Supporting pupils with specific learning difficulties

There are a variety of ways of achieving this, depending on each student's special educational needs, by:

- introducing new words explicitly, e.g. the starter activities often suggest writing key terms and definitions on the board

- letting students present their work in a different way, thus making allowances for their special needs, e.g. completing a mind-map instead of writing a fact sheet, recording pair or group discussions instead of making notes on points discussed

- encouraging students to use visual representations to make useful points (there are plenty of activities that provide opportunities for this, e.g. designing a poster, making a leaflet, watching a video)

- allowing students to present their ideas orally where possible, e.g. through spoken quizzes so that the students do not have to read the questions and during which pupils can also answer questions orally instead of writing their answers down

- not presenting large amounts of text to students who have low reading ages (too much text will easily lead to frustration and boredom and will lower their self esteem)

- encouraging students to word process their work so that they can check grammar and spelling easily, as well as improving presentation (improving presentation can help to boost students' confidence and self esteem)

- choosing appropriate activities from the file that suit the needs of the class and pupils with special educational needs

- liaising with the SENCO to acquire information on pupils' reading ages in your groups, plus any additional information on pupils with special educational needs

- reviewing the needs of the students with special education needs regularly to ensure their needs are being met in the Citizenship and PSHE lessons.

Integrating learning support

Teacher assistants in the classroom provide a vital way of supporting and integrating students with special educational needs, e.g. by helping to clarify instructions; motivating and encouraging students in group work activities; assisting in weak areas such as language, behaviour, reading, spelling, planning and drafting writing activities; and by helping students to concentrate and complete tasks. In addition to this, they can help by establishing a supportive relationship with the students and in encouraging the acceptance and integration of students with special educational needs.

Good liaison between Citizenship and PSHE staff and teaching assistants prior to lessons will enable pupils' needs are determined, as well as any resource implications such as devising complementary learning activities.

Involving teacher assistants fully in the aims, content and strategies and outcomes will prove extremely effective in helping pupils with special educational needs to participate fully in the Citizenship and PSHE lessons.

UNIT 1 You and your feelings – anxieties and worries

Lesson 1 *Your Life Student Book 1*, pages 6–7
Personal wellbeing – managing your emotions

Objective: To understand feelings of anxiety about school and to explore ways of dealing with these feelings.

Resources

Copies of the plan of the school and of the school rules

Copies of Copymaster 1 'Feeling stressed and unhappy'

Starter

Introduce the topic by asking the students to think about the things that have made them anxious during their first days at secondary school. Then read the advice on 'Settling in' (page 6). Which piece of advice do they think is the most useful?

Suggested activities

- Ask the students, in pairs, to familiarise themselves with: the school layout by studying the school plans; their timetables by discussing what they need to bring to school on particular days; and the school rules by discussing what particular rules there are, e.g. on school uniform. Conclude the activity with a class discussion about rules, why schools have them, and how rules make it possible for the school to operate as a community.

- Ask groups to decide who is the best person to help them in a crisis (see 'Students with problems', page 6), then share their views in a class discussion.

- Read 'Manjit's story' on page 7. Discuss how she overcame her anxiety. Then invite pairs to discuss the advice they would give to someone anxious about giving a talk, before acting out the role play.

- Read 'Terry's story' on page 7. Discuss who Terry should tell about his problem and what advice you would give to help him to deal with it.

Plenary

Discuss what the students have learned about feeling anxious and worried at school, and about particular problems and how to deal with them.

Extension activities

Ask students to write about their feelings about starting secondary school, describing their anxieties and worries, any problems they have faced and how they have dealt with them.

Hand out copies of Copymaster 1. By discussing the letters and advice and preparing their replies to Estelle's letter, the students can demonstrate their understanding of how to cope with anxieties and worries. They can then look for examples of similar letters in magazines and discuss the advice that is given.

Feeling stressed and unhappy

Agony aunt
replies

I'm feeling desperate

I'm 11 and I've just started at my secondary school. We moved house in the summer and I miss my friends from the village where we used to live. My new school is so much bigger than the village school and I have difficulty in finding my way around it. I find it confusing going from lesson to lesson and we get so much homework. I have to get up early to catch the bus, as my new school is the other side of town. I'm getting tired and bad-tempered. Everyone in the family says they're fed up with me being so moody. They don't seem to understand why I'm so depressed. I'm beginning to feel desperate.

Starting at a new school is difficult, especially when you've just moved house. It often takes time to settle in, but with help you'll learn to cope. Your family are probably taking time to adjust to the move too and may not be able to offer the support and encouragement you need. Go and talk to your tutor or guidance teacher. Tell them what's troubling you. They should be able to help you find a way of coping.

If you go on feeling stressed out and still find that you can't talk to your parents about it, go and see your family doctor. The doctor can help you to explain your feelings to your parents and make them see that you need their help.

If you need someone to talk to and feel that there's no one available, you can call **ChildLine** free on **0800 1111**. Pressure can feel overwhelming, but with support you'll learn to deal with it.

School is Getting Me Down

My problem is that since I started secondary school I haven't been able to make friends with anyone in my class. The teachers often ask us to work in pairs or groups and I'm the one who's always left without a partner. So I have to stand there feeling embarrassed while the teacher finds me someone to work with. I dread lessons like science and drama. It's really getting me down, especially as I find the work difficult in many lessons and I keep forgetting to take the right things to school each day. I was so looking forward to starting secondary school, but it all seems to be going wrong. Please help me. I hate going to school at the moment and long for the weekends.

Estelle

In groups

1 Read the 'Agony aunt' column. Discuss the problems this person is having and how he or she is feeling. Talk about the advice that is given to them and what you learn from it about how to deal with feeling stressed and unhappy.

2 Study the letter 'School is getting me down' and together draft a reply offering advice on how to cope with Estelle's problems.

UNIT 1 You and your feelings – anxieties and worries

Your Life 1/Year 7

Lesson 2 *Your Life Student Book 1*, pages 8–9
Personal wellbeing – managing your emotions

> **Objective:** To understand how to deal with anxiety, in particular anxiety caused by feelings of rejection, shyness and grief.

Starter

Discuss what it means to feel rejected, to feel a lack of confidence because of shyness and to feel grief. Talk about how each of these feelings can cause anxiety and how it is important to learn how to deal with them.

Suggested activities

- Read the three letters and the advice given in the article on page 8. Focus on each letter in turn. Encourage students who are willing to do so to share their own experiences of these feelings. Discuss how helpful they find the advice. What is the most useful piece of advice? What is the least useful? What other advice would they offer on how to deal with the anxieties caused by these feelings?

- Read the article 'Packing up your cares and woes' (page 9). Invite pairs and groups to discuss the questions about sharing their worries and to talk about whom they could share their worries with.

Plenary

Discuss what the class has learned about anxieties and how to deal with them in a class discussion. Emphasise the importance of sharing their worries if their anxiety is getting on top of them. Explain that if they do not feel they can talk to someone face to face, they can always call a helpline such as ChildLine (Freephone 0800 1111).

Extension activities

Ask the students to write a story about someone whose worries get on top of them. Explain that they could, if they wish, base it on their own experience of a time when they were anxious because of feelings of rejection, shyness or grief.

Explain what a counsellor does. If your school has a counsellor, ask them to talk to the students about their role. Suggest the students use the internet to research counselling services that are available for young people.

UNIT 2 You and your body – growing and changing

Your Life 1/Year 7

Lesson 1 – *Your Life Student Book 1*, pages 10–11
Keeping healthy – understanding puberty

Objective: To understand what puberty is, the physical changes that occur during puberty and what causes those changes.

Resources

Copies of Copymaster 2 'Periods'

Starter

Explain what puberty is and how the release of either female or male hormones causes a person's body to change during puberty. Ask the students how a girl's body changes and how a boy's body changes, and compile lists on the board.

Suggested activities

- Read the article 'Becoming a woman' (page 10). Ask groups to discuss the questions on the article and to compare the list the class made of how a girl's body changes with the list of changes described in the article.

- Invite individuals to prepare a reply to Christy's question 'Am I normal?' (page 10), and then to use a computer to draft a reply.

- Read the article 'Becoming a man' (page 11). Ask groups to discuss the questions on the article and to compare their list of how a boy's body changes with the list of changes described in the article.

Plenary

Discuss how some people get embarrassed by the changes that happen to their bodies, and how others become worried because the changes occur later to their bodies than to the bodies of their friends. Emphasise that the changes are natural and nothing to get embarrassed about, that it is perfectly normal for the changes to happen to different people at different ages, and that it is hurtful to tease a person about the fact that their body has or has not changed. Finally, introduce the idea of the questions box ('Puberty problems', page 11) and explain how they can ask anonymously any question they would prefer not to ask publicly.

Extension activities

Discuss and answer the questions the students put into the box. Use any questions about periods as a way of introducing and discussing the information on Copymaster 2. Focus in particular on the advice that is given on how to cope with PMS and painful periods.

Students can find more information about what happens during puberty on the internet, e.g. at www.kidshealth.org/kid/grow.

If your school has a nurse, ask him or her to talk to the students.

Periods

▶ WHAT IS A PERIOD?

A period occurs each month as the body prepares itself for a possible pregnancy. An egg is released from one of the ovaries and travels down the fallopian tube to the womb. While the egg moves down the tube, the womb prepares for the egg's arrival by lining its walls with tissue. If the egg is not fertilised by joining up with a sperm (which it won't be if sex has not taken place) the lining breaks down and starts to flush itself out. A period is, therefore, a mixture of blood (2–3 tablespoons, though it looks much more), womb lining and fluid. Periods can last for up to 5 days, sometimes more.

▶ MENARCHE

A girl's first period is known as menarche and can start at any age. It usually begins after your breasts and pubic hair have grown, though this very much depends on your own personal body clock. The exact time you begin your periods will be dictated by your hormones and genetic make-up.

▶ REGULAR AND IRREGULAR PERIODS

Once you've started, don't expect your periods to begin at the same time every month. For the first 2 years, your periods are likely to be irregular, and sometimes non-existent. This is completely normal because periods take time to regulate. As your ovaries mature, your periods will probably fall into a 28-day cycle (sometimes longer, sometimes shorter).

▶ COUNTING YOUR CYCLE

A cycle begins from the first day you start your period. For instance, if you begin bleeding on the 15th of January, you count 28 days on from then, which makes the projected start of your next period (the first day you actually bleed) the 12th day of February.

▶ PAINS, PMS AND WHAT TO DO

It is estimated that 90% of women suffer from pre-menstrual syndrome (PMS) and period pain at some time in their lives. PMS is caused by hormones, and sufferers may find themselves with a variety of symptoms including: bloating, moodiness, spots, tearfulness and headaches, to name but a few.

Period pain or cramps are thought to be contractions of the muscles of the womb as they push the lining out.

You can help yourself by:

▶ Eating a healthy diet, making sure you eat lots of fresh fruit and vegetables.

▶ Cutting out sugar, fizzy drinks, coffee and fatty foods. All these things slow down your digestive system and can make an uncomfortable period feel worse.

▶ Placing a hot-water bottle on your stomach, which will help relax the muscles.

▶ Exercising. This may be the last thing you feel like doing, but exercise releases endorphins (the body's natural painkillers), which will help to relieve period pain.

▶ You can buy painkillers at the chemist which should help, but check with your pharmacist or doctor before you start taking them.

UNIT 2 You and your body – growing and changing

Lesson 2 *Your Life Student Book 1*, pages 12–13
Keeping healthy – understanding puberty

Objective: To understand the emotional changes that take place at puberty and how to manage these changes in a positive way.

Starter

Recap on what puberty is and explain that the increase in the levels of hormones causes changes in a person's feelings, as well as physical changes. Explain that someone can have positive feelings and negative feelings. Make lists on the board of positive and negative feelings and discuss how certain feelings, such as anger, can be positive or negative, depending on how they are dealt with. Explain to the class that the aim of this lesson is to help them to be able to recognise their feelings and to learn how to manage them.

Suggested activities

- Read the article 'Getting in touch with your feelings' (pages 12–13). Either ask the students to work in pairs, identifying what they consider to be the main points in the article, then discussing the points in groups or as a class; or work on the article with the whole class. The key things to focus on are the three basic rules stated in the middle section of the article (page 13).

- Ask groups to carry out the discussion activity on the four statements quoted on page 13, then to share their views in a class discussion. Focus in particular on the second statement, stressing the need to learn how to follow your feelings and to say 'No' if you really don't want to join in and do something that everybody else wants you to do.

Plenary

Ask: 'What have you learned about positive ways of dealing with your feelings, and negative ways of dealing with them?' Discuss how it is positive to be able to recognise the reasons for certain feelings, to let feelings out and to follow them when making decisions. Talk about how it is negative to wallow in feelings without exploring the reasons for them, to bottle up feelings, and to ignore them when taking action. Finally, remind the students of the types of feelings that are normal during puberty (see the end of the article on page 13) and how these are a normal part of growing up.

Extension activities

Challenge the students to do the role plays (see page 13) to demonstrate their skills at saying 'No'. Then hold a debriefing session to discuss how they felt when they said 'No' and any difficulties they faced when doing so. Encourage them to discuss any strategies they may have used to help them to resist the pressure that the friend put on them.

UNIT 3 You and your responsibilities – beliefs, customs and festivals

Your Life 1/Year 7

Lesson 1 *Your Life Student Book 1*, pages 14–15
Social education – respecting other cultures

Objective: To understand that Britain is a diverse society, and that it is important to respect the wide variety of beliefs and customs which are part of life in Britain.

Starter

Read the introductory paragraph 'What do you believe?' (page 14). Discuss: 'What influences your beliefs? Your family? Your neighbours? People who share your religion? Your school friends and school teachers? People who write the books you read? People you admire? Things you hear on television and the radio? Things you read in newspapers and magazines?'

Talk about the communities to which the students belong and how their views and beliefs are influenced by people in those communities and by the media.

Suggested activities

- Ask the students to study the list of statements under 'I believe' (page 14), to record their scores and to compare them in groups.

- Hold a class discussion and explain that people who belong to certain religions groups hold a number of the listed beliefs, e.g. many Muslims believe statements 2, 7, 8, 9 and 14. Many Jewish people believe statements 6 and 15. Many Jehovah's Witnesses believe statement 16. Conclude this discussion by stressing that in a diverse society people hold a wide range of different beliefs.

- Explain that dress customs may be based on beliefs. Talk about how the wearing of religious symbols and clothing is banned in schools in France. Discuss the different views expressed about the ban (page 15) and then hold a vote on whether the class would support a ban in British schools.

Plenary

Write the words 'discrimination' and 'prejudice' on the board. Explain that prejudice means intolerance of, or dislike of, people who come from a particular race or who have particular beliefs. Explain that discrimination means the unfair treatment of a person or group of people based on prejudice.

Read 'Freedom from discrimination' (page 15). Discuss PC Singh's story and re-emphasise the importance of respecting different customs and beliefs.

Extension activity

Ask the students to write a paragraph to explain why it is important to respect other people's beliefs.

UNIT 3 You and your responsibilities – beliefs, customs and festivals

Your Life 1/Year 7

Lesson 2 *Your Life Student Book 1*, pages 16–17
Social education – respecting other cultures

Objective: To understand how food customs can be based on religious beliefs and to research festivals based on religious beliefs.

Resources

Copies of Copymaster 3 'Obon'

Starter

Introduce the topic of food customs with a short discussion on vegetarianism. Encourage anyone in the class who is a vegetarian to explain why they are a vegetarian, if they wish to do so. Discuss how being a vegetarian and refusing to eat meat is often based on the belief that it is wrong for humans to eat animals.

Suggested activities

● In pairs, ask the students to read 'Jewish food laws' (page 16), then to perform the role play to show their understanding of how religious beliefs can determine what people eat.

● Read 'Salim comes to tea' (page 16) and ask groups to discuss the questions, then to report their views in a class discussion.

● Read the paragraph on 'Easter' (page 17) and either ask groups to draw up a calendar of Christian festivals or work together as a class to draw up the calendar. Be aware that students may find this difficult and will need to have many of the main days of the Christian calendar explained to them, e.g. Shrove Tuesday, Ash Wednesday, Palm Sunday, Good Friday, Easter, Whit Sunday.

Plenary

Recap what they have learned from the lesson about food customs based on religious beliefs. Read the paragraph on 'Janmashtami' (page 17) and set up the extension activity to research a religious festival.

Extension activities

Ask the students to work either individually or in pairs to research a religious festival, and to prepare a factsheet on it for a class 'A–Z of festivals'.

In groups, ask the class to study Copymaster 3, to discuss what they learn from it about Obon, and what message about people's religious beliefs is conveyed by Barrie Wade's poem. Then ask the students to share their views in a class discussion.

3 Obon

Ask the students to work – either individually or in pairs – to research a religious festival, and to prepare a factsheet on it for a class 'A–Z of festivals'.

In groups, ask the class to study Copymaster 3, to discuss what they learn from it about Obon, and what message about people's religious beliefs is conveyed by Barrie Wade's poem. Then ask the students to share their views in a class discussion.

The Visitors

'Twenty-seven lamps is what it takes,' he said,
setting his little candles on the stairs,
'to light the way and welcome back the dead.'
I helped him light their little welcome flares

because he's my best mate. His Dad and Mum
were Buddhists and I know his Obon feast
means food set out for visitors to come
seeking *Nirvana* which, he says, is *peace*.

'At Obon we invite them to return
and visit us.' He paused with eyes alight –
like mine, I guess, on Christmas Eve, when wine
is left for Santa Claus. 'They'll come tonight.'

I know his grandad and his mother drowned,
with nearly everybody from their junk,
under the China Seas when bandits rammed
their overcrowded boat. He would have sunk

but for his Dad and sister who took turns
to hold him up. I reckon one who's
rescued from a hell like that soon learns
what welcome lights we can't afford to lose.

'We'll burn the paper lantern now,' he said.
'Grandad used to make them out of lotus
leaves, but this will have to do instead.'
I pray and hope it helps them reach us

in these flats. I watch his eyes go still and wide
with peaceful welcome. In the flickering glare
his face is like a beacon lit to guide
the old man and his daughter up the stair.

Barrie Wade

In groups

Read and discuss Barrie Wade's poem about celebrating Obon.

1 Why does the writer of the poem pray even though he is not a Buddhist?

2 What message about people's religious beliefs does the poem convey?

Appoint a spokesperson to share your ideas in a class discussion.

Your Life 1/Year 7

Lesson 1 *Your Life Student Book 1*, pages 18–19
Personal wellbeing – time management

Objective: To encourage students to assess their management of their time, and to help them to understand the importance of planning and organisation in their personal lives.

Resources

Copies of Copymaster 4 'How good are you at managing your time?'

Starter

Explain to students that the purpose of the lesson is to look at how they manage their time. Ask: 'How well do you think you manage your time?' Ask them to give themselves a mark out of ten for their time-management and to explain the reasons why they gave themselves that mark.

Suggested activities

- Give out copies of the quiz and ask the students to complete the quiz on their own.

- In pairs, invite students to share what they have learned from the activity about how good they are at planning and organising their lives and making the best use of their time.

- Compare what the activity tells the class about their use of their time, with their own assessment of their use of time given in the Starter. Had they given themselves a true assessment? Do they need to alter the mark they gave themselves in the light of what the quiz has revealed?

- Together, study the list of 'Time-saving tips' (page 19), and then ask students to decide on up to three things each of them could do that would improve their management of time.

Plenary

Hold a class discussion, focusing on the time-saving tips. What other time-saving tips can they suggest? Which do they think are the most useful tips? List the tips on the board, then appoint someone to copy down the list and type it out on a computer for display on the classroom wall. You could print out copies for the students to put in their files, too.

Extension activity

Ask the students to write the letter to Darren, advising him on how to manage his time (see 'For your file' page 19), in order to demonstrate their understanding of how they can manage their time effectively.

How good are you at managing your time?

How good are you at managing your time?

Check your time-management skills by putting a circle round your answers. Then discuss with a partner what the quiz tells you about how you manage your time.

A test-yourself quiz

1 When you make an arrangement to do something, do you write the details on a calendar or in a diary?

a *Usually*　　**b** *Sometimes*　　**c** *Never*

2 When you want to find something in your bedroom, can you find it immediately?

a *Usually*　　**b** *Sometimes*
c *Never*

3 Do you put out the books and equipment you'll need for school next day, and pack your bag, before going to bed?

a *Usually*　　**b** *Sometimes*　　**c** *Never*

4 Do you plan when you're going to do your homework, rather than just doing it when you feel like it?

a *Usually*　　**b** *Sometimes*　　**c** *Never*

5 Do you make sure what time the buses run, so that you don't spend lots of time waiting at bus stops?

a *Usually*　　**b** *Sometimes*　　**c** *Never*

6 If someone rings up when you are busy doing something, do you tell them you'll ring them back?

a *Usually*　　**b** *Sometimes*　　**c** *Never*

7 When you have finished using something, do you put it away in the place where it is kept?

a *Usually*　　**b** *Sometimes*　　**c** *Never*

8 Do you waste time each day looking for things because you can't remember where you put them?

a *Usually*　　**b** *Sometimes*
c *Never*

9 Do you plan what TV programmes you are going to watch and fit in your other activities around them?

a *Usually*　　**b** *Sometimes*　　**c** *Never*

10 Do you work out beforehand exactly how you are going to spend the weekend, rather than wait to see what comes up?

a *Usually*　　**b** *Sometimes*　　**c** *Never*

11 Do you always check the opening times before you go somewhere, such as to the ice rink or swimming pool?

a *Usually*　　**b** *Sometimes*　　**c** *Never*

12 Do you always know exactly what homework you've got each night?

a *Usually*　　**b** *Sometimes*　　**c** *Never*

Your Life 1/Year 7

Lesson 2 *Your Life Student Book 1*, pages 20–21

Personal wellbeing – time management

Objective: To explore homework habits and to discuss problems with homework and how best to handle them.

Starter

Introduce the topic of homework by asking the class: 'How good are you at getting your homework done?' Talk about problems with homework. Ask: 'What is the main problem?' (Finding the time to do it? Forgetting what it is? Finding somewhere to do it? Not being able to do it? Getting interrupted all the time? Not being able to find the books/equipment needed? It taking so long that it can't be completed?) Make a list on the board of homework problems. Explain that the purpose of the lesson is to look at attitudes towards homework and how to deal with homework problems.

Suggested activities

- Read the views about homework of the four students (pages 20–21). You could invite four students to read aloud the statements of Salima, Tristan, Gary and Abby.

- Ask groups to discuss the follow-up questions on page 21 and to draw up a list of advice on how to cope with homework.

- Hold a class discussion in which the spokesperson from each group takes it in turn to report the group's ideas on how best to cope with homework.

- Ask pairs of students to study the list of homework problems (page 21) and to decide what advice they would give to each person. Encourage the students to share their ideas in a group or class discussion.

Plenary

As a class, make a list of 'Top Ten Tips on How to Handle Homework'. Either ask the class to copy out the list as you write it up on the board or ask someone to put the list on the computer, so that you can print copies for the students' files.

Extension activity

Invite the students to act out the role play (page 21) in which one of a group of friends refuses to give in to pressure to go out, and says that they have set aside the time to do their homework. Then hold a debriefing session to discuss how the person felt when saying 'No' and what they can do in such situations to help them not give in to pressure.

UNIT 5 You and your values – right and wrong

Objective: To develop students' own sense of values and responsibility towards others by sharing their views on right and wrong behaviour and on the seriousness of various forms of antisocial behaviour.

Resources

Copies of Copymaster 5 'Which is most serious?'

Copies of Copymaster 5A 'Understanding your values'

Starter

Discuss how, as members of society, we all have responsibilities about how we behave, and how our behaviour depends on what we believe to be right and wrong. Talk about how members of religious communities have guidelines about behaviour (e.g. Christians believe we should follow The Ten Commandments, such as 'Thou shalt not kill'). Ask the children, either individually or in pairs, to brainstorm a list of basic rules which they think everyone should live by today.

Suggested activities

- Read 'My ten rules for today' (page 22). In groups, discuss Stefan's list of rules and compare them with the lists they have written. Ask each group to agree on their list of ten rules for today, then to share their views in a class discussion.

- Read '25% of teenagers think cheating is OK' (page 23). Ask students to discuss their views on cheating in exams, travelling without a ticket and shoplifting. Ask groups to perform the role plays, then hold a class discussion of the arguments used in the role plays to try to persuade people to do the right thing.

- Invite individuals to complete the activity on Copymaster 5, which lists a number of different examples of antisocial behaviour and asks students to decide on their level of seriousness. Then ask groups to compare their views and to put the antisocial actions into a rank order.

Plenary

Ask groups to report their views on the seriousness of different antisocial actions and on how they ranked them. Discuss any major differences of opinion. Ask why they ranked some actions as more serious than others. Ask: 'What would society be like if these antisocial activities were regarded as acceptable behaviour?' Point out that it is the responsible behaviour of the majority of people who avoid such antisocial actions that underpins society.

Extension activity

Encourage individuals to complete the writing activities suggested in 'For your file' (page 23).

Assessment

Use Copymaster 5A to assess students' learning by asking them to write their own guidelines, entitled 'Ten rules for today' (see 'For your file' on page 22). They must give a reason for each of their rules.

Which is most serious?

ACTION		LEVEL OF SERIOUSNESS				
1	stealing	1	2	3	4	5
2	swearing	1	2	3	4	5
3	blackmail	1	2	3	4	5
4	joyriding	1	2	3	4	5
5	name-calling	1	2	3	4	5
6	taking drugs	1	2	3	4	5
7	vandalism	1	2	3	4	5
8	spitting	1	2	3	4	5
9	writing graffiti	1	2	3	4	5
10	shoplifting	1	2	3	4	5
11	beating someone up	1	2	3	4	5
12	cruelty to animals	1	2	3	4	5
13	spreading rumours	1	2	3	4	5
14	killing someone	1	2	3	4	5
15	lying	1	2	3	4	5
16	trespassing	1	2	3	4	5
17	forging a signature	1	2	3	4	5
18	breaking into a house	1	2	3	4	5
19	dropping litter	1	2	3	4	5
20	riding on a bus without paying	1	2	3	4	5
21	fighting	1	2	3	4	5
22	borrowing something and not returning it	1	2	3	4	5
23	bullying	1	2	3	4	5
24	mugging	1	2	3	4	5

Study this list of actions which most people would agree are wrong and decide which you think are the most serious and which are the least serious. Rank each of them on a five-point scale by circling the number in the right-hand column: 1 extremely serious, 2 very serious, 3 serious, 4 not very serious, 5 trivial.

In groups

Compare how you have ranked the actions. Then work together to list them from 1 to 24 in order of seriousness, starting with 1 – the most serious – and ending with 24 – the least serious.

5A Understanding your values

Draw up your list of ten rules for today. After each rule, write one or two sentences giving the reason why you believe that it is important for people to follow that rule.

Rule 1	
Reason	
Rule 2	
Reason	
Rule 3	
Reason	
Rule 4	
Reason	
Rule 5	
Reason	
Rule 6	
Reason	
Rule 7	
Reason	
Rule 8	
Reason	
Rule 9	
Reason	
Rule 10	
Reason	

UNIT 5 You and your values – right and wrong

> **Objective:** To examine the moral issue of whether it is right or wrong to tell on someone, and to discuss a number of situations involving a moral judgement.

Starter

Begin with a class discussion. Write the words 'informer', 'tell-tale', 'grass' and 'sneak' on the board. Ask: 'Why do people despise anyone who tells tales? Are they right to do so?' 'Does whether to tell depend on the circumstances, e.g. the seriousness of the incident?' 'Is telling on someone who has attacked another person different from telling on someone who has stolen something?' 'Does it make a difference if the person responsible is a relative or a friend?' 'Does it make a difference if you've promised not to tell?' 'Are there circumstances in which you should break such a promise?' End the discussion by emphasising that when faced with a difficult decision, each of us has to make up our mind about the right thing to do.

Suggested activities

● Read 'The right thing?' (page 24). In groups, discuss what the writer says about the difficulty of deciding when to tell or not to tell. Ask: 'Which of his statements do you agree with?' 'Which do you disagree with?' Invite students to share their own experiences of any dilemmas they have faced, but stress that they can choose whether or not to do so. Encourage them to share their views in a class discussion, and ask: 'Do you think it often takes more courage to tell than not to tell?'

● Ask groups to discuss the ten situations described in the section 'What should you do if …?' (page 25). Point out that different people in the group may make different decisions and that the purpose of the activity is to help them to make up their own minds rather than to agree as a group.

Plenary

Ask the students to share their views on what to do in the ten situations. Talk about the pressure that a person can come under in difficult situations – sometimes from other children, sometimes from adults. Ask: 'In such a situation, is there anyone you can turn to for advice or do you always have to rely on your own judgement?' 'Can talking to a helpline or an independent adult, such as a counsellor, help?'

Extension activity

Ask the students to write their own essay entitled 'The right thing?' (see 'For your file' on page 25).

UNIT 5 You and your values – right and wrong

> **Objective:** To understand what manners are, and how, in a diverse society, people from different cultures have different customs which are important to respect.

Starter

Explain what manners are and draw two columns on the board, labelling one 'Good manners' and the other 'Bad manners'. Ask the students to suggest types of behaviour, which are considered good manners and bad manners, and list their suggestions under the columns on the board. Then ask: 'Do you know of any behaviour that is regarded as good manners in our society, but considered bad manners in another society?' 'Do you know of any behaviour that is regarded as good manners in another society, but bad manners in our society?' Discuss any examples the class can think of, then read the first paragraph on page 26.

Suggested activities

- Ask individuals to look at the nine statements about manners (page 26) and, for each statement, to decide whether they a) agree with the statement, b) disagree with it, or c) are not sure. Then invite them to share their views as a class.

- Read the information about table manners on page 27. Ask the students to work in groups to design the layout of either a leaflet or a page for a magazine for 10- to 11-year-olds on the subject of table manners. Encourage them to be creative. For example, in addition to text giving information, they could also include cartoons and/or a comic strip or a story about a character called 'Billy Badmanners'. Ask the groups to share their ideas in a class discussion.

Plenary

Ask the students to look again at the lists of good manners and bad manners, which they compiled at the start of the lesson. Add any other examples that have been discussed during the main activities. Focus on the list of bad manners. Ask: 'Do you think some acts of bad manners are worse than others?' Focus on the list of good manners. Discuss why good manners are important.

Extension activities

Ask groups to produce their leaflet or magazine page on table manners.

Students interview a number of older people to find out their views on manners (see 'In pairs' page 26). Then ask individuals to write a statement saying how important they think good manners are (see 'For your file' page 26).

Ask students to choose a different society, e.g. Japanese society, and find out about manners in that society.

UNIT 6 You and your family – getting on with others

Your Life 1/Year 7

Lesson 1 *Your Life Student Book 1*, pages 28–29
Personal wellbeing – family relationships

> **Objective:** To explore the causes of tension between young people and their parents, and to understand that parents and children have different feelings and perspectives.

Starter

Ask the students to brainstorm the causes of arguments between them and their parents or carers. Then make a class list of the causes on the board. Tell them that the top five causes of arguments are: money, clothes, going out, helping at home and school. Explain that the aim of the lesson is to look at the causes of arguments and to discuss the different viewpoints that children and parents have.

Suggested activities

- Study 'Problems with parents' (page 28). Read the article 'I need my own space' and then, either in groups or as a class, discuss Laura's problem and the issue of parents giving their children enough privacy.

- In groups, ask students to read and discuss 'What causes arguments?' (page 29), before sharing their thoughts in a class discussion.

- Ask individuals to read 'Doing your share of the chores' (page 29), and to make a note of how often they help with each of the tasks. Then ask groups to compare how much they help and how much they think children should be expected to help.

Plenary

Recap the main points that students made in the class discussion about quarrels over clothes and going out. Focus on the different viewpoints that parents and children have and why they are different. Try to encourage the class to agree on the ages at which children should be able to a) choose their own clothes, b) go out without telling their parents where they are going, or c) decide the time they should come in. Then try to reach agreement on how much children should be expected to help adults with the chores.

Extension activities

Ask students to write their views on how much children should help with the household chores (see 'For your file' page 29).

Ask students to act out the role play (page 29), then hold a debrief in which they discuss their feelings and the alternative responses.

UNIT 6 You and your family – getting on with others

Your Life 1/Year 7

Lesson 2 *Your Life Student Book 1*, pages 30–31
Personal wellbeing – family relationships

Objective: To discuss ways of behaving that can help young people deal with difficulties in their relationships with parents, brothers and sisters.

Resources

Copies of Copymaster 6 'How to cope with brothers and sisters'

Starter

Recap the causes of arguments between young people and their parents discussed in the previous lesson. Ask: 'What are the main causes of arguments between you and your brothers and sisters?' Explain that there are different ways of behaving when conflicts occur in families, and that the aim of the lesson is to discuss strategies for dealing with difficult situations.

Suggested activities

● Read the top ten tips on page 30. Ask the students to discuss the questions in groups, then to share their ideas in a class discussion.

● Read Annabel's problem and the advice she is offered (page 31). Ask groups to discuss her problem and decide what advice they would give her.

● Ask pairs or groups to draw up a list of tips on how to cope with their brothers and sisters, then to compare their list with the tips given on Copymaster 6. Ask: 'Which of the tips from the two lists are the most helpful?'

Plenary

Write the words 'communication', 'consideration', 'co-operation' and 'compromise' on the board. Discuss what each word means and how they each suggest a way of behaving that can be useful in ensuring that the students maintain a good relationship with other members of their families.

Extension activities

Ask students to write a paragraph for their files to show their understanding of why following the four cs is a good way of behaving towards family members.

Ask pairs to develop role plays about arguments between brothers and/ or sisters, showing different ways of reacting to the situation. Then hold a debrief in which they discuss their feelings and talk about the most constructive responses.

Ask pairs each to write a letter (either real or imaginary) to a magazine's agony aunt from someone who is having a problem with a brother or sister, then swap their letters and write the agony aunt's reply. Share the letters and replies in a group or class discussion.

6 How to cope with brothers and sisters

How to cope with brothers and sisters –
make them your mates

- **T**reat them the way you'd like them to treat you. If you're thoughtful about their feelings and try to stay calm when they're looking for a fight, you might be surprised at the change in them.

- **G**ive each other space! Even your best friend would get on your nerves eventually if you had to spend hours every day sharing everything from the TV to the bathroom and maybe even a bedroom. Give each other time for privacy to read/ study/ talk to your mates and stick to it!

- **Y**ou can't have it both ways – you can't expect to boss your kid brother or sister around one minute like you're a grown-up, then throw a babyish tantrum the minute they do something you don't like! Try to remember what you were like at their age and make a few allowances if you can.

- **S**peak to them! You've got a ready-made mate in your brother or sister so don't shut them out. Chat to them like you would a new friend and find out what you've got in common – there must be something!

 **In groups**

Discuss the advice in the article on how to get on with your brothers and sisters. Which do you think is the most helpful tip? Suggest other things you might do to help you to get on better with your brothers and sisters.

UNIT 7 You and your body – smoking

Your Life 1/Year 7

Lesson 1 *Your Life Student Book 1*, pages 32–33
Keeping healthy – smoking

> **Objective:** To understand how smoking affects the health and appearance of people, and what the risks and the costs of smoking are.

Starter

Introduce the subject of smoking by asking students to say whether or not they are concerned about smoking ('I am/am not very concerned about smoking') and how high they think the risks from smoking are ('I think the risks from smoking are high/not very high'). Then explain that the lesson is going to examine how smoking affects people's health, the risks from smoking and the costs of smoking, and that you are going to ask them again about their attitudes to smoking at the end of the lesson to see whether they have changed their views.

Suggested activities

- Read 'Smoking – the facts' (page 32). Then ask the students to work in pairs to design a 'True or false' fact-check quiz about smoking. Help them to get started by giving them an example of a question: Less than 50% of lung cancer deaths are related to smoking. True or false? When they have finished, ask them to form groups of four and encourage each pair to do the other pair's quiz.

- Ask pairs to role play the scene (page 32) in which a non-smoker uses the information from 'Smoking – the facts' to try to persuade someone who has started smoking to give up.

- Read 'The high costs of smoking' (page 33) then ask the students to plan a 30-second TV advert as part of an anti-smoking campaign (see 'In groups' page 33).

Plenary

Ask students to think of three facts about smoking that they have learned from the lesson. Hold a class discussion in which they share the facts they have learned. Finally, ask them the same questions as you asked about attitudes to smoking at the beginning of the lesson. Have they changed their minds in any way as a result of what they have learned?

Extension activity

Ask students to demonstrate their understanding of smoking facts by designing a leaflet entitled 'Ten facts you should know about smoking'. They can use the internet to provide them with extra facts about smoking. Useful websites to look at include www.cancerresearchuk.org and www.ash.org.uk.

UNIT 7 You and your body – smoking

Your Life 1/Year 7

Lesson 2 *Your Life Student Book 1*, pages 34–35
Keeping healthy – smoking

Objective: To consider the reasons why people smoke, to examine the issue of passive smoking and to discuss the laws about tobacco.

Resources

Copies of Copymaster 7 'Smoking crossword'

Starter

Draw two columns on the board. Label one 'Reasons for smoking' and the other 'Reasons for not smoking'. Hold a class discussion and write the reasons students suggest in the appropriate column. Then explain what is meant by passive smoking, and why the issue of passive smoking causes people to have strong views about where people should be allowed to smoke. Smokers argue that they have a right to smoke wherever they want, while non-smokers argue they should be able to avoid having to inhale other people's smoke.

Suggested activities

- Read 'What do you really think about smoking?' (page 34). Ask groups to discuss the questions on page 34 and to appoint someone to note down their views and then to report them in a class discussion.

- Read 'Electronic cigarettes' and 'Tobacco and the law' (page 35). Ask groups to discuss the questions and to report their views in a class discussion.

Plenary

Hold a debrief in which you look again at the list of reasons for smoking and reasons for not smoking which they drew up at the beginning of the lesson. Add any new ideas that have arisen during the lesson.

Extension activities

Ask students to complete the crossword (Copymaster 7) to demonstrate their knowledge and understanding of smoking. Answers, across: 1 Cancer, 5 Places, 8 Bronchitis, 9 Inhale, 11 Nails, 14 Teeth, 17 Start, 18 Tar, 22 Oxygen, 23 Drug, 24 Quit, 25 Baby; down: 1 Carbon monoxide, 2 Nicotine, 3 Rich, 4 Death, 5 Passive, 6 Air, 7 Smoke, 10 ASH, 12 Sixteen, 13 Hair, 14 TV, 15 Emphysema, 16 Warning, 19 Mucus, 20 Cough, 21 Heart.

Invite groups to investigate attitudes to smoking by designing a questionnaire and carrying out a survey. Ask them to analyse the completed questionnaires and to report their findings to the rest of the class.

Suggest individuals put their own views on smoking issues in an email to a magazine or newspaper.

Smoking crossword

Clues across

1. Ninety per cent of deaths from this type of lung disease are smoking-related. (6)
5. Anti-smokers want smoking banned in all public _____. (6)
8. A lung disease which is often caused by smoking. (10)
9. What you do when you breathe in tobacco smoke. (6)
11. These may become stained if you are a heavy smoker. (5)
14. These may become stained too! (5)
17. Begin to smoke – don't do it! (5)
18. This mixture of chemicals is deposited in your lungs when you smoke. (3)
22. When you smoke, less of this is carried round your body by your blood. (6)
23. Nicotine is a very powerful one. (4)
24. Stop smoking, which lots of smokers would like to do. (4)
25. This may be smaller and underweight if a pregnant mother smokes. (4)

clues down

1. Poisonous gas in tobacco smoke. (6, 8)
2. Drug in tobacco smoke which can be addictive. (8)
3. What tobacco companies become by selling tobacco. (4)
4. You are more likely to have an early one if you are a smoker. (5)
5. Type of smoking in which you breathe in other people's smoke. (7)
6. Tobacco smoke pollutes this. (3)
7. What you do when you have a cigarette. (5)
10. Action on Smoking and Health – an organisation that campaigns against smoking. (3)
12. The age at which you can legally buy cigarettes. (7)
13. After being in a smoky atmosphere this may smell of smoke. (4)
14. Smoking adverts are banned on this. (1, 1)
15. Disease caused by smoking which progressively destroys the walls of the air sacs in the lungs. (9)
16. Cigarette packets have to carry one. (7)
19. The irritants in tobacco smoke cause smokers to produce lots of this liquid. (5)
20. What smokers do to get rid of 19 down. (5)
21. Smoking is a major cause of diseases of this organ. (5)

Your Life 1/Year 7

Lesson 1 *Your Life Student Book 1*, page 36
Citizenship – understanding the law

Objective: To understand why we have laws and that different countries have different laws.

Starter

Hold a class discussion on the question 'Why do we have laws?' Write the reasons the students suggest on the board. Then read the section 'Why do we have laws?' (page 36). Discuss how different countries have different laws, and how laws not only protect your rights but also define your responsibilities. Read the section 'Knowing and respecting the law' (page 36).

Suggested activities

● Ask groups to discuss what rules they would make for a group of people shipwrecked on a desert island.

● Invite each group to list their rules and to appoint a spokesperson to explain the reasons for their rules in a class discussion.

● Encourage the class to agree on a set of rules, based on the suggestions made by the groups.

● Discuss the rights that each rule protects and the responsibilities each rule puts on every member of the shipwrecked group.

Plenary

Hold a class discussion of how they would ensure that the people on the desert island kept to the rules.

Encourage them to consider the following questions:

How would they deal with lawbreakers?

Would they have a system of courts? How would they decide who were to be judges? Would they have a jury system?

How would they settle disputes between individuals?

What would they do to try to stop people breaking the rules?

Would they have a police force?

Extension activities

Ask students to write an article for a magazine aimed at Year 6 children, explaining why we have laws and what this means in terms of our rights and responsibilities.

Explain that in some countries the law of the land can be used to take away people's rights rather than to protect them. For example, a dictator may pass a law that denies people the right to free speech, making it an offence to criticise the government. In a democracy such as Britain, a law may be passed which affects your human rights. Suggest students use the internet to research the views of the human rights organisation Liberty and to find out its concerns about existing laws and proposed new laws, e.g. the introduction of identity cards (www.liberty-human-rights.org.uk).

UNIT 8 You and the law – why we have laws

Your Life 1/Year 7

Lesson 2 *Your Life Student Book 1*, page 37
Citizenship – understanding the law

Objective: To understand the difference between criminal law and civil law.

Starter

Explain that there are two types of laws – laws about criminal offences, called 'criminal laws', and laws about private matters called 'civil laws' and that there are separate systems of courts – criminal courts and civil courts. Criminal offences are dealt with in magistrates' courts and the Crown Court, and civil cases in county courts and the High Court.

Suggested activities

● Read about civil law and criminal law on page 37. Discuss the types of cases that are dealt with in civil courts, e.g. family disputes such as divorce and custody cases, financial and property disputes, contract cases and cases involving libel and slander.

● Ask the class to talk about what a solicitor does and discuss why it is a good idea to have a solicitor to represent you if you are accused of a crime, or if you are involved in a county court case.

● Invite the students to perform the role play (page 37) and then discuss what the two people decided to do.

Plenary

Ask groups to discuss the two views about whether or not it is a good idea to go to court or to settle out of court (see 'In groups' page 37), then to share their opinions in a class discussion.

Your Life 1/Year 7

Lesson 3 *Your Life Student Book 1*, pages 38–39
Citizenship – understanding the law

Objective: To explore laws concerning neighbours' behaviour and to discuss Antisocial Behaviour Contracts.

Resources

Copies of Copymaster 8 'An Acceptable Behaviour Contract'

Starter

Discuss how people's behaviour can affect their neighbours. Ask the class to suggest the types of behaviour that can interfere with a neighbour's life and list their suggestions on the board. Then read the first two paragraphs on page 38.

Suggested activities

- Read the sections on different kinds of nuisance – noise, trespass, pets and animals, bonfires and harassment – and discuss what the law is on each type of nuisance (pages 38–39).

- In groups read the emails sent to 'Ask Erica' (page 39) and draft Erica's replies.

- Invite students to study the section on anti-social behaviour and share their views on acceptable behaviour contracts in a class discussion. Then ask pairs or groups to use Copymaster 8 to draw up the contract that they would ask Adam to sign.

Plenary

In a class discussion, compare the acceptable behaviour contracts that they would ask Adam to sign.

An Acceptable Behaviour Contract

Study the details of Adam Pointer's behaviour, then in the space below draw up the Acceptable Behaviour Contract that you would ask Adam to sign.

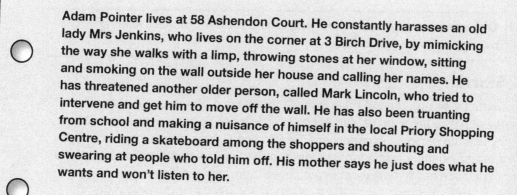

Adam Pointer lives at 58 Ashendon Court. He constantly harasses an old lady Mrs Jenkins, who lives on the corner at 3 Birch Drive, by mimicking the way she walks with a limp, throwing stones at her window, sitting and smoking on the wall outside her house and calling her names. He has threatened another older person, called Mark Lincoln, who tried to intervene and get him to move off the wall. He has also been truanting from school and making a nuisance of himself in the local Priory Shopping Centre, riding a skateboard among the shoppers and shouting and swearing at people who told him off. His mother says he just does what he wants and won't listen to her.

UNIT 9 You and other people – bullying

Your Life 1/Year 7

Lesson 1 *Your Life Student Book 1*, pages 40–41
Personal wellbeing – bullying

Objective: To explore what bullying is, to discuss the different kinds of bullying and who gets bullied.

Starter

Begin by setting ground rules for the discussion of the issue. Explain that the aim is to investigate bullying by looking at some examples, rather than by sharing personal experiences. Therefore, no one is allowed to talk about another person's experiences unless that person has first spoken about them, and no one has to talk about experiences in front of the class.

Ask: 'What is bullying?' Invite students to brainstorm what they think bullying is and collect their ideas on the board. Then read the statements in 'What is bullying?' (page 40). Discuss the three questions that follow on page 40, either in groups or with the whole class. List on the board all the types of behaviour that they consider to be bullying and classify them according to whether they are physical, verbal or emotional bullying.

Suggested activities

- Read 'Cyber bullying' (page 41), then ask groups to do the discussion activity and to report their views in a class discussion.

- Ask pairs to do the two role plays. Afterwards, discuss how the bully tried to defend their actions and the arguments the adult used to try to convince them that it was a very serious matter. Then discuss what advice the person offered the victim of cyber bullying.

Plenary

Explain that there is no such thing as a 'typical' victim, and read and discuss 'Who gets bullied?' (page 40). End by recapping the different types of bullying that they identified at the start of the lesson and discuss whether some types of bullying are more serious than others.

Extension activity

Ask the students individually or in pairs to design a poster offering advice on what to do if you are the victim of cyber bullying.

UNIT 9 You and other people – bullying

Your Life 1/Year 7

Lesson 2 *Your Life Student Book 1*, pages 42–43
Personal wellbeing – bullying

Objective: To explain why people bully, what it feels like to be bullied and to explore what to do if you are bullied.

Starter

Ask the students: 'Why do some people bully others?' Encourage them to brainstorm their ideas and collect them on the board. Suggestions might include: 'To have fun at the victim's expense', 'To make themselves feel powerful', 'Jealousy', 'Spite', 'Because they are racist'. Explain that many bullies are people who have problems that they take out on others (e.g. they are insecure and unhappy, either at home or at school, and bullying is a way of giving themselves some status). Evidence suggests that people who bully have often been bullied themselves.

Suggested activities

- Read 'Lana's story' (page 42) and 'Stephen's story' (page 42). Ask groups to discuss why they were bullied. Share the groups' views in a class discussion and ask: 'How do these stories make you feel about bullying?'

- Read and discuss the poem 'It hurts' (page 42). Ask: 'What is the message of the poem?' Ask students to do the writing activity (see 'For your file' page 42).

- Ask pairs to study the eight situations described on page 43, to decide what they think is the best way of responding in each situation, then to share their views in a group discussion, followed by a class discussion. During the discussions, ask students to focus on the consequences of each type of action. Which action would help to defuse the situation? Which action would escalate the situation? Which action would be most likely to bring an end to the bullying? Which action would let the bullying continue?

Plenary

Reread 'Stephen's story'. List the choices that Stephen has: to do nothing; to tell a teacher; to tell his parents; to talk to someone else; to ring a helpline. Ask students to imagine that they are the editor of a problem page and that Stephen has written to them – what would they say to him? Discuss their suggestions, before explaining that in the next lesson they will be exploring what to do if they are bullied.

Extension activities

Ask groups to perform the role play (page 42). Think carefully about the composition of the groups as you might want to keep certain children apart. Invite groups to present their role plays. Discuss how they show Stephen reacting and what they think is the best way for him to respond.

Students can explore bullying issues on the internet. Information and advice on bullying can be found on these websites: The Anti-bullying Network (www.antibullying.net); ChildLine (www.childline.org.uk); Kidscape (www.kidscape.org.uk).

UNIT 9 You and other people – bullying

Your Life 1/Year 7

Lesson 3 *Your Life Student Book 1*, pages 44–45
Personal wellbeing – bullying

Objective: To explore the different ways of reacting to bullying and to discuss what to do if you are being bullied.

Resources

Copies of Copymaster 9 'The truth about bullying'
Copies of the school's policy on bullying

Starter

Write the words 'aggressive', 'assertive' and 'passive' on the board and explain what they mean. Talk about how the way you react to bullying may be aggressive, assertive or passive. Explain that the purpose of this lesson is to investigate the advantages and disadvantages of the different ways of reacting to bullying.

Suggested activities

- Read 'How to beat the bullies' (page 44). Ask pairs to identify what they consider to be the three most useful pieces of advice. Compare their views in a class discussion and focus on the importance of speaking out, reinforcing the views expressed in the article that it is not telling tales, and that everyone has a right to feel safe and happy. Read and discuss 'Stay SMART online'.

- Read the advice given on 'Fogging' (page 44). Discuss what it is and how it works. Ask students to rank its value as a strategy on a scale of 1–10 (1 not very useful, 10 extremely useful) and to give reasons for their views.

- Study the advice Liz gives to Sarah and Jasbinder in 'Don't suffer in silence' (page 45) and ask groups to discuss how useful they think it is. Then ask them to draft the advice they would give to Clare, Thurston and Darren in 'Bullying problems' (page 45).

Plenary

In groups, students should draft a class bullying policy (see page 44). If copies of the school's bullying policy are available, as an alternative activity, they could study it critically, discuss how effective they think it is and suggest any alterations to make it more effective.

Extension activities

Study Copymaster 9. Ask students to compare the advice given in this article with the advice given on 'How to beat the bullies'. Which pieces of advice are the same? What other advice does this article give? Which do they find more useful?

Ask students to demonstrate their understanding of the issue of bullying by saying what they would plan to include in an article on bullying for a teenage magazine, then to draft the article.

The truth about bullying

"It's only real bullying if they push you around – calling names and stuff is just teasing and you have to get used to it."

Once in a while we have to put up with being the butt of a joke or a bit of teasing, but if this is deliberately meant to hurt you then it's bullying. Bullying doesn't just have to mean physical violence – it can be verbal violence (things said to hurt you) or even just threatening looks or gestures.

"It's too embarrassing to own up to anyone that you're being bullied."

Bullying can, and does, happen to anyone. It's not something you deserved or asked for, and it certainly isn't something to be ashamed of. Besides, having the courage to speak up and ask for help is proof that you're a strong and confident person – not the weak little victim the bullies would like to feel you are.

"The only way to deal with bullies is to stand up to them."

Trying to beat bullies at their own game often just isn't the way. Bullies see it as a victory if they can make you lose your temper or lash out (and it gives them an excuse to hit back even harder). If the bullying is of the name-calling, teasing type, it can be much more effective to laugh it off, or ignore it. In most cases, 'standing up to bullies' should mean refusing to give in, and speaking out.

"If I tell a teacher, it'll just get worse."

Bullies rely on you being too afraid to tell anyone in order to get away with it. The more fuss you make and the more people who know about your problem, the harder the bullies will find it to get near you and cause trouble. If your school has an anti-bullying policy, follow the guidelines for reporting trouble, otherwise go to your Year Head and have the facts clear in your head before you start.

"If I told my mum, she'd go round to the bullies' houses and try to sort them out – it would make it worse."

You can't blame parents for feeling angry and upset and wanting to protect you. But you have to tell them that the best way they can support you is to put pressure on your school to deal with the bullying, and maybe help out in other ways like meeting you after school, or just giving you a cuddle at home when you're feeling bad.

"Moving schools is the best way out."

Sometimes, in very serious cases, that does turn out to be the best option. But since it means leaving behind friends, disrupting your education AND the strain of being the new girl or boy somewhere else when your confidence is already low, it's a last resort. Give yourself and the school a fair chance at fixing the problem first. Remember that bullying often fizzles out after a while when the novelty wears off or the bullies realise they're being 'watched'.

Who to go to for help …
- Friends, parents
- Form teacher
- Year Head
- School Bullying Committee (if your school has one)
- Head Teacher
- Board of School Governors
- ChildLine (0800 1111, 24 hours)

UNIT 10 You and the media – the power of television

Your Life 1/Year 7

> **Objective:** To discuss the influence of television on people's lives and to examine whether it presents a fair and realistic picture of people and of life.

Resources

Copies of Copymaster 10 'TV – What do you think?'

A recording of an episode from a TV soap (optional – for extension activity only)

Starter

Ask the students: 'How big an influence do you think television has on you?' 'Do you think its influence is sometimes exaggerated?' Read 'Television and its influence' (page 46). Either in groups or as a class, discuss the six statements in turn. Conclude the discussion by asking for a show of hands: 'Who thinks the influence of television is exaggerated?' 'Do you think TV plays too big a part in your lives?'

Suggested activities

- Explain what a 'stereotype' is (a standardised image of a type of person). Give an example of stereotyping, e.g. anyone with red hair has a quick temper. Then read 'TV isn't fair' (page 46) and discuss whether TV presents a fair picture of all sections of society. In addition to the questions on page 46, ask: 'What sort of picture of teenagers does TV give?' 'Is it a fair picture?'

- Introduce the topic of how realistic TV dramas are by asking students which soaps they watch. 'Do you think that people actually behave like the characters in their favourite soaps?' Read 'Fact or fiction?' (page 47) and discuss what students learn about how realistic soaps are from a) the writer, b) the actress and, c) the director.

- Give out copies of Copymaster 10 and ask the students in groups to share their views on the various statements.

Plenary

Invite individual students to share their views on the statements on the copymaster in a class discussion.

Extension activities

Organise a debate on the motion 'Television does more harm than good'. Begin by asking individuals to list what they consider to be the good points and the bad points about television. Then suggest they work in groups to draft speeches for the debate.

Show a recording of an episode from a TV soap. Discuss it critically in the light of the comments from the writer, the actress and the director. Then ask students to do the writing task (see 'For your file' page 47).

10 TV – What do you think?

H.
TV never did anyone any harm. Young people should be allowed to watch whatever they want whenever they want.

A.
I think parents should control which programmes young people watch and limit the number of hours they watch TV.

B.
The storylines in TV soaps are far-fetched. People seem to forget that they are watching actors and start talking about the characters as if they are real people.

G.
The influence of TV is exaggerated. You get your views and values from your family, your friends and your school rather than from TV.

C.
I think TV presents a fair and balanced picture of society and that minority groups are represented.

F.
TV is the most powerful influence that exists in our society. It shapes people's opinions and values.

E.
You learn a lot about real life from watching TV soaps. They're informative as well as entertaining.

D.
I don't think that TV presents a fair picture of certain groups, such as older people, people with disabilities and people from ethnic minorities.

 In groups

Discuss these different views on television,
saying why you agree or disagree with them.

UNIT 10 You and the media – the power of television

Your Life 1/Year 7

Lesson 2 *Your Life Student Book 1*, pages 48–49
Social education – understanding the media

Objective: To explore the issues of bias and viewpoints in TV programmes.

Resources

Copies of old newspapers/recording of a TV news broadcast (optional – for extension activities only)

Copies of Copymaster 10A 'Understanding television'

Starter

Write the words 'bias', 'objective' and 'subjective' on the board and explain their meanings. Discuss how we expect journalists to be unbiased and objective in their news reporting. Explain that, nevertheless, it is easy for a report to be biased, because of the viewpoint from which it is presented and through the language the reporter uses. Explain that the lesson is about bias in TV programmes.

Suggested activities

- Before studying the picture of the soldier (page 48), ensure that the students know who Saddam Hussein is and why the Americans and British remained in Iraq after the war to overthrow him. Draw attention to the use of emotive language ('tyrannical rule', 'invaded') which increases the bias. Then focus on the rainforest picture and discuss the bias in the two alternative commentaries.

- Read 'The hero's point of view' (page 49). As a class, discuss what it says about seeing the action in dramas and sitcoms from a particular viewpoint. Discuss the final two paragraphs and what they say about news programmes.

Plenary

Read 'Viewpoint matters' (page 49). Ask: 'What does it say about the effect of camera angles in news reports?' List on the board what people need to be aware of when watching TV news reports in order to detect bias.

Extension activities

Ask students to find pictures in old newspapers and to prepare two alternative commentaries on them. They could display them.

Watch a recording of a TV news broadcast. Discuss how the stories are presented.

Assessment

Use Copymaster 10A to assess students' understanding of television and its messages.

10A Understanding television

On a separate sheet, answer these questions as fully as you can, giving reasons for the statements you make and, wherever possible, supporting them with examples.

1. How much influence do you think television has on people's views and values: A little? Quite a lot? A huge amount?
Give reasons for your view.
(See 'Television and its influence' on page 46.)

2. Do you think television programmes present a fair and balanced view of all sections of society? Think about older people, people with disabilities and ethnic minorities, and give reasons for your views.
(See 'TV isn't fair' on page 46.)

3. How true to life are TV soaps? In what ways are the characters and stories in soaps different from people and events in real life?
(See 'How true to life are soaps?' on page 47.)

4. How are the messages you get from the pictures you see in TV news broadcasts influenced by the viewpoint of the news reporter and what the reporter says?
(See 'Every picture tells a story' on page 48.)

5. How can the camera angle from which a news picture is taken alter the message the picture gives?
(See 'Viewpoint matters' on page 49.)

6. How does the point of view from which a drama or a comedy programme is presented influence your attitude towards the characters and their behaviour?
(See 'The hero's point of view' on page 49.)

UNIT 11 You and your money – pocket money, budgeting and saving

Your Life 1/Year 7

Lesson 1 *Your Life Student Book 1*, pages 50–51
Citizenship/Economic wellbeing and financial capability – money management

> **Objective:** To discuss students' money-management skills by exploring how they handle their pocket money.

Starter

Write the words 'spendthrift' and 'miser' on the board and explain that a spendthrift is someone who spends money extravagantly, while a miser is someone who hoards their money. Ask the students to think about how they handle their money – are they a spender or a saver? Encourage them to rank themselves on a scale of 1–10 (1 = a spendthrift, 10 = a miser), and to explain to a friend why they gave themselves the ranking they did. Then explain to the class that you are going to ask them to complete a quiz and to see whether the results support their view of how they handle their money.

Suggested activities

- Ask the students to do the quiz on pages 50–51, taking time to think about each question and to answer honestly. Tell them to count up to see whether their answers are mostly **a**s, **b**s or **c**s, then to read the section 'What your answers say about how you handle your money'. Ask: 'How does your self assessment compare with what the quiz says about how you handle your money?'

- Ask pairs to discuss their money-management skills and to suggest anything either of them needs to do in order to improve the way they handle their money.

Plenary

Read and discuss 'Money-management tips' (page 51). How helpful do students think the tips are? Can they suggest any other useful tips? Explain that the focus of the next lesson will be on pocket money problems and how to develop money-management skills by budgeting.

Extension activity

Ask students to research people's views on pocket money. Ask them to draw up a questionnaire aimed at either young people or parents and carers. Then encourage them to analyse the results and to present their findings in the form of a magazine article.

UNIT 11 You and your money – pocket money, budgeting and saving

Your Life 1/Year 7

Lesson 2 *Your Life Student Book 1*, pages 52–53

Citizenship/Economic wellbeing and financial capability – money management

Objective: To develop money-management skills by exploring pocket money issues and explaining how to work out a budget plan.

Resources

Copies of Copymaster 11 'Who should pay?'

Starter

Introduce the topic by reading the first paragraph on page 52. Then ask students, 'What should your pocket money be for?' and draw a spidergram of their suggestions on the board.

Suggested activities

- Hand out copies of Copymaster 11 'Who should pay?' for the students to complete and then to compare their answers in groups. Alternatively ask them to do the 'In groups' activity 'What should your pocket money be for?' (page 52).

- Ask groups to discuss the questions in 'What do you do with your pocket money?' (page 53). Ask them: 'What conclusions can you draw from your discussions about how you spend your money?' 'Do most of you spend it on the same things?' 'Do most of you spend it all rather than save any of it?'

- Explain what a budget is and ask individuals to follow the steps in the flowchart in the section 'Planning a budget' (page 53). Challenge them to plan a budget for someone who will have a total of £15 available over the four weeks. Then ask them to discuss their budget plans in pairs. How would their plans be different if the person had £25 rather than £15?

- Ask pairs to read 'Pocket money problems' (page 52), then discuss the problems. Ask them what they would say in a letter to one of the children offering advice on how to deal with the problem. Share ideas in a class discussion.

Plenary

Ask the students to imagine they are planning an article on pocket money for a magazine for people of their own age. What would be their 'Top tips on how to handle your cash'? Hold a class discussion and list their ideas on the board.

Extension activities

Ask pairs to role play the scene 'I've spent my school trip money' (page 53). Invite some of them to perform their role plays and discuss what they suggest the person should do.

Write an article for a teenage magazine about how to plan a pocket money budget.

Who should pay?

Study this list and decide which things you think your parents or guardian should pay for and which things you should think you should pay for out of your own money.

Put a tick in the appropriate column. If you can't decide, put a question mark in both columns. Then compare your answers in groups, explaining why you put question marks against any of the items.

	Things I should pay for	Things my parents or guardian should pay for
Food for meals		
Snacks and sweets		
School uniform		
Everyday clothes		
Shoes and trainers		
Sports kit and sports equipment		
Toiletries (e.g. soap, toothpaste)		
Make up		
Haircuts		
DVDs and computer games		
Tickets for cinema/sports events		
Bus/train fares		
School trips		
Holidays and outings		
Comics/magazines		
Stationery		
Books		
Presents for you to give other people at birthdays/festivals		
Telephone calls/text messages		

UNIT 12 You and the law – children's rights

Your Life 1/Year 7

Objective: To explain what children's rights are at home and what parents' responsibilities are.

Resources

Copies of Copymaster 12 'Smacking – what do you think?'

Starter

Ask the students: 'What is the difference between a right and a responsibility?' Write definitions and examples on the board: a right is something which you are entitled to, e.g. children have the right to be fed and clothed; a responsibility is something that you should do, e.g. parents have a responsibility to protect their children from harm.

Read the two paragraphs on 'Parents' duties and children's rights' (page 55). Discuss what is said about the responsibilities that parents have to care for their children and about what can happen if parents neglect their children or treat them cruelly.

Suggested activities

● Read 'Your rights at home' (page 54). Ask pairs to do the true/false quiz on page 55. Then hold a class discussion in which you give the answers: 1 True, 2 True, 3 False, 4 False, 5 True, 6 False, 7 False (but your views may be taken into account), 8 False (you have the right to go on seeing your dad, but in practice your mum may make it impossible for you to do so), 9 False, 10 False.

● Ask groups to discuss the statements on choice of schools, smacking and medical treatment on page 55. Then ask them to report their views in a class discussion.

Plenary

Summarise what the students have learned about parents' duties and children's rights by making lists on the board. You could then transfer the lists onto posters to display in the classroom.

Extension activity

Organise a class debate on the issue of smacking. Give out copies of Copymaster 12. Then split the class into four groups and ask two groups to prepare the arguments in support of smacking and two groups to prepare the arguments against smacking. Ask the groups to appoint a spokesperson to present their views. After the four representatives have given their speeches, invite contributions from the rest of the class. Then hold a vote to decide whether the class is for or against smacking. They can then write emails to a magazine giving their individual views.

Your Life 1/Year 7

12 Smacking – what do you think?

All about smacking

What the law says

As the law currently stands, parents in the UK can get away with belting and beating children – even with a stick or an electric flex. This is because it can be ruled in court that a parent has used 'reasonable chastisement'. But that may be about to change. The European Court on Human Rights has ruled that a British boy's human rights were breached when he was repeatedly beaten by his stepfather, even though the stepfather had been acquitted of assault in a UK court. In response, the UK government has agreed that the law needs to be changed. Although the government is opposed to a total ban on smacking, many Labour MPs want the law tightened to outlaw punishment that causes 'mental or physical harm'.

Smacking facts

- Physical punishment of children is illegal in Austria, Croatia, Cyprus, Denmark, Finland, Latvia, Norway and Sweden. Germany is also intending to outlaw physical punishment.

- In countries where physical punishment against children is banned, attitudes towards violence have changed, and there are fewer prosecutions for violence, and fewer children in care.

WHAT CHILDREN SAY ABOUT SMACKING

An adult like my daddy, he can smack you very hard … He can smack you like a stone … And you'll cry. (Wayne, aged 7)

It hurts and it's painful. Inside, it's like breaking your bones. (Gilly, aged 7)

If they changed the law, then a lot of people will realise what they have done to their child. If they don't change the law, adults will think: 'Oh well, the child doesn't mind, so we can keep on smacking.' (Tara, aged 7)

WHAT ADULTS SAY ABOUT SMACKING

There are much better ways of teaching children how to behave than giving them a smack.

I don't approve of smacking children all the time, but I think it's OK once in a while if they've done something very serious or dangerous.

I think parents who smack their children do it out of anger and frustration rather than because they think it's the best way to discipline them.

Smacking doesn't help children to understand why they've done wrong. It only makes them resentful.

In groups

1. What do you learn from this page about the law on smacking in the UK and in other countries? Discuss the views expressed by the children and adults. What do you think of smacking as a way of disciplining children?

2. 'I'd rather be given a smack than be grounded or have my pocket money stopped.' Discuss this view.

UNIT 12 You and the law – children's rights

Your Life 1/Year 7

Lesson 2 *Your Life Student Book 1*, pages 56–57
Citizenship – understanding the law

> **Objective:** To examine the law regarding the ages at which children are allowed to do things, and the law concerning children being taken into care.

Resources

Copies of Copymaster 12A 'Understanding children's rights'

Starter

Explain that the law in the UK aims to protect children by not allowing them to do certain things until they are considered old enough. Ask the students to write down the minimum ages at which they think the law allows them to a) open a bank account, b) buy a pet, c) go into a bar, d) buy an alcoholic drink, e) buy cigarettes, f) vote in local and parliamentary elections, g) drive a car, h) get married, i) choose their own doctor, j) join the armed forces.

Suggested activities

- Ask pairs to read 'Children and the law' (page 56) and to check whether or not the answers they wrote down were correct. Then, in groups, invite them to discuss the questions at the bottom of page 56, before holding a class discussion about what changes (if any) they think should be made to the law. Make a list on the board of the changes they suggest.

- Read 'Children in care' (page 57) and ask groups to discuss the questions. (Note: Be aware that there may be children in the group who are in care, and so the activity may need careful handling. In such circumstances, it may be better to hold a class discussion rather than group discussions.)

Plenary

Ask the students to write a short statement giving their views on the laws concerning children and whether any of them should be changed (see 'For your file' page 56). Remind them to refer to the list you wrote during the main activity to help them.

Extension activities

Suggest the students interview a number of adults to find out their views on the laws concerning the ages at which children can do certain things. Hold a class discussion in which they report their findings. Do the adults' views differ from their views? If so, why do the students think this is?

Choose an issue on which the students feel very strongly that the age should be changed. Ask them to draft an email to their local MP stating their arguments on why that particular law should be changed.

Assessment

Use copies of Copymaster 12A to assess understanding of children's rights. (Answers: All the statements are false with the exception of statement 7 and statement 10.)

ASSESSMENT
COPYMASTER

12A | # Understanding children's rights

Use this quiz to check your knowledge of the laws about children's rights.

Decide which of these statements are true and which are false, and put a tick in one of the boxes.

		TRUE	FALSE
1.	You can leave home without your parents' permission at 16.	☐	☐
2.	Once you are 13 you can work for four hours on any day.	☐	☐
3.	From the age of eight you can be held responsible for any crime you commit.	☐	☐
4.	You need your parents' consent to join the armed forces if you are under 18.	☐	☐
5.	At 16 you can buy yourself alcohol to drink with a meal in a pub or restaurant.	☐	☐
6.	You have to be 21 before you can vote in a parliamentary or local election.	☐	☐
7.	Your parents have no legal duty to give you pocket money.	☐	☐
8.	Your parents have the right to smack you as hard and as often as they like.	☐	☐
9.	Parents must take children's views into consideration when choosing a school for them.	☐	☐
10.	Your parents can choose which religion you are brought up in.	☐	☐
11.	Foster parents have all the same rights and responsibilities as natural parents.	☐	☐
12.	Adopted children aged 14 and over have the right to see their birth records.	☐	☐

UNIT 12 You and the law – children's rights

Your Life 1/Year 7

Lesson 3 *Your Life Student Book 1*, pages 58–59
Citizenship – understanding the law

Objective: To explore what rights children have, to explain the laws concerning child employment in the UK and to examine child labour in the developing world.

Starter

Write up on the board: 'All children should be allowed to work whatever age they are'. Ask the students whether they agree or disagree with this statement. Ask: 'Why aren't children allowed to work?' 'Up to what age should children be prohibited from working?' 'Should there be limits on the times when children can work and on the hours they work?' 'What are the laws in the UK?' Read 'Child employment in Britain' (page 58) and discuss what the law is. Explain that the laws are designed to protect children, and that the aim of the lesson is to look at children's rights and at how child workers are exploited in many parts of the world.

Suggested activities

- Read 'The rights of the child' (page 58). Ask: 'Do you think any of the rights are more important than others? Why?' 'What other rights do children have?' Ask groups to draw up a charter of children's rights. Then hold a class discussion and, on the board, list the rights they agree all children have.

- Read 'Child labour in the developing world' (page 59). Discuss the different types of jobs done by children in the developing world, then read and discuss 'Sawai's story' (page 59). Talk with the class about how different Sawai's life is from theirs and how they would feel if they were in her position. Encourage them to imagine what it would be like to be a child labourer and to tell each other about a typical day in their life.

Plenary

Recap the list of rights, which the class agreed all children have. Refer to the charter of children's rights that you wrote on the board and ask them to copy it for their files.

Extension activities

Talk about organisations which exist to protect children's rights. Explain that the National Society for the Prevention of Cruelty to Children (NSPCC) works to protect children from abuse in the UK and that Anti-Slavery International campaigns throughout the world to stop children being forced to work for little or no money. Ask pairs to use the internet to research the work of the NSPCC (www.nspcc.org.uk) and Anti-Slavery International (www.antislavery. org). Ask them to make notes and to write a short report about how these organisations try to protect children's rights.

UNIT 13 You and the world of work – developing a product

Your Life 1/Year 7

Lessons 1–4 *Your Life Student Book 1*, pages 60–61
Citizenship/Economic wellbeing and financial capability – understanding industry

Objective: To involve the students in an enterprise activity in order to help them to understand how a new product is developed.

Resources

Copies of Copymaster 13 'Market testing questionnaire'

Starter

Read 'Invent a new game' (page 60) and discuss the rules of the competition. Explain that the task is for groups to prepare an entry by developing a product and that the process of development is similar to that followed by any manufacturing company.

Suggested activities

- Lesson 1. Carry out the brainstorming activity (see 'Stage 1 Deciding on an idea'). Then explain what market research is and read 'Stage 2 Market research'. Ask students to carry out their market research for homework.

- Lesson 2. Ask them to share with other members of the group what they each found out in their market research and to follow the steps in the flowchart to design and produce a sample copy of their game (see 'Stage 3 Designing your product').

- Lesson 3. Ask them to market test each other's games (see 'Stage 4 Market testing or piloting') and to complete the questionnaires (Copymaster 13) about the games they tested. Encourage them to make any changes to their game as a result of what they have learned from piloting it. Ask them to prepare a market presentation for homework (see 'Stage 5 Market presentation').

- Lesson 4. In turn, invite groups to give their market presentation. Discuss whose presentation was the most effective and why. End the lesson with a plenary in which you emphasise the importance of each of the five stages they have gone through in developing their games.

13 Market testing questionnaire

Name of the game: _____

1. What do you think the good points of the game are? Why?

_____

_____

_____

2. What do you think the bad points of the game are? Why?

_____

_____

_____

3. Are the instructions easy or difficult to follow? Why?

_____

_____

_____

4. Did you enjoy playing the game? Why?

_____

_____

_____

5. How do you think the game could be improved?

_____

_____

_____

6. Is the game suitable for the target age-range? Give reasons for
your answer.

_____

_____

_____

7. Do you think the game is more or less enjoyable than other
similar games?

_____

_____

_____

UNIT 13 You and the world of work – developing a product

Lesson 5 *Your Life Student Book 1*, page 62

Citizenship/Economic wellbeing and financial capability – understanding industry

Objective: To understand that risks are involved in manufacturing a product for sale and in setting a price for it.

Starter

Explain that anyone selling a product takes a risk. They have to work out a price for the product, taking into account the cost of producing it and to ensure that they set a price that people are prepared to pay for it. Often they will take out a loan to cover the initial costs of production. Then read the introductory paragraph of 'Selling your product – taking a risk'.

Suggested activities

- Read 'The cost of production'. Then in their groups ask students to discuss what things they need to consider when deciding which materials to use to make the game and the packaging for it.

- Read the case study 'Setting the price' and discuss why Jack's group chose to set a price of £10. Then discuss in groups what they estimate the costs of producing their game will be and what price they need to set for it. Ask them to decide whether or not it would be worth the risk of borrowing £100 to enable them to manufacture and sell it.

Plenary

Ask each group to feed back their decision on whether or not they would be prepared to take the risk of borrowing £100.

UNIT 13 You and the world of work – developing a product

Lesson 6 *Your Life Student Book 1*, page 63
Citizenship/Economic wellbeing and financial capability – understanding industry

> **Objective:** To explore the different ways that companies advertise their products.

Starter

Ask: 'What is the point of advertising your product?' Elicit the point that advertising has two main purposes – to try to persuade potential buyers and to give consumers information about the product.

Suggested activities

- Read 'Advertising your product'. Make sure that students understand the importance in advertising campaigns of stressing a product's 'unique selling points' (USPs). Discuss the need to target particular groups of potential customers when deciding what form your campaign should take.

- Ask groups to draw up an advertising strategy for their game. What are its USPs? How are they going to persuade people to buy it? What form will the adverts take? Ask them to choose a spokesperson to report their ideas in a class discussion.

Plenary

Ask the class: 'What makes an effective advertising campaign?' List the points they suggest on the board.

Extension activities

Ask students to study leaflets or a catalogue advertising toys and games and to say in a class discussion which adverts they think are the most effective and why.

Encourage them to carry out their advertising campaign by producing adverts for their game.

UNIT 14 You and your body – drugs and drugtaking

Your Life 1/Year 7

Lesson 1 *Your Life Student Book 1*, pages 64–65
Keeping healthy – drugs and drugtaking

Objective: To consider why some drugs are socially acceptable and others illegal, to discuss what drug abuse is and to understand the effects illegal drugs have.

Resources

Copies of Copymaster 14 'The language of drugs'

Starter

Introduce the topic by explaining that when we talk about drugs we often mean illegal drugs, but that there are other kinds of drugs. What other kinds of drugs can the students think of? Talk about drugs which are medicinal and drugs which are socially acceptable. Read and discuss 'What do we mean by 'drugs'?' (page 64). Discuss the view that if alcohol and tobacco had only recently been discovered, they would be banned (see 'In pairs' page 64).

Suggested activities

● Read the two statements in 'What is drug abuse?' (page 64). Ask groups to draft their own definitions of drug abuse, then compare them in a class discussion.

● Ask groups to read the information on 'How drugs can affect you' and 'Drugs can kill' on page 65. Invite them to show their understanding of the effects drugs can have by preparing a list of 'Ten ways drugs can affect your life'. Then ask individuals to write a statement saying how dangerous they think drugtaking is.

Plenary

Ask the students: 'Do you think the dangers of drugtaking are exaggerated?' 'Why are adults so concerned about drugtaking?' Ask individuals to read their statements about how dangerous they think drugtaking is, and discuss their views.

Extension activities

Ask students to design a poster to warn people of their age about the dangers of drugtaking.

Encourage them to demonstrate their knowledge and understanding of the terms used when discussing drugs and drugtaking by completing the matching exercise on Copymaster 14.

14 The language of drugs

Study the list of ten terms (below) that are often used when people discuss drugtaking. Then write the correct term against its definition in the table. Check your answers in a class discussion.

Addiction

Depressants

Hallucinogenic

Hard drugs

Physical dependence

Psychological dependence

Soft drugs

Stimulants

Tolerance

Withdrawal symptoms

	Term	Definition
1		These drugs increase the activity of the brain and make people feel more alert, energetic and awake. Examples are caffeine, speed and ecstasy.
2		This is when a drug is craved so much that it is impossible to stop taking it.
3		These are drugs which are taken for social purposes (also known as recreational drugs), such as cannabis. They do not have withdrawal symptoms when given up. However, such drugs are not safe.
4		A term used to describe drugs, such as LSD, that distort the senses. They can cause users to see and hear things that are not really there.
5		This is when someone needs to keep taking a drug to feel okay and cope with their life, even though their body is not physically dependent.
6		This is when the body gets so used to a drug that larger and larger amounts of the drug are needed in order to maintain the same feeling.
7		These drugs, such as heroin, slow down the activity of the brain, creating a feeling of relaxation, sleepiness and a loss of anxiety.
8		Physical and mental reactions to a drug being denied to a user, for example, shaking, sweating, vomiting, night terrors and anxiety.
9		These drugs, such as heroin and cocaine, have powerful effects. They are addictive and hard to give up.
10		This is when drugs have to be taken on such a regular basis that the body needs regular doses to avoid withdrawal symptoms.

UNIT 14 You and your body – drugs and drugtaking

Lesson 2 *Your Life Student Book 1*, pages 66–67
Keeping healthy – drugs and drugtaking

Objective: To explore why people start to take drugs and to discuss attitudes towards drugs and drugtaking.

Starter

Recap what the students learned about the effects drugs can have on a person's life (see Lesson 1). Explain that although people are aware of the dangers, some people take drugs. Explain that a focus for this lesson is on why they start to take drugs. Read the extract from Drugs by Anita Naik on page 66 and make the point that there isn't one single reason why people take drugs.

Suggested activities

- Ask students to read the statements on page 66 alone, and to rank the reasons given at the foot of the page in order, starting with what they consider to be the main reason. Tell them to include any other reasons that they can suggest. Point out, however, that the focus is on the recreational use of drugs and that sports people taking drugs to enhance their performance is a separate issue. Invite students to share their views in a group discussion and to produce a group statement to share with the rest of the class.

- Read Cannabis: the dangers (page 67), and ask groups to discuss the advice given to Fay and the question of what you should do if you find that your brother or sister is taking drugs.

Plenary

Read Sammy's statement 'People are pressurised into drugs' (page 67). As a class, discuss the points she makes and why they agree or disagree with them.

Extension activities

Ask students to complete the writing activity (see 'For your file' page 67), explaining their attitude towards drugs and drugtaking. Then organise a drugs forum in which you chair a discussion of the issues raised in the lesson. Ask individuals to form a panel and to start the debate by reading out what they have written.

Suggest students use the internet to research information about, and attitudes towards, drugs and drugtaking. For information on the subject for 11- to 14-year-olds, see www.talktofrank.com.

UNIT 15 You and the community – being a good neighbour

Lesson 1 *Your Life Student Book 1*, pages 68, 70
Social education – respecting your neighbours

Objective: To explore what being a good neighbour involves and to examine the problem of vandalism.

Resources

Copies of Copymaster 15 'How good a neighbour are you?'

Copies of Copymaster 15A 'Understanding what being a good neighbour means'

Starter

Explain that as a neighbour you have responsibilities as well as rights. Ask: 'What makes a good neighbour?' Prompt pairs to brainstorm their definition of a good neighbour. Then ask groups to compare their definitions, to discuss the comments on page 68 and to draft a group statement about what makes a good neighbour to share with the rest of the class.

Suggested activities

- Ask pairs of students to discuss their ideas on how to be a good neighbour. Then invite them to compare their ideas with Hassan and Philip's list, to do the ranking activity (see 'How to be a good neighbour', page 68), and to discuss their views in groups.

- Suggest the students complete the quiz on Copymaster 15, then compare their answers in a group discussion.

- Explain what antisocial behaviour is and how vandalism is just one form of antisocial behaviour. Read 'Vandalism – a costly problem' (page 70). Ask students to discuss the four questions in groups, then to share their views in a class discussion.

Plenary

Discuss what the students have learned from the lesson about their rights and responsibilities as neighbours, and compile lists on the board.

Extension activities

Ask students to write a short statement for their files to show their understanding of what rights they have as a neighbour and what responsibilities they have.

Ask groups to discuss how serious they think graffiti writing is. They can then work individually to write their views on graffiti writing.

Ask students to either write a story about an act of vandalism which leads to someone getting hurt or to design a poster about vandalism, pointing out how dangerous and costly it is (see 'For your file', page 70).

Ask your Police Community Support Officer (PCSO) to come into school and talk to the students.

Assessment

Use Copymaster 15A to assess students' understanding of what being a good neighbour involves.

15 How good a neighbour are you?

Do this quiz about you and your neighbours.
Circle **a**, **b** or **c** in answer to each question.

1 You are playing football and your ball goes over a fence into a neighbour's garden. Do you:

a climb the fence and get it back

b go round and ask for it back

c wait for your neighbour to find it and throw it back?

2 One of your neighbours has an accident and cannot take their dog out for its walks. Do you:

a offer to take the dog out as a favour

b offer to take the dog out if they'll pay you

c not offer to help because it'll be too much trouble?

3 You see someone coming out of a neighbour's house and think they look suspicious. Do you:

a go up and ask them what they are doing

b find an adult and tell them about it

c ignore it in case you're making a mistake and they are not doing anything wrong?

4 You are walking past a neighbour's house when you see one of them struggling to unload something heavy. Do you:

a stand and watch to see what happens

b offer to help

c walk past and leave them to it?

5 A neighbour complains about the noise you are making because they work nights and are trying to sleep. Do you:

a say it's none of their business and go on playing

b go on playing and try to keep the noise down

c pack up your game and go and play somewhere else?

6 You see some younger children scrawling graffiti on a bus shelter. Do you:

a go and join in because they are having a laugh

b try to persuade them to stop and say you'll tell someone if they don't

c do nothing because you don't want to get involved?

7 The local youth centre is organising a rota of litter-pickers to keep your area free of litter. Do you:

a volunteer to take part

b wait to see whether your friends volunteer and do what they do

c refuse to join in because you think it's the council's job to keep the area free of litter?

8 You see some friends of yours bullying someone in the park. Do you:

a intervene and try to stop them

b go and tell an adult

c ignore it because it's none of your business?

9 A new boy or girl moves into your neighbourhood. Do you:

a make a deliberate attempt to befriend them

b wait to see if they speak to you

c ignore them?

10 Your school asks for volunteers to deliver parcels to old people in your neighbourhood. Do you:

a agree to deliver some parcels after school

b agree to deliver them only if it means missing some lessons

c let other people do it because it would take up too much of your time?

In groups

Compare your answers and discuss what you think a good neighbour would do in each of these situations.

15A Understanding what being a good neighbour means

Draw up a list of ten 'Dos' and 'Don'ts' on how to behave in order to be a good neighbour.

1	
2	
3	
4	
5	
6	
7	
8	
9	
10	

UNIT 15 You and the community – being a good neighbour

Your Life 1/Year 7

Lesson 2 *Your Life Student Book 1*, pages 69 and 71

Social education – caring for the local environment

Objective: To discuss how the neighbourhood might be improved and to explore how to take community action to improve it.

Starter

Remind the students that one of the points you identified in the previous lesson about being a good neighbour is to take care of the environment. Explain that this means not only avoiding antisocial behaviour, such as dropping litter or vandalism, but also taking steps to try to improve the neighbourhood.

Explain what an assessment is and how, in order to help them identify what needs to be done in the neighbourhood, they will start by assessing existing facilities and services and the current state of the environment.

Suggested activities

- Ask groups to carry out the discussion activities on 'Facilities and services', 'Safety' and 'Appearance' (page 69). Write the headings 'Facilities and services', 'Safety' and 'Appearance' on the board and, during a class discussion of their ideas, make lists of their suggestions for improvements.

- Read the article 'Street Scene Champions' (page 71). Then invite students to discuss the questions in groups, before holding a class discussion to share their views on the idea of having 'Local Environment' champions.

Plenary

Explain that identifying what you think needs to be done is only the first step. Next you need to check that it is what people want. Read and explain the various steps involved in developing a community action project (see the flowchart on page 71). Discuss how to tackle the next step – drafting a questionnaire.

Extension activities

Ask groups to follow the steps in the flowchart, beginning with drafting a questionnaire and carrying out the survey. After they have analysed the survey, students can either draft an action plan as suggested or, alternatively, write a report of their findings for the local newspaper.

Suggest students research how to set up or join a youth action group to try to improve their neighbourhood by visiting the National Youth Agency website: www.nya.org.uk.

UNIT 16 You and your money – you as a consumer

Lesson 1 *Your Life Student Book 1*, pages 72–73
Citizenship/Economic wellbeing and financial capability – consumers and their rights

Objective: To understand what it means to be a consumer and to explore factors which influence people when they are buying goods.

Resources

Copies of Copymaster 16 'What influences you?'

Starter

Ask each student to write a definition of what a consumer is. Share their definitions in a class discussion, then look at the definition of a consumer on page 72.

Suggested activities

- Talk about how, as consumers, we buy goods for ourselves. Discuss the difference between 'needs' and 'wants', then in pairs ask students to draw up lists of needs and wants and to compare their lists in either a group or class discussion.

- Read the section on 'Services' on page 72 and discuss how we pay for some services directly and other services indirectly. Get them to suggest further examples. Then ask them to write a statement for their files about what being a consumer means.

- Explain that there may be various factors which influence what they buy. Read 'Who influences what you buy?' (page 73) and explain that there are also influences on where we buy things. Ask them individually to complete the questionnaire on Copymaster 16, then to share their answers in a group discussion, followed by a class discussion.

Plenary

Discuss what they have learned about their shopping habits and what influences them when they are being consumers.

Extension activity

Discuss what impulse buying is. Get the students to perform the role play on page 73, then to write Erica's reply to Imogen (see 'For your file' page 73). Ask some of them to read out their replies and discuss ways of resisting peer pressure when they are out shopping.

16 What influences you?

What influences what you buy?

	A lot	Quite a lot	Not much	Not at all
Advertising – You have been made to believe that a product is worth having or that you will only be accepted if you have it.				
Friends – Your friends put pressure on you to get what they have got.				
Fashion – You model your style on someone you admire.				
Quality – You only buy certain brands or from certain stores because you think they are reliable.				
Value for money – You can't resist a good bargain.				

What influences where you buy?

	A lot	Quite a lot	Not much	Not at all
Shop name – You go to a certain shop because it's well known and you think it's fashionable.				
Good after-sales service – You go to certain shops because they are aware of your legal rights and are prepared to change goods if you aren't satisfied with them.				
Good range of items – You prefer to go to one large shop as you know they stock a good range of items.				
Convenience – You go to a shop near your home because it's more convenient or you prefer to shop from home, buying from catalogues, the internet or by satellite TV.				
The best price – You compare prices and buy from wherever offers the best price.				

Complete this questionnaire on your own. Then discuss what you learn from it about what influences you when you go shopping.

Write a statement about your shopping habits and what things influence you when you go shopping.

UNIT 16 You and your money – you as a consumer

Lesson 2 *Your Life Student Book 1*, pages 74–75
Citizenship/Economic wellbeing and financial capability – consumers and their rights

Objective: To understand the rights and responsibilities that consumers have.

Starter

Explain that consumers have rights. Ask students to suggest what these rights are. Make a list of their suggestions.

Suggested activities

- Read 'What are my rights?' on page 74. Ask the students individually to rank the rights they have as a consumer in order of importance, then to compare their rankings in a group discussion.

- Discuss what the right to redress means, then read the section on 'Consumer protection laws' on page 75. Share their experiences of making complaints about items they have bought.

Plenary

Refer to the list of rights which they suggested consumers have at the start of the lesson. How is it similar to/different from the rights described in the section 'What are my rights?'

Extension activities

Talk about what Trading Standards departments do. Invite someone from the local Trading Standards department to come into school to explain what their rights as consumers are. Prepare for their visit by getting the students in groups to draw up lists of questions to ask them.

Produce a poster to advise people of your own age about your rights when you are shopping.

UNIT 17 You and your opinions – how to express your ideas

Your Life 1/Year 7

Lesson 1 *Your Life Student Book 1*, pages 76–77
Social education – communication skills

Objective: To develop the communication skills that will enable students to express their opinions effectively in exploratory group discussions.

Starter

Introduce the topic by asking: 'What is the purpose of group discussions?' Collect the students' ideas on the board, then read the introductory section on page 76 and explain the aim of the lesson.

Suggested activities

- Ask students: 'How do you organise a good group discussion?' 'What guidelines can you follow to make sure that you have a successful discussion?' Read the guidelines 'Taking part' (page 76) and discuss them with the whole class.

- Explain that it is important always to appoint a chairperson to organise and control the discussion. Read and discuss the role of the chair in 'Chairing the discussion' (page 76). Explain that it is important also to appoint a secretary/reporter to write down the main points people make, so that they can then be reported in a class discussion.

- Read the articles about battery hens (page 77), then encourage groups to discuss their opinions about battery hens and to report their views in a class discussion.

Plenary

Ask students to reflect on the process of taking part in group discussions by inviting at least one member of each group to say how successful or unsuccessful their group discussion was, explaining the reasons why.

Extension activity

Ask students to perform the role play activity (page 77). Choose four students to be members of the panel, then split the class into four groups and ask them to assist the panel members in preparing their different views. Either act as the presenter yourself or choose a student who will perform the role effectively.

UNIT 17 You and your opinions – how to express your ideas

Your Life 1/Year 7

Lesson 2 *Your Life Student Book 1*, page 78
Social education – communication skills

Objective: To develop their ability to prepare a speech, expressing and justifying an opinion.

Resources

Copies of Copymaster 17 'Shooting and fishing – what do you think?'

Starter

Explain that when you are asked to give a speech expressing an opinion, you have to do three things: 1) research the issue, 2) prepare the speech and 3) deliver the speech. Talk about how you can research the topic (see 'Helpful hint' page 78) and how it is important to identify the arguments for and against a topic, so as to be able to argue an opinion effectively.

Suggested activities

- Read 'Preparing your speech' (page 78) and ask groups to add other arguments for and against boxing to Tony's list 'Boxing should be banned'. Then invite them to draw up their own lists for and against blood sports.

- Read 'Planning your speech' and discuss how Prisha used a flowchart to plan her speech. Draw attention to the structure of her speech: an introductory paragraph, followed by three paragraphs stating her arguments against zoos, then two paragraphs saying why the arguments for zoos are flawed, and a final paragraph in which she sums up her viewpoint.

- Ask students to use the rest of the lesson to plan a speech expressing their opinion on an animal rights topic such as zoos or battery hens. You could distribute copies of Copymaster 17 for them to read the articles and to plan a speech expressing their views on shooting and fishing.

Plenary

Conclude the lesson by getting students to share the flowcharts they drew up while planning their speeches.

17 Shooting and fishing – what do you think?

Shooting – a test of skill or a barbaric ritual?

For many people, shooting game birds – such as pheasant, partridge, grouse, duck, woodcock or snipe – is a test of skill and an opportunity to learn about the countryside. They emphasise, like the huntsman, that they derive no pleasure from the act of killing.

Their critics condemn in particular the custom of rearing birds for shooting. Enthusiasts argue that this is no different from rearing chickens, turkeys or any other livestock for food. And at least a game bird has a chance to survive.

They also claim that birds killed by a clean shot suffer less than the many which die from starvation in the winter. Only the surplus is shot, leaving a full breeding population for the future. And shooting plays an important part in shaping and preserving the rural landscape, from which all wildlife benefits.

> **"**Without the conservation management provided by country shooting, all this beautiful countryside and everything that it contains, the flowers, the wildlife and the songbirds, would have disappeared a long time ago.**"**
>
> — David Bellamy, conservationist

Fishing – a gentle pastime?

Fishing is popular all over the world. People go fishing for many reasons: to test their powers of observation and skill, to find solace in the countryside, or simply to be alone with their thoughts. Many fishermen return their catch to the water. And they generally argue that fish, being cold-blooded, do not suffer.

Critics argue, however, that fish appear to feel pain. Their lips and mouths are particularly sensitive. And many people maintain that returning fish to the water is even more cruel than killing them. The fisherman uses the animal as a plaything; most fish suffer physical damage and die as a result, or are doomed to a period of suffering.

Fishermen are also accused of disturbing wildlife and damaging the countryside. Nylon lines and hooks left on river banks can harm animals. And many swans die from hook and line injuries as well as lead poisoning from discarded weights.

In groups

Study the articles on shooting and fishing, then discuss these questions:

1. Shooting is an expensive sport: people who shoot grouse pay a lot for the privilege. But many people do not regard shooting as a sport. What are your views? Do you think it is wrong to rear birds specially for shooting?

2. Discuss the issues raised in the article on fishing. What are your views on fishing?

For your file

Write an article for a magazine column called 'In My Opinion', expressing your views on shooting and fishing.

UNIT 17 You and your opinions – how to express your ideas

Your Life 1/Year 7

Lesson 3 *Your Life Student Book 1*, page 79
Social education – communication skills

Objective: To understand how to deliver a speech effectively.

Resources

Copies of Copymaster 17A 'Assessing your speaking skills'

Starter

Read page 79 and discuss the list of points to remember when delivering a speech.

Suggested activity

- Ask some of the class to deliver their speeches. Invite the rest of the class to use the list of points to assess their delivery, giving marks out of ten. Stress that the aim of the assessment is firstly to give the speaker credit for what they did well, then to point out the things they could work to improve on next time they give a speech.

Plenary

Ask the students to discuss what they have learned from the lesson about how to deliver a speech effectively.

Extension activity

Organise a class debate. Either ask the class to choose their own topic and draft their own motion, or suggest a motion such as 'This house believes that boxing should be banned'. Choose four main speakers (a proposer and seconder, and an opposer and seconder). Help them to prepare their speeches. Open the debate with the proposer and their seconder, followed by the opposer and their seconder, then invite contributions from the rest of the class, before taking a vote.

Assessment

Using Copymaster 17A to assess their speaking skills.

17A Assessing your speaking skills

On your own, think about your speaking skills. Rate each skill as either good, quite good or not very good. Then join up with a partner and discuss what your strengths and weaknesses are, and which skills you need to work on improving.

Taking part in group discussions

	Good	Quite good	Not very good
Joining in and contributing to the discussion	☐	☐	☐
Listening to what other people say	☐	☐	☐
Waiting your turn and not interrupting	☐	☐	☐
Supporting your views with reasons and examples	☐	☐	☐
Sticking to the subject	☐	☐	☐
Introducing new ideas	☐	☐	☐
Helping to keep the discussion focused	☐	☐	☐
Summarising ideas and opinions	☐	☐	☐
Reporting the group's views in a class discussion	☐	☐	☐

Making speeches

	Good	Quite good	Not very good
Starting with an introduction which grabs the audience's attention	☐	☐	☐
Developing your arguments and supporting them with reasons	☐	☐	☐
Arguing against opposite points of view	☐	☐	☐
Emphasising key points by varying your tone	☐	☐	☐
Keeping eye-contact with the audience	☐	☐	☐
Speaking clearly and loudly enough	☐	☐	☐
Speaking fluently and not too fast	☐	☐	☐
Standing up straight and using your body language to suggest confidence	☐	☐	☐
Using technical and visual aids to put points across	☐	☐	☐
Ending your speech with an emphatic conclusion	☐	☐	☐

On a separate sheet, write a statement saying what you have learned about your speaking skills from this activity, commenting on what your strengths are and which skills you need to work on improving in the future.

UNIT 17 You and your opinions – how to express your ideas

Your Life 1/Year 7

Lesson 4 *Your Life Student Book 1*, pages 80–81
Social education – communication skills

Objective: To develop their ability to express and justify their opinions in writing.

Starter

Write the words 'purpose' and 'audience' on the board. Discuss how when you are writing to express an opinion your purpose is to persuade and how you structure and organise your writing will depend to a certain extent on your audience. Talk about how the audience will also affect your style and the language you use. For example, a letter to a friend will be more informal than a letter to a magazine, and an article for an adult audience may be written in different language to one for a teenage magazine.

Suggested activities

- Read the three emails in the section 'In my opinion' (page 80), then allow groups time to discuss which one they think should win the prize as Email of the Week. Share the reasons for their choice in a class discussion. Then ask them to work individually to write a reply to one of the emails (see 'For your file' page 80).

- Read and discuss with the class the advice given in the flowchart on how to write an article or essay (page 81). Discuss Dominic's plan for an article on Bonfire Night, drawing attention to how he has an introductory statement, followed by a separate paragraph for each point of his argument, and a final paragraph summing up his opinion. Then ask the students, in pairs, to draw up a flowchart for an article, giving their opinion on whether parents should be allowed to smack their children.

Plenary

Recap the step-by-step guidelines on how to write an article or essay and ask students to make a copy of the flowchart for their file.

Extension activity

Ask individuals to write an article for a newspaper for young people, either on a subject on which they hold a strong opinion or on one of the topics suggested in 'For your file' (page 81).

UNIT 18 You and your body – eating and exercise

Your Life 1/Year 7

Lesson 1 *Your Life Student Book 1*, pages 82–83
Keeping healthy – eating and exercise

Objective: To understand what a healthy diet is and why it is important to eat a balanced diet.

Starter

Talk about how if we eat too little food we may become ill through undernourishment, and how if we eat too much food we can become overweight. Define 'obesity' (being extremely overweight) and explain how it is linked with eating too much fat and sugar, and how it can lead to health problems, such as heart disease and diabetes. Define 'a balanced diet' (eating the right amount of a variety of different foods) and explain that the aim of the lesson is to discuss what constitutes a healthy diet.

Suggested activities

- Read 'Healthy eating facts' (page 82) and discuss, first in groups and then as a class, what it says about the different foods your body needs. Draw attention to the fact that many people eat too much fat, sugar and salt, and point out that many junk foods contain high amounts of these.

- Ask groups to read and discuss what the four children had for lunch (page 82). Then, as a class, discuss why Francesca's lunch is the healthiest, followed by Lauren's, with Sam and Darren having the least healthy meals. Ask groups to compare how healthy their own lunches are.

- Ask groups to read and discuss 'Trudy's eating diary' (page 83) and to report their views in a class discussion (see 'In pairs'). Plus points they should make include: she has three good meals a day at weekends; her lunches and suppers always include foods containing protein. Minus points include: she doesn't always have breakfast on schooldays; she needs to eat more fruit as she doesn't like vegetables; she needs to think about eating healthier snacks as cakes and biscuits are full of sugar and crisps contain too much salt.

Plenary

Read 'Healthy eating tips' (page 83) and discuss with the class the reason for each piece of advice. List on the board any further suggested tips.

Extension activities

Ask students to demonstrate their understanding of healthy eating by designing a leaflet offering advice to other students on what they should eat in order to have a healthy lunch.

Ask students to keep a food diary similar to 'Trudy's eating diary' and to rate their diet on a scale of 1–10 (1 = very unhealthy, 10 = very healthy). Discuss in groups how healthy they think their diet is and what they could do to improve it.

UNIT 18 You and your body – eating and exercise

Lesson 2 *Your Life Student Book 1*, pages 84–85

Keeping healthy – eating and exercise

Objective: To understand the importance of exercise to a healthy lifestyle and of developing a healthy attitude to your body shape.

Resources

Copies of Copymaster 18 'How healthy are you?'

Starter

Introduce the topic by asking: 'Why is it a good idea to exercise?' List the reasons the students suggest on the board, e.g. it's fun; it helps you to relax; it keeps you fit; it stops you getting fat; it's a good way of meeting people and making friends. Then read the introductory paragraph on page 84.

Suggested activities

- Read 'Some good reasons for taking exercise' (page 84) and discuss the various ways that exercise helps to keep your body in good condition. Then ask students to show their understanding of the value of exercise by preparing a reply from a magazine's agony aunt to a letter from Sam, a self-confessed couch potato who thinks exercise a waste of time, explaining to her why she should take exercise regularly.

- Read the first three paragraphs on page 85 about body shape and discuss the factors which determine it, explaining what is meant by the term 'metabolic rate'.

- Discuss Jessica Ennis's view that strong can look good.

- Read 'Losing weight' (page 85) and talk about the pressures to conform to a certain shape. Discuss whether boys are under as much pressure as girls and, if not, why there is more pressure on girls.

Plenary

Read and discuss the advice given in the article 'Going on a diet' (page 85). Then recap what eating a balanced diet means and repeat the reasons why it is important to get enough exercise.

Extension activities

Challenge individuals to complete the quiz 'How healthy are you?' on Copymaster 18. Then ask them to write a comment saying what their answers tell them about how healthy their diet is and whether they are taking enough exercise.

Ask individuals to keep an exercise diary for a week, and then to set themselves a realistic target for getting themselves fitter if they discover that they need to do so (see 'In pairs', page 84).

Organise a debate either on the motion: 'This house believes that exercise is a waste of time' or 'This house believes there should be twenty minutes compulsory PE every school day.'

18 How healthy are you?

Do you have a healthy diet? Do you take enough exercise to keep you fit?

Look at this quiz. Circle either 'a' or 'b' in answer to each question, then check what your answers tell you about how you eat and how you exercise.

 1 What's your idea of a brilliant breakfast?
a a big fry-up with eggs and bacon
b cereal, toast and fruit juice

 2 How do you usually get around?
a take the bus or ask Dad for a lift
b walk or cycle

 3 How often do you eat fresh fruit?
a less than once a day
b once a day or more

 4 What do you do when you've got a PE lesson?
a do as little as you can get away with
b really go for it and work up a sweat

 5 What type of bread do you usually eat?
a white
b brown or wholemeal

 6 What do you do when you go swimming?
a mess around on the flumes or relax in a whirlpool
b swim a few lengths or race your friends

 7 What do you usually eat for a quick snack?
a a bar of chocolate or a packet of crisps
b a sandwich or a piece of fruit

 8 What do you usually do when you go to the park?
a sit around chatting to friends
b play football or run around

 9 Which do you eat more often?
a chips
b jacket potatoes

 10 What's your idea of a good Sunday morning?
a having a long lie-in
b playing your favourite sport

 11 Do you enjoy sugar in tea or coffee or on cereal?
a most of the time
b sometimes or never

 12 How well do you know your local sports centre?
a you sometimes go there to meet your friends in the café
b pretty well – you go there a lot

 13 Do you ever eat snacks in bed?
a yes, quite often
b no, hardly ever

 14 Which do you spend more time doing?
a watching TV
b playing your favourite sport

What your answers say about how you eat and exercise

Mostly 'a's You'd rather take it easy than rush around being sporty. There's nothing wrong with that, but you perhaps ought to think about taking more exercise. You don't want to let yourself become a couch potato! And think about your diet, too. Yours isn't as healthy as it might be.

A mixture of 'a's and 'b's Some of your habits are healthier than others. So you need to think a bit more about what you're eating. And if you want to get really fit, then you'll have to take a bit more exercise.

Mostly 'b's You take good care of your body. You're aware of which foods it's healthy to eat and you're getting plenty of exercise. But don't overdo it. Make sure you have time to relax and that you get enough rest, and you'll stay fit and healthy.

UNIT 19 You as a citizen – how Britain is governed

Lesson 1 *Your Life Student Book 1*, pages 86 and 88
Citizenship – understanding Britain's government

> **Objective:** To understand what Parliament is and what the monarch's role is in Britain's government.

Resources

Copies of Copymaster 19 'Should the monarchy be abolished?'

Starter

Ask the students: 'What sort of system of government does Britain have?' 'What other forms of government are there in other countries?' Explain that Britain is a parliamentary democracy and point out how this is different from countries which are totalitarian states, such as China, and dictatorships, such as North Korea.

Suggested activities

- Discuss how Parliament is made up of the House of Commons, the House of Lords and the British Sovereign, then read the first two paragraphs on page 86.

- Explain that the power in Parliament has passed over the centuries from the monarch and the House of Lords to the House of Commons. Then read 'Who runs Parliament?' (page 86).

- Explain that Britain is a constitutional monarchy. Read 'What is a constitutional monarchy?' (page 88) and discuss what the monarch's role is in Britain's government.

- Invite groups to discuss the views on whether or not the monarchy has a place in 21st century Britain (page 88). Use Copymaster 19 and encourage groups to draw up lists of arguments For and Against keeping the monarchy.

Plenary

Recap on what the monarch's role is in Britain's government and hold a class discussion of their views on the monarchy.

Extension activity

Encourage individuals to research the history of how the House of Commons has become the most powerful part of Parliament by using the internet and drawing the timeline suggested in 'For your file' (page 86).

19 Should the monarchy be abolished?

YES

The monarchy is an anachronism. The royal family has no place in a modern democracy.

No one elected the monarch. The head of state should be elected for a set number of years. It is ridiculous to have a hereditary monarch, who is there for life.

The monarchy costs a lot of money and is funded by the taxpayer. The cost of security for the royal family is exorbitant.

The monarch has too much power and shouldn't be involved in Parliament at all.

To say that the royal family encourages tourism isn't entirely correct. We would attract more tourists if Buckingham Palace were open to the public and all the art treasures owned by the royal family were on public display.

The royal family should keep their views to themselves and not involve themselves in politics at all. Too much publicity is given to what Prince Charles and other royals do and say. We'd be better off without them.

NO

The monarch has no real power, but plays an important part in government that would otherwise have to be played by a president.

It is crucial to have an institution at the centre of British society that is politically neutral.

The royal family represents Britain's culture and attracts tourism.

The royal family take their role seriously and do a lot of good through their charity work.

Having a president would cost as much as having a monarch. The royal family provides value for money.

The monarchy is traditional and royal occasions provide a focus for national celebrations and pride in being British.

 In groups

In groups, discuss these views, then hold a class debate and vote on the motion that this house believes that the monarchy should be abolished.

UNIT 19 You as a citizen – how Britain is governed

Your Life 1/Year 7

Lesson 2 *Your Life Student Book 1*, pages 87 and 89
Citizenship – understanding Britain's government

> **Objective:** To understand how a government is formed, what Parliament does and how laws are also made by the European Union and regional governments.

Resources

Copies of Copymaster 19A 'Understanding Britain's government'

Starter

Ask: 'What happens after a general election?' 'How is a government formed?' Read 'What happens after a general election' (page 87), explaining step-by-step what happens.

Suggested activities

- Ask the students to read 'What does Parliament do?' (page 87) and discuss how important each of its functions are. Talk about how individuals can take up individual issues with their local MP at their regular surgeries. Ask: 'Who is the local MP?' 'Where and when does s/he hold a surgery?'

- Read 'What is the civil service?' (page 87) and talk about what civil servants do.

- Discuss what the European Union is and how Great Britain is part of the EU, then read the paragraph about Britain's membership of the EU (page 89).

- Read the section on 'Regional government' on page 89. Discuss what devolution is and how Scotland, Wales and Northern Ireland have different types of regional governments.

Plenary

Either invite the students in pairs to draw up their own Test Yourself quizzes or use Copymaster 19A to assess what the students have learned about Parliament and how Britain is governed.

Extension activity

Encourage groups to research the arguments for and against an independent Scotland (see 'In groups' page 89), then hold a class debate on the motion: 'That this house believes that Scotland should remain a part of the United Kingdom'.

ASSESSMENT COPYMASTER

19A Understanding Britain's government

Choose the correct ending and write **a** or **b** in the box.

1. Britain's system of government is
   a) an elective dictatorship.
   b) a parliamentary democracy.

2. Parliament consists of
   a) MPs, peers and the Sovereign.
   b) MPs and civil servants.

3. At a general election people vote to choose who will sit in
   a) the House of Commons.
   b) the House of Commons and the House of Lords.

4. A general election has to be held
   a) once every 3 years.
   b) once every 5 years.

5. The House of Lords is
   a) less powerful than the House of Commons.
   b) more powerful than the House of Commons.

6. The Sovereign
   a) can refuse to give approval to new laws.
   b) can not refuse to give approval to new laws.

7. The monarch
   a) can support which ever political party she chooses.
   b) must remain politically neutral.

8. The Head of State in Britain is
   a) the Prime Minister.
   b) the monarch.

9. MPs are appointed to the Cabinet by
   a) the Prime Minister.
   b) the head of the civil service.

10. In Britain,
   a) the constitution was written in the 19th century.
   b) there is no written constitution.

UNIT 20 You and the world of work – attitudes to work

Your Life 1/Year 7

Lesson 1 *Your Life Student Book 1*, pages 90–91
Citizenship/Economic wellbeing and financial capability – understanding work

Objective: To share views on what work is and to discuss the different reasons why people work.

Starter

Ask the students to think about what the word 'work' means, then share their ideas in a class discussion. Draw a spider diagram showing their different ideas.

Suggested activities

- Read 'What is work?' (page 90). In groups get them to discuss the teenagers' views of what work is and to agree on a definition of work, then to share their definitions in a class discussion.

- Explain that while it is true that most people work in order to get money, there may be other reasons too. Read 'Why do people work?' on page 91. Hold a class discussion of the different reasons why people work.

Plenary

Remind students of what they said work is at the start of the lesson by referring to the spider diagram. Have they altered their views as a result of their discussions?

Extension activity

Ask them to imagine that they have been asked to write an article for a teenage magazine about what work is and why people do it. Tell them to interview a number of adults with different jobs and to include quotes of what they say during the interviews.

UNIT 20 You and the world of work – attitudes to work

Your Life 1/Year 7

Lesson 2 *Your Life Student Book 1*, pages 92–93
Citizenship/Economic wellbeing and financial capability – understanding work

Objective: To understand that work has both advantages and disadvantages and to explore students' views on what they want from work.

Resources

Copies of Copymaster 20 'Comparing jobs'

Starter

Introduce the idea that work has both advantages and disadvantages. Draw two columns on the board, labelled advantages and disadvantages. Hold a class discussion in which students suggest what some of the advantages and disadvantages of work are.

Suggested activities

● Read 'The advantages and disadvantages of work' (page 92). Ask students to think of three different jobs which they currently think they might like to do. Get them to complete Copymaster 20 'Comparing jobs', then to share what they have learned about the advantages and disadvantages of the jobs in a class discussion.

● Discuss the differences between being employed and being self-employed. Ask: 'What do you see as the advantages and disadvantages of being self-employed?'

● Read 'What do you want from work?' (page 93), then ask the students to write a brief statement about what they would want from work, before sharing their views in a group discussion (see 'In groups' page 93).

Plenary

Look again at the list of advantages and disadvantages of work that the students suggested at the beginning of the lesson and add any further points that have come up during the course of the lesson.

Extension activity

Ask the students to choose a job that a family member or family friend does and to talk to them about the benefits and drawbacks of the job. They then write about what they see as the advantages and disadvantages of that job (see 'For your file' page 92).

Comparing jobs

What are the advantages and disadvantages of different jobs?

Choose three jobs and list the advantages and disadvantages of each job. Things to think about:

well paid/low paid

repetitive/varied

uninteresting/very interesting

high status/low status

no responsibility/high responsibility

long training/short training

opportunity for career development/little opportunity for career development

working with others/working on your own

heavy work/light work

shift work/not shift work

of great benefit to society/not of great social benefit

stressful/not stressful

Job	Advantages	Disadvantages
1		
2		
3		

UNIT 21 You and the community – taking action: raising money for charity

Objective: To discuss raising money for a charity and to decide from a group of charities which one to support.

Resources

Leaflets produced by the charities which they are considering (optional)

Starter

Read out this statement: 'I know I should give money to charity, but I hate it when I see a charity collection in the street and feel guilty if I don't give anything'. Ask: 'What's your view of giving money to charity?' Invite students to share their views in a class discussion.

Suggested activity

● Ask groups to read the information about the eight different charities on pages 94–95 (together with any leaflets that you have been able to obtain from the charities) in order to decide on which two charities they recommend should be supported. Write on the board a list of points for them to consider:

Do you want to support a charity that helps –

- animals or people?
- people in the UK or in developing countries?
- conservation of the environment?
- people with disabilities?
- the homeless?
- people whose lives are in danger?

● Invite students to prepare a statement giving their first and second choices of charity, using the description of what the charity does to help support their decision. Then share their views in a class discussion before voting on which two charities they would choose to support.

Plenary

Discuss together the reasons why students rejected some charities and preferred others. How difficult was it for them to choose? What were the particular reasons for choosing the two charities they decided to support?

Extension activity

Ask students to imagine that someone has offered to donate £50 to one of the eight charities described on these pages. Suggest students write an email to the person, explaining which of the charities they think they should support and why.

UNIT 21 You and the community – taking action: raising money for charity

Your Life 1/Year 7

Lesson 2 *Your Life Student Book 1*, pages 96–97

Citizenship – being an active citizen

Objective: To choose a local charity to support, to decide on and plan a fundraising activity.

Resources

Copies of Copymaster 21 'How to hold a committee meeting'

Copies of Copymaster 21A 'How to organise a fundraising event'

Starter

Introduce the idea of raising money for a local charity by asking for suggestions of local charities the students might support. Read the two introductory paragraphs on page 96, then make a list of suggested charities on the board. Be prepared to prompt, if necessary, by making a list of possible charities prior to the lesson.

Suggested activities

- Ask groups to discuss the list of local charities and to choose one which they would like to support. Invite them to share their views in a class discussion.

- Study the 'Fundraising activities' on page 96. Can the class suggest any others? Add them to the list, then have a class discussion and hold a vote to choose one.

- Read 'Organising a fundraising event' on page 97 and discuss which jobs the class decided needed doing when organising a second-hand sale. Talk about the groups they set up and what the responsibilities of each group were. Ask the class to make a similar list of jobs that need to be done for their planned event and to list in detail the responsibilities of the group in charge of each job.

Plenary

Discuss the steps you would need to take in order actually to organise the event. Introduce the idea of setting up a planning committee (see 'The planning committee' on page 97). Discuss together whether or not it is practicable to organise the events and make a decision on whether or not you are going to go ahead.

Extension activities

Read and discuss Copymaster 21. Discuss the responsibilities of a) the chairperson, b) the secretary and c) all the committee members. Then ask groups to draw up an agenda for the meeting of a planning committee organising either the event the class chose or a sale of second-hand books and toys.

Plan and hold your fundraising event for a local charity.

Assessment

Use Copymaster 21A to assess understanding of organising a fundraising event.

21 How to hold a committee meeting

When you are holding a fundraising event, you will need to set up a planning committee. To ensure that everything gets done, the committee will need to have formal meetings. This sheet explains how to hold a committee meeting.

Once you have decided who is going to be on the committee, you need to appoint someone to be the **chairperson** and someone to be the **secretary**. The chairperson and secretary are responsible for calling and organising the meetings.

The secretary is responsible for:
1. Before the meeting – giving a copy of the agenda to all the committee members.
2. During the meeting – taking notes of the most important points made in the discussions and of any decisions that are made.
3. After the meeting – writing up a record of the meeting in the form of a set of 'minutes', and sending a copy of the minutes to each committee member.

It is the responsibility of all committee members:
1. To attend all the meetings or send their apologies in advance to the secretary.
2. To join in the discussions, listening to other people's views without interrupting and waiting for the chairperson to invite them to speak.
3. To ensure that they stick to the point when they speak and that the points they make are connected to the particular agenda item that is being considered.

The chairperson is responsible for:
1. Drawing up the agenda (in consultation with the other committee members). The agenda is a list of the items to be discussed at the meeting.
2. Beginning the meeting once everyone is present.
3. Introducing each agenda item and controlling the discussion by inviting members to take turns at commenting on the item. For example, they might give an update on what action has been taken, or make suggestions as to what else needs to be done.
4. Organising a vote by asking for a show of hands on a proposal, if there is disagreement about whether a particular course of action should be taken.
5. Making sure that not too much time is spent discussing one item, so that all the items on the agenda are discussed before the end of the meeting.
6. After all the agenda items have been discussed, asking members to raise any other items under what is known as 'any other business'.
7. Closing the meeting by arranging the date of the next meeting.

 In groups

Imagine that your class has decided to organise a sale of second-hand books and toys to raise money for charity. Draw up an agenda for the first meeting of your planning committee.

21A | How to organise a fundraising event

Explain how to organise a fundraising event for a charity by either writing a step-by-step guide or drawing a flowchart. Include advice on:

● how to decide what sort of fundraising event to hold

● how to plan and organise the event

● how to present your donation to the charity

● how to review the project.

UNIT 22 You and other people – people with disabilities

Your Life 1/Year 7

Lesson 1 *Your Life Student Book 1*, pages 98–99
Social education – understanding disability

Objective: To understand what is meant by disability, to explain how people become disabled and to explore what it is like to have a disability.

Resources

Copies of Copymaster 22 'Becoming disabled'

Starter

Ask the students: 'What do you understand by the term 'disability'?' Read 'Defining disability' (page 98) and discuss the difference between the two definitions. Then read 'What is a disability?' (page 98) and explain the point it makes about how physical and social barriers disable a person with an impairment from participating fully in the community.

Suggested activities

● Read 'Becoming disabled' (page 98) and discuss the various ways that impairments occur. Read and discuss the information on Copymaster 22 about the most common medical conditions which cause an impairment. Invite pairs to show their understanding of the information by compiling a quiz, then to swap their quiz with another pair.

● Read 'What is it like to have a disability?' (page 99). Discuss in groups, then as a class, what they learn from the statements about how people with a disability feel about the attitudes of able-bodied people towards them.

Plenary

Read 'In groups' (page 99) and discuss how the language people use when discussing disabilities can be negative and discriminate by stereotyping people. Recap what the students have learned about what it is like to have a disability. Emphasise that people with disabilities want the able-bodied to recognise them as individuals and as people, rather than to stereotype them or pity them because of their impairment.

Extension activity

Invite individuals or pairs to use the internet to research one of the medical conditions which can cause an impairment. They can then either produce a fact sheet on it or prepare a short talk about it to give to the rest of the class.

22 Becoming disabled

This sheet gives general information about some of the most common medical conditions which can cause physical or mental impairment. It is important to remember that the degree to which each person's life is affected will depend on the individual, his or her personal circumstances and the social conditions he or she faces.

Autism
- Research suggests that this is a physical problem which affects the parts of the brain which process language and information received from the senses.
- May be caused by a chemical imbalance in the brain.
- Affects a person's communication and development skills.

Brain Damage
- The brain is responsible for controlling everything that happens to the body.
- Damage either before birth or as a result of an accident can lead to a variety of impairments, both physical and mental, depending on which part of the brain is affected and how badly.

Cerebral Palsy
- Caused by *brain damage* occurring at birth or in young children.
- May result in problems of movement, *sensory impairment*, learning difficulties or *epilepsy*.
- Effects vary from an unsteady walk to multiple disabilities.

Cystic Fibrosis
- Passed on genetically.
- Causes the mucus in the body to thicken, blocking the air passages, making breathing difficult.
- People with cystic fibrosis will cough frequently, which helps to clear the lungs. They may need to do special exercises and take plenty of rest breaks.
- Exercise and medical drugs can help control the condition.

Down's Syndrome
- Caused by an irregularity in the cells of a baby during pregnancy.
- People with Down's Syndrome may have unusual facial features and have specific physical or mental impairments, such as poor hearing or vision and difficulty in learning.

Epilepsy
- A disorder of the nervous system, which causes people to have seizures or fits which may take the form of a sudden loss of consciousness or uncontrollable movements.
- The frequency and length of these attacks varies from person to person, and they may be brought on by specific factors, such as flashing lights.

Multiple Sclerosis (MS)
- A disease of the central nervous system which causes damage to the protective covering around the nerves.
- The signals from the nerves to the brain and spine are not transmitted properly, resulting in a range of physical problems, from difficulty in moving to visual impairment.

Muscular Dystrophy
- An inherited condition which becomes more severe as a child grows older.
- Causes a gradual breakdown of the muscle fibres, leading to a weakening of all the muscles.
- A person may eventually need to use a wheelchair or a brace to keep the spine straight.

Sensory Impairments
- *Aural impairment* is the term to describe any kind of hearing problem, from being 'hard of hearing' to total deafness.
- *Visual impairment* refers to a serious loss of sight which cannot be corrected.
- *Speech or language impairment* means difficulty with speech.
- Sensory impairments may be due to a problem before birth, or may be the result of disease or damage to a particular part of the body.

Spina Bifida
- A condition which means that the bones of the spine are incomplete.
- Usually results in some paralysis, depending on the severity of the damage to the spine.
- A person with spina bifida may have no feeling in parts of the body below the point at which the damage to their spine has occurred.

Spinal Injury
- An inability to move a particular part of the body.
- May occur for a variety of reasons, usually through some form of damage to the spinal cord, either through disease or accident.
- The two most commonly heard words used to describe the different forms of paralysis are *paraplegia* – paralysis affecting the legs only – and *quadriplegia* – where all limbs are affected.

Stroke
- A sudden loss of brain function, caused by a brief interference to the brain's blood supply.
- Can be fatal, but many people make good recoveries.
- Some people may be left with permanent physical impairment, such as loss of speech or paralysis of part of the body.

UNIT 22 You and other people – people with disabilities

Your Life 1/Year 7

Lesson 2 *Your Life Student Book 1*, pages 100–101
Social education – understanding disability

> **Objective:** To understand the needs of people with disabilities and to challenge the stereotyped view of people with disabilities.

Starter

Ask the students to consider the following: 'What would it be like to be unable to use your arms or your legs? To be in a wheelchair? To be blind? To be unable to hear or speak?' 'What would you need in order to be able to live a full and independent life?' Brainstorm and list what the special needs of people with disabilities are. Then read the introductory paragraph on page 100.

Suggested activities

● Read the sections about 'Meeting the needs of people with disabilities' on page 100. Hold a class discussion and encourage students to talk about people they know who have disabilities and how their needs are met.

● Encourage groups to discuss the questions in 'Transport and access in your area' (page 100), to keep notes of their discussions and to report their suggestions in a class discussion. Then ask them to work together to draft an email to the local paper, explaining any problems they have identified and making suggestions about what could be done about them.

● Read the articles on page 101. Ask students to talk about people they know with disabilities who have achieved successes, and about famous people with disabilities and their achievements (e.g. ex-Home Secretary David Blunkett, physicist and author Stephen Hawking, and wheelchair athlete Tanni Grey-Thompson). Discuss how much media coverage is given to people with disabilities. Is it true that they are 'largely invisible' because they are under-represented on TV, newspapers and magazines?

Plenary

Conclude by discussing these two myths: 1) People with disabilities can't take care of themselves; 2) People with disabilities can't have successful careers. Discuss how with the right support and facilities, people with disabilities are quite capable of leading full, independent lives and achieving success.

Extension activities

Ask the students to invite someone with a disability to come and talk to the class. Prepare for the visit by getting them to draw up a list of questions they want to ask.

Suggest students interview a person with a disability, and write an article about them based on the interview. Collect the articles into a booklet.

UNIT 23 You and global issues – resources, waste and recycling

Your Life 1/Year 7

Lesson 1 *Your Life Student Book 1*, pages 102–103
Citizenship – understanding global issues

> **Objective:** To understand why reducing waste is a global issue and to discuss the benefits of recycling.

Resources

Copies of Copymaster 23 'Are you a waste watcher?'

Copies of Copymaster 23A 'Understanding recycling'

Starter

Explain that we live in a throwaway society. Each year, every household throws away on average one tonne of rubbish. Ask: 'What happens to our rubbish?' Explain that most of it is either dumped as landfill or burned in incinerators. Discuss what recycling is and how much of our rubbish consists of paper, metal and plastics that could be recycled.

Suggested activities

- Read 'Stop talking rubbish, start thinking about reducing waste' and 'Recycling facts' (page 102). Challenge pairs to show understanding of the articles by making a list of ten key facts they learn from the articles about waste and recycling.

- Read 'Incineration and landfill' (page 103). Discuss the reasons given in the article to suggest that both incineration and landfill are bad for the environment. Then ask groups to discuss whether they would support or oppose the building of a new incinerator near their home.

- Invite groups to list their ideas about what they could do at home to reduce waste and to increase the amount of waste that they could recycle. Then share their ideas in a class discussion.

Plenary

Ask individuals to make a short statement answering 'Why I am concerned about waste' and to list their reasons on the board.

Extension activities

Ask students to design a poster to encourage young people to get involved in recycling.

Challenge individuals to complete the quiz on Copymaster 23, to check their scores, then to discuss in pairs what each of them needs to do to become more of a 'waste watcher'.

Ask students to use the internet to find out further information on recycling. Visit the websites of pressure groups, such as Friends of the Earth (www.foe.co.uk).

Assessment

Use Copymaster 23A to assess understanding of recycling.

Answers: Across – 1. green, 2. reduce, 4. pollution, 5. skip, 6. energy, 9. cans, 11. plastic 13. incinerator. Down – 1. gases, 3. conserve, 4. paper, 7. glass, 8. recycle, 10. acid, 12. iron.

23 Are you a waste watcher?

Circle your answers to these questions, then check your score.
Discuss with a partner the ways in which you need to change your
habits in order to become a waste watcher.

 Do you recycle your old comics and magazines rather than just throw them out?

a Usually **b** Sometimes **c** Never

 Do you insist on cycling or walking short distances instead of going in the car?

a Usually **b** Sometimes **c** Never

 Do you recycle cans?

a Usually **b** Sometimes **c** Never

 Do you refuse unnecessary packaging, for example, when someone offers to put a single item of shopping in a bag?

a Usually **b** Sometimes **c** Never

 Do you switch off the TV when nobody is watching it?

a Usually **b** Sometimes **c** Never

 Do you take a bag with you when you are sent out to do the shopping?

a Usually **b** Sometimes **c** Never

 Do you give your old toys to second-hand shops or jumble sales rather than throw them away?

a Usually **b** Sometimes **c** Never

 Do you make sure that your family recycles glass bottles and jars?

a Usually **b** Sometimes **c** Never

 When you are the last person out of a room, do you switch off the light?

a Usually **b** Sometimes **c** Never

 Do you switch the tap on and off while you clean your teeth rather than leave it running all the time?

a Usually **b** Sometimes **c** Never

 Do you try to get the rest of the family to buy recycled products, for example, toilet rolls made from recycled paper?

a Usually **b** Sometimes **c** Never

 When your family uses the washing machine do you try to make sure that there is a full load?

a Usually **b** Sometimes **c** Never

Score check

Mostly 'a's – Keep up the good work! You've clearly declared war on waste.

Mostly 'b's – You're doing something to cut down on waste. But you could be doing more!

Mostly 'c's – Either you can't be bothered or you don't care. You've got a lot to do before you can call yourself a waste watcher.

23A Understanding recycling

Complete this word puzzle to check your knowledge about recycling.

Clues across

1. The name of the political party whose main policies are to take care of the environment. (5)

2. Recycling schemes _ _ _ _ _ _ waste. (6)

4. Recycling schemes cut down the _ _ _ _ _ _ _ _ _ that results from burying waste in landfill sites. (9)

5. You can put your old newspapers in one at a recycling centre. (4)

6. Recycling uses less _ _ _ _ _ _ than producing things from new materials. (6)

9. Aluminium _ _ _ _ have a high scrap value. (4)

11. Soft drinks containers made of this can be recycled as filling in such things as sleeping bags. (7)

13. Waste can be burned in one. (11)

Clues down

1. Decaying waste in landfill sites produces _ _ _ _ _ such as methane. (5)

3. Recycling schemes help to _ _ _ _ _ _ _ _ the Earth's natural resources. (8)

4. Recycling this saves trees, by cutting down the amount of wood pulp that has to be imported to make it. (5)

7. Bottles made of this can be washed and reused or crushed and recycled. (5)

8. To reclaim things for further use. (7)

10. Saving energy by recycling reduces the release of gases that contribute to this sort of rain. (4)

12. Recycling steel cans means we use up less of the Earth's supply of _ _ _ _ ore. (4)

Your Life 1/Year 7

Lesson 2 *Your Life Student Book 1*, pages 104–105
Citizenship – understanding global issues

> **Objective:** To carry out an audit of how the school manages waste and conserves energy and to explore ways of increasing the amount it recycles.

Resources

Copies of the school's recycling policy

Starter

Explain what an audit is and that the first step towards reducing waste at school is to carry out an audit.

Suggested activities

- Get the students to complete the questionnaire in pairs (pages 104–105) and to decide whether the school is an environmental success or an environmental disaster, then to compare their scores. Hold a class discussion and decide where the school scored well and where it might be doing more.

- Hand out copies of the school's recycling policy. Encourage them to suggest ways in which it could be made more effective.

- Read 'Recycling is fashionable at local school' (page 105). Get students in groups to visit the local council's website to find out about its recycling schemes, to discuss what it is doing and whether there are any schemes that the school might get involved in.

Plenary

Summarise their suggestions for making the school's recycling policy more effective and choose someone from the class to present their views to a school council meeting.

Extension activity

Ask students individually to draft an article for a local newspaper explaining what the school is doing to reduce waste, to recycle materials and to save energy and why they think it is important to do so.

UNIT 24 You and your achievements – reviewing your progress

Your Life 1/Year 7

Lesson 1 *Your Life Student Book 1*, pages 106–107
Personal wellbeing – reviewing your progress

> **Objective:** To review your progress and achievements in Year 7 and to set yourself targets for the future.

Resources

Copies of Copymaster 24 'Your skills'

Starter

Explain that the lesson is the first part of a three-step process: 1) Thinking about your achievements; 2) Discussing your achievements and progress with your tutor and setting targets for Year 8; 3) Writing a statement for your Progress File.

Suggested activities

- Read 'Your subjects' (page 106) and ask the students to use the five-star system to give themselves grades, before writing a statement about their progress in each subject.

- Read 'Your skills' (page 106) and ask the students to study Copymaster 24, then to write a statement reviewing their progress in each of the skills.

- Read 'Your activities' (page 106) and ask the students to write a statement about their most significant achievements in their activities during the year.

- Read 'Your attitude and behaviour' (page 107) and ask the students to write a statement summing up their attitude and behaviour during the year.

Plenary

Allocate times for individuals to meet with you to discuss their statements and set targets, allowing them further time in tutor time (as necessary) to complete their statements.

Extension activities

Hold the discussion meetings with individuals. During the discussion, encourage them to note down any points you make, especially when agreeing targets at the end of the discussion (see 'Discussing your progress'/'Setting targets', page 107).

Ask the students to draft statements to go in their Record of Achievements (see 'Recording your achievements', page 107).

24 Your skills

Study the list of skills (below) and write a short comment on each one, saying how much you think you have improved that skill during the past year (A lot? Quite a lot? or Only a little?). Support your statement by referring to something you have done during the year.

For example, here's what Paul wrote about his study skills:

> My study skills have improved a lot. I've learned how to pick out the main points when I take notes, rather than just copy everything out.

Communication skills

* Has your written work improved? Are you better at conveying information, and at presenting arguments and using evidence to support your views?

* Has your reading ability developed? Can you read and understand more complex information? Have you improved your ability to analyse and interpret different types of text?

* Have your speaking and listening skills improved? Do you join in group discussions more? Are you more confident about presenting a report or arguing a point of view?

Numeracy skills

* Has your ability to handle numerical information improved?

* Has your ability to collect and present numerical information in different ways improved?

Study skills

* Have your skills at doing projects improved? Are you better at finding information from different sources and at making notes?

* Have your skills at organising your homework improved?

* Are you better at doing revision and preparing for tests?

Problem-solving skills

* Has your ability to plan investigations and enquiries improved?

* Has your ability to ask questions and make observations improved?

* Are you better at analysing results, forming opinions and drawing conclusions?

* Are you better at making suggestions and offering solutions to problems?

Personal and social skills

* Have you settled in well? Has your ability to deal with new situations developed and your self-confidence improved?

* Have you worked well in groups during the year? Has your ability to be a good team member developed?

* Are you better at listening to and understanding other people's points of view?

* Has your knowledge of your own strengths and weaknesses increased?

ICT skills

* Are you better at thinking of ways to use computers to solve problems?

* Have your word processing skills improved?

* Are you better at finding information that is stored in computers?

* Are you better at using computers to store and process information?

UNIT 1 You and your feelings – self-esteem

Your Life 2/Year 8

Lesson 1 *Your Life Student Book 2*, pages 6–7
Personal wellbeing – developing self-esteem

Objective: To understand what self-esteem is, why it is important and how to build up self-esteem.

Starter

Write these words on the board: 'self-esteem', 'self-confidence', 'self-centredness', 'self-consciousness', 'self-importance' and 'self-possession'. Explain to the students what they mean, then draw two columns and list those which describe positive qualities (self-esteem, self-confidence and self-possession) and those which describe negative qualities (self-centredness, self-consciousness and self-importance). Then read 'Self-esteem' (page 6). Discuss why self-esteem is important and how having self-esteem is different from being conceited.

Suggested activities

- Explain that identifying your strong points is one way you can build up your self-esteem. Ask individuals to make lists of their own strengths and weaknesses, then to discuss them in pairs (see 'Know yourself' page 6).

- Read 'Feeling confident' (page 6) and Erica Stewart's tips on how to build your self-esteem (page 7). Invite groups to discuss Erica Stewart's advice and to report their ideas in a class discussion.

- Ask groups to discuss the six statements on page 7, to say why they agree or disagree with the statements, then to share their views in a class discussion.

Plenary

Recap the importance of developing self-esteem by asking students to suggest the reasons why self-esteem is important and listing them on the board. Talk about how people with high self-esteem are likely to be happier and to get into less trouble than those with low self-esteem. Explain how having low self-esteem can lead people into trouble by acting foolishly in order to try to impress other people and win popularity, or by taking out their negative feelings about themselves through bullying or other forms of antisocial behaviour.

Extension activity

Ask individuals to write statements aimed at building up their self-image by reflecting on positive aspects of themselves.

Eight Positive Things About Myself

- Two things people say they like about me
- Two things which I'm good at
- Two things I've successfully achieved
- Two reasons friends value my friendship

Individuals can then choose whether to share what they write with others or to keep it confidential.

UNIT 1 You and your feelings – self-esteem

Objective: To develop self-confidence by discussing what causes shyness and how to cope with it and how to deal with and learn from mistakes.

Resources

Copies of Copymaster 1 'Say goodbye to being shy!'

Starter

Write the words 'introvert' and 'extrovert' on the board and explain that an introvert is someone who is inward looking, quiet, thoughtful and often rather shy, while an extrovert is outward looking, lively, boisterous and outgoing. Talk about how no one is a complete introvert or extrovert. Explain that if you're more of an extrovert you probably find coping with social situations easier than if you're more of an introvert. However, whatever type of person you are, there are times when you may feel shy or embarrassed, so you need to know how to deal with such feelings.

Suggested activities

- Read 'Coping with shyness' (page 8). Ask groups to discuss situations in which people are likely to feel shy and the advice on how to deal with shyness, then to share their ideas in a class discussion.

- Read the articles on 'Coping with classroom mistakes' and 'Learning from your mistakes' (page 9). Ask groups to identify three key pieces of advice given in the articles and to explain in a class discussion why they think those are the most important points.

Plenary

Ask individuals to write a short statement for their files about making mistakes, explaining what they have learned about how to cope with mistakes. Then invite some of them to share their statements with the rest of the class.

Extension activity

Read the article 'Say goodbye to being shy!' on Copymaster 1. Ask groups to discuss the advice, then to demonstrate what they have learned about how to cope with shyness by preparing replies to the two letters, offering advice on how to overcome shyness.

Say goodbye to being shy!

So you're shy? Help yourself to beat it!

Most of us are shy in certain situations – even the people who seem really confident. Their secret is that they've learned how to deal with shyness. With effort and practice, you can overcome shyness too so you control it, instead of it controlling you …

If you feel like everyone's watching you every time you walk into a room – tell yourself they're not and believe it. People may look over out of curiosity – you probably do the same yourself – but they'll soon lose interest unless you're doing cartwheels or something like that!

Be brave. You'll never overcome shyness if you don't make a real effort, so you have to try to speak to people. You don't need to be fantastically funny or intelligent – even just saying hello and talking about the weather is a step in the right direction.

If you're naturally quiet-natured, it's no use trying to turn yourself into a loud, exciting person. It's unlikely to work out and you'll just come across as being really false. Just try to be yourself, but talk a bit more.

Asking a question is always a great way to re-start a conversation. Most people like the chance to talk about themselves, and while they're talking it gives you time to gather your thoughts and think what to say next.

Learn to laugh at yourself! Most of us make a fool of ourselves at sometime or other and if you can laugh it off, it means other people won't make a big deal out of it. Even if you don't really think it's funny and are cringing inside, your reaction can make all the difference to the way others think of you.

Take care over your appearance. It may sound strange, but if you don't feel good about how you look, it makes you even more self-conscious and shy.

Work out what makes you most shy and find a way to overcome it – then practise, practise, practise. Some people get embarrassed reading aloud in class and find that practising it at home helps build their confidence.

Lots of people get embarrassed because shyness makes them blush. But the more you get annoyed or embarrassed about it, the more you seem to end up blushing! So try your best not to get worked up about it and you'll find that blushing goes away much more quickly.

In groups

Discuss the advice that is given in the article on how to cope with shyness. Which do you think are the three most helpful tips?

Write a reply to Shara's and Tristan's emails (right) offering them advice on how to overcome their shyness.

> Whenever I go somewhere I get really worked up. I feel shy and nervous and never know what to do. I've started turning down invitations, because I don't want to end up just standing there on my own with no one to talk to. What can I do? – Shara

> When I walk into a room I feel as if everyone's looking at me. Then if someone starts talking to me I get tongue-tied, which makes me even more embarrassed. What makes things really awful is that I blush easily. I hate being so shy. – Tristan

UNIT 2 You and your body – drugs and drugtaking

Your Life 2/Year 8

Lesson 1 *Your Life Student Book 2*, pages 10–11
Keeping healthy – drugs and drugtaking

> **Objective:** To explore myths about drugtaking, and to understand the risks of taking cannabis and taking ecstasy.

Resources

Copies of Copymaster 2 'How much do you know about ecstasy?'

Starter

Explain what a myth is (something which people believe which is not fact but fiction) and that there are lots of myths about drugs and drugtaking. Tell the students that you are going to read an article about drug myths. Before giving out the books, read out the four statements from 'Drugs – facts and fictions' (page 10). Ask each student to write down whether or not they think each statement is a myth or not.

Suggested activities

- Look at 'Drugs – facts and fictions' (page 10) and check whether or not students answered correctly. Then read the article, pausing after each section to discuss the comments on the statement. Emphasise that anyone who takes drugs is gambling with their health.

- Read 'Is cannabis safe?' (page 10). Then ask pairs, working with the books closed, to write down three effects that heavy use of cannabis can have.

- Ask pairs to read and study 'Ecstasy factfile' (page 11) and to make a list of the most important facts explained in the article. Then discuss as a class what the risks of taking ecstasy are.

Plenary

Hold a class discussion in which you discuss the statements of the three young people (see 'In groups', page 11).

Extension activities

Ask pairs to role play either the scene between two teenagers or the scene between the doctor and a teenager (see 'Role play', page 11).

Challenge individuals to demonstrate their knowledge and understanding of ecstasy by writing an article for a teenage magazine, entitled 'Ecstasy – is it worth the risk?' In addition to using the information on these pages, ask them to find out more about ecstasy by researching it on the internet, using websites such as www.drugscope.org.uk and www.talktofrank.com.

Organise a visit from a police officer to discuss drugs and drugtaking with the class. Before the visit, ask students to prepare questions to ask and, afterwards, hold a discussion about what they learned from the visit.

Check their understanding of the facts about ecstasy by getting them to complete the questions on Copymaster 2 'How much do you know about ecstasy?'

How much do you know about ecstasy?

On your own decide whether these statements about ecstasy are TRUE or FALSE. Put a tick in one of the boxes, then join up with a partner, compare your answers and look at page 11 of *Your Life Student Book 2* to see whether your answers are right or wrong.

		TRUE	**FALSE**
1.	Ecstasy is a class A drug, so the courts can give heavy penalties for possessing or supplying it.	☐	☐
2.	Ecstasy tablets all look the same, so it's very easy to recognise them.	☐	☐
3.	Ecstasy is a stimulant which gives a person an energy buzz.	☐	☐
4.	The effects of ecstasy wear off very quickly – within an hour or so.	☐	☐
5.	Ecstasy has exactly the same effect on anyone who takes it.	☐	☐
6.	Ecstasy lowers the body temperature, making it easier to dance in a hot atmosphere.	☐	☐
7.	People who dance for a long time after taking ecstasy can get dehydrated.	☐	☐
8.	When the effects of taking ecstasy wear off, users can feel tired and depressed and may find it hard to sleep.	☐	☐
9.	Research suggests that there are no long-term ill-effects from heavy use of ecstasy.	☐	☐
10.	Around 50 deaths a year occur as a result of taking ecstasy.	☐	☐

UNIT 2 You and your body – drugs and drugtaking

Your Life 2/Year 8

Lesson 2 *Your Life Student Book 2*, pages 12–13
Keeping healthy – drugs and drugtaking

Objective: To understand the laws about drugs and to explore how to deal with pressure to experiment with drugs.

Starter

Introduce the topic by discussing the difference between drugs that are legal and drugs that are illegal. Remind students of the distinction between medicinal drugs (drugs prescribed by doctors and drugs considered safe enough to be sold as medicines at chemist's, e.g. aspirin), social drugs (drugs in everyday use which are not illegal – caffeine, nicotine, alcohol) and illegal drugs (drugs which it is against the law to possess because they are considered dangerous).

Suggested activities

- Read 'Drugs and the law' (page 12). Ask individuals to write answers to questions 1–4 (see 'In groups', page 12). Then ask them to discuss questions 5 in groups and to report their views in a class discussion, before writing their answers to those two questions.

- Introduce the issue of peer pressure to experiment with drugs by asking the students to imagine a teenager, Zed, who is at a party. Ask: 'How might his friends put pressure on him to try drugs? What might they say or do?' 'What can Zed say or do to resist this pressure?' Then read and discuss 'How to turn down drugs and stay friends' (page 13). Ask students to work individually to write down the piece of advice they think is the most helpful, then to share their views in a group or class discussion.

- Ask groups to show their understanding of how to say no to drugs by acting out or scripting a scene in which a teenager, like Zed, resists the pressure from a group of friends to experiment with a drug.

Plenary

Ask groups to act or read out their scenes and discuss which of the tactics used to say no they think are the most effective.

Extension activity

Ask individuals to write a statement giving their views on the drug laws (see 'For your file' page 12).

UNIT 3 You and your responsibilities – other cultures and lifestyles

Your Life 2/Year 8

Lesson 1 *Your Life Student Book 2*, pages 14–15

Social education – recognising stereotyping

Objective: To understand that the United Kingdom is a diverse society, and to explore what ethnic stereotyping is and how it creates a false image of people.

Resources

Copies of Copymaster 3 'Do you stereotype people?'

Starter

Explain what 'multicultural' means and how in Britain today there are people from many cultures with different ideas, beliefs, values and traditions. Talk about how these people come from different ethnic groups, explaining that an ethnic group has racial, religious, linguistic and other features in common, and that Britain is a diverse society, in which there are people from many different ethnic groups. Explain how people have been coming to Britain for centuries and that the makeup of present-day society is a result of the immigration that took place during the 20th century.

Suggested activities

- Read 'Britain – a diverse society' (page 14). Ask individuals to make notes on what it tells them about a) immigration during the 1950s and 1960s and in more recent times and b) the ethnic population of Great Britain. Then, as a class, discuss what they have learned from the article.

- Ask students: 'What are the benefits of living in a diverse society?' Ask them individually to think about such things as food, clothes, music, art, festivals, sport, travel and people, and to write one or two sentences saying what they like best about living in a diverse society. Then share their views in a class discussion.

- Explain what ethnic stereotyping is (thinking that a person behaves in a particular way because they belong to a certain ethnic group). Read the paragraph 'Ethnic stereotyping', the comments by Nazrah and Tariq and the poem 'Stereotype' (page 15). Ask groups to do the three discussion activities (see 'In groups', page 15), then to share their views in a class discussion.

- Ask individuals to complete Copymaster 3 'Do you stereotype people?' then to compare their answers in either a group or a class discussion.

Plenary

Recap what ethnic stereotyping is and discuss the negative effects it can have by sticking inappropriate labels on people.

Extension activity

Ask students to think of people from ethnic minorities who have made significant contributions to society. Build up a list on the board, e.g. broadcaster Sir Trevor McDonald, actress Meera Syal, novelist Zadie Smith, sports stars Mo Farah, Christine Ohoruogu, Lewis Hamilton and Rio Ferdinand and rap poet Benjamin Zephaniah. Ask students to choose a person from an ethnic minority who has achieved success and to research what they have achieved on the internet, and then to explain to the rest of the class why they admire them. The 100 Great Black Britons campaign could be one starting point (www.100greatblackbritons.com).

3 Do you stereotype people?

On your own, look at each of the following statements. Decide whether you agree or disagree with it and put a tick in one of the boxes. Then form groups and compare your answers. Discuss as a class what you learn from this activity about what stereotyping is.

		Agree	**Disagree**
1.	You can tell what a person is like by the way they dress.	☐	☐
2.	You can often tell where people come from by their accent.	☐	☐
3.	People who speak a dialect are less intelligent than people who speak Standard English.	☐	☐
4.	Everyone from the West Indies likes cricket and reggae.	☐	☐
5.	All Scotsmen wear kilts and like highland dancing.	☐	☐
6.	People with red hair are more quick-tempered than other people.	☐	☐
7.	A person's hairstyle tells you exactly what sort of person they are.	☐	☐
8.	English people are less emotional than people from other European countries.	☐	☐
9.	People who wear glasses are more academic than other people.	☐	☐
10.	You can tell what a person is like by the music they like.	☐	☐

UNIT 3 You and your responsibilities – other cultures and lifestyles

Your Life 2/Year 8

Lesson 2 *Your Life Student Book 2*, pages 16–17
Social education – stereotyping in the media

Objective: To investigate images and stereotypes of ethnic groups in the media.

Starter

Remind them what stereotyping is (see Lesson 1). Explain what negative stereotyping is and note that it may occur as a result of how people are presented in the media. Ask: 'Can you think of any examples of people from an ethnic minority being stereotyped in the TV programmes you watch?' Explain that the focus of the lesson is on the images of ethnic minorities presented in the media.

Suggested activities

- Read 'Ethnic minorities still shown as stereotypes in films' (page 16). Talk about what the study found. Ask: 'Do you agree that black characters don't get enough good guy roles?' 'Is it true that films present stereotypes of Asian families and Eastern Europeans?' Talk about film stars from ethnic minorities and the roles they have played in recent films.

- Invite groups to read 'TV programmes don't reflect real life' (page 16) and to discuss whether they agree that broadcasters are guilty of tokenism. As a class discuss the arguments for and against including scenes that involve racism.

- Ask groups to carry out activity 4 (see 'In groups', page 16) and to write out their plans, then to explain them to the rest of the class.

- Read 'Does the media stereotype Muslims?' (page 17). Discuss what Dr Awad and Mariam Rafa say about the media's image of Muslims. Ask: 'Do you agree with their views?' Share their opinions in a class discussion.

- Study 'Young gifted and black'. Ask: 'Does the media focus too much on black youths involved in criminal activities rather than including stories about young black people's achievements?'

Plenary

Recap what they have learned from this lesson about how the media presents ethnic minorities. Encourage the students to write a short statement saying what they think the media should be doing to make sure they do not reinforce stereotyping.

Extension activity

Challenge students to show their understanding of the issues raised on these pages by writing an email to a newspaper expressing their views.

UNIT 4 You and Your Money – making the most of your money

Your Life 2/Year 8

Lesson 1 *Your Life Student Book 2*, page 18
Citizenship/Economic and financial capability – money management

Objective: To understand how items that we spend our money on can be divided into necessities and luxuries and which household expenses their parents or guardians have to budget for.

Resources

Copies of Copymaster 4 'Household expenses'

Starter

Write the headings Necessities and Luxuries on the board and explain how the things we spend our money on can be divided into two groups. Ask students to suggest some necessities and luxuries. List their suggestions on the board. Then read the first two paragraphs on page 18 and add any other items it mentions that are not on their lists.

Suggested activities

- Ask pairs or groups to complete the activity on Copymaster 4. Talk about how many people use banks to make regular payments for them from their accounts. Explain what a standing order is and what a direct debit is.

- Encourage the students to think about what they spend their money on, to make a list and to decide which are necessities and which are luxuries. Then get them to discuss in pairs which luxuries are most important to them and which they would be prepared to give up in order to save money.

Plenary

Ask the students to read 'Petra's problem' (page 18) and then to write a paragraph offering her advice. Get some of them to share what they have written in a class discussion.

Household expenses

In groups, study this list of household expenses and decide which are necessities and which are luxuries. Discuss whether they are regular or occasional expenses. Which are weekly expenses and which can be paid monthly, quarterly or annually?

		Necessity	Luxury
Mortgage repayments/rent			
Utility bills	electricity/gas		
	water		
Council tax			
Insurance	house		
	contents		
Food			
Clothes			
Telephone	line rental/calls		
	mobile calls/texts		
Computer – internet access			
TV licence			
TV subscriptions			
Transport costs	bus/train fares		
	road tax		
	car insurance		
	petrol		
Newspapers/Magazines			
Books			
Toiletries			
Household cleaning items			
Membership subscriptions, e.g. sports clubs			
School trips			
Birthday/Christmas presents			
Meals out/Days out			
Cinema/Concert tickets			
Pocket money			

UNIT 4 You and Your Money – making the most of your money

Your Life 2/Year 8

Lesson 2 *Your Life Student Book 2*, page 19
Citizenship/Economic and financial capability – money management

Objective: To explore ways that young people can increase their income.

Starter

Ask the class to suggest ways that a young person can increase their income and list their suggestions on the board.

Suggested activities

- Read Ian Ashendon's article (page 19). In groups, discuss the advice he gives on finding jobs to increase your income. Ask: 'Which of his suggestions is the most helpful?'
- Discuss the advice he gives on selling items. Invite the students to share their experiences of selling items. In their experience where is it best to advertise items for sale? How can you ensure that you get a fair price for your unwanted goods?

Plenary

Compare the list of ideas they suggested with those Ian Ashendon suggests.

Discuss the view that it is better to ensure you have enough money for your needs by cutting down your expenditure rather than trying to increase your income by working or selling things you no longer want.

UNIT 4 You and Your Money – making the most of your money

Your Life 2/Year 8

Lesson 3 *Your Life Student Book 2,* pages 20–21
Citizenship/Economic and financial capability – money management

Objective: To explore ways in which young people can make the most of whatever money they have

Starter

Explain the 80/20 rule (see paragraph one of Erica Stewart's article, page 20). Ask the students for their views on this idea. Is it a good idea in principle, but one that is hard to put into practice?

Suggested activities

● Invite students to read and discuss each of the twelve suggestions that Erica Stewart makes in her article. They should say how valuable they think each idea is by ranking it on a 5-star scale, with one star being not very useful and five stars being extremely useful. Then list the twelve ideas in order of usefulness, starting with the most useful.

Plenary

Ask students to compare lists in a class discussion.

UNIT 5 You and your values – where do you stand?

Objective: To understand how your beliefs and values influence the way you behave, what your ambitions are and who you admire.

Resources

Copies of Copymaster 5 'What influences how you behave?'

Starter

Talk about how your behaviour is influenced by what your beliefs and values are. Ask the students: 'What's the most important thing that influences you when making a decision about how to behave?' 'Is it: a) What your parents will think? b) Whether or not you'll get into trouble? c) Whether or not it's right or wrong? d)Whether or not you'll benefit from your actions? or e) Whether or not your actions will hurt someone?' Ask each of them to write a short statement saying what most influences how they behave.

Suggested activities

● Ask individuals to do the ranking activity 'What influences how you behave?' (see page 22 or use Copymaster 5). Then ask them to share their views in a group discussion, comparing their statements with what other group members think should be the most important influences.

● Study the list of things which young people said were important when asked to state their ambitions (see 'Your ambitions', page 22). Ask students to discuss the list and to share their views on what they consider to be important.

● Read the article 'Idols or heroes?' (page 23). Ask groups to discuss whether or not they agree with Derek Stuart's views, to decide on their definition of a hero and to propose some heroes to include in a class 'Hall of fame'. Then hold a class discussion and agree a class list of top ten heroes.

● Ask individuals to think about someone they know personally whom they admire (see 'Someone you admire', page 23) and to explain to a partner who it is and why they admire the person.

Plenary

Talk about how society often rewards pop stars, TV personalities and sports stars more than people who make other contributions to society, such as nurses, doctors, police officers and fire officers. Ask: 'Has society got its values right? Who should we value more – the Premier League footballer or the ambulance driver?'

Extension activity

Suggest individuals write an email to the editor of the magazine in which 'Idols or heroes?' (page 23) might have appeared, replying to Derek Stuart's views and saying why they agree or disagree with them.

5 What influences how you behave?

The way you behave is influenced by what your beliefs and values are. For example, in some situations your behaviour might depend on how important you think it is to impress people, compared to doing what you believe to be right.

What plays the most important part in influencing how you behave? Here are some possibilities. On your own, rank them in level of importance on a five-point scale by circling the number in the right-hand column – 1 for extremely important, 5 for not at all important.

		1	2	3	4	5
1	Trying to avoid arguments	1	2	3	4	5
2	Standing up for what you believe is right	1	2	3	4	5
3	Making sure your actions don't hurt other people	1	2	3	4	5
4	Trying to impress people	1	2	3	4	5
5	Listening to what your parents and teachers say	1	2	3	4	5
6	Keeping out of trouble	1	2	3	4	5
7	Doing what your religion says you should do	1	2	3	4	5
8	Keeping your temper	1	2	3	4	5
9	Following the latest fashion	1	2	3	4	5
10	Behaving with courtesy	1	2	3	4	5
11	Telling the truth	1	2	3	4	5
12	Looking after your own interests	1	2	3	4	5
13	Imitating the behaviour of your idols	1	2	3	4	5
14	Respecting other people's opinions and beliefs	1	2	3	4	5
15	Keeping your promises	1	2	3	4	5
16	Doing what your friends want you to do	1	2	3	4	5

In pairs

Compare with a partner how you have ranked the things that influence your behaviour. Then work together to list them from 1 to 16 to show what you think the most important influences should be. Start with 1 – the most important influence – and end with 16 – the least important influence.

UNIT 5 You and your values – where do you stand?

Objective: To consider some of the issues that make news and to discuss which are the most important.

Resources

Copies of Copymaster 5A 'Understanding your values'

Starter

Ask the students: 'What are the major issues that face us in the world today?' Make a list of their suggestions on the board, e.g. terrorism, global warming, poverty, cloning, deforestation, pollution, AIDS, human rights, weapons of mass destruction and racism. Ask: 'If you had £100 million to spend on one of these issues, which would you choose to spend it on?' Invite them to share their views in a class discussion. Talk about how their views differ according to their values and beliefs.

Suggested activities

- Explain that the class is going to do a ranking exercise. Ask pairs to read and study the reports on pages 24–25, then to rank them in order of the importance of the issue they raise. Ask them to compare their views in a class discussion, inviting individuals to explain why they consider some issues to be more important than others.

- Ask individuals to choose one of the issues on which they have a strong opinion and to write an email expressing their views on the issue.

Plenary

Share some of their emails.

Extension activities

Choose an issue that particularly interests the class. Suggest they research the issue on the internet and then either to organise a debate on the issue or to role play a TV discussion of the issue.

Ask students to cut out newspaper reports that raise issues about which they are concerned and to write comments expressing their opinions on the issues. Ask the students either to put them in their files or to mount them and make a display on topical issues.

Assessment

Use Copymaster 5A to assess understanding of what their values are.

5A Understanding your values

Study the list of issues and rate how concerned you are about each one by putting a tick in the appropriate column.

	Concerned	Very concerned	Not concerned
Hunting			
Drug dealing			
Cloning			
AIDS			
Recycling			
World hunger			
Sex discrimination			
Experiments on live animals			
Pollution			
Euthanasia			
Racial prejudice			

Which three issues concern you the most? Write a statement saying which three issues you are most concerned about and why.

Your Life 2/Year 8

Lesson 1 *Your Life Student Book 2*, pages 26–27

Personal wellbeing – family relationships: coping with separation and divorce

Objective: To explore the reasons why parents separate and the feelings that this can cause and to understand who decides whom children live with.

Resources

Copies of Copymaster 6 'It's all my fault!'

Starter

Introduce the topic by setting ground rules for discussion and stressing that no one needs to talk about their own experiences if they do not want to. Explain that there are many reasons why relationships break up. What different reasons can the class think of? Make a list on the board, such as: money problems, affairs, domestic violence, drug or alcohol addiction, incompatibility or stress (caused by unemployment, bereavement, long-term illness or unfulfilled expectations). Discuss how there are often a combination of factors, rather than one single cause.

Suggested activities

- Read 'Dealing with divorce' (page 26). Ask groups to discuss what the three children say about their parents' divorce and then share their views in a class discussion.

- Ask individuals to study the eight statements (see 'In groups', page 26), to write down whether or not they agree with them, then to share their views in a group discussion.

- Read 'A mixture of feelings' (page 27). Discuss with the class the different feelings that the young people describe. Ask: 'Who is the best person to talk to about your feelings?'

- Read 'Who decides who you live with?' (page 27). Make sure students understand what a residence order and a contact order are. Invite pairs to discuss the view that children should always have the final say. Ask: 'Does it depend how old the child is?' Then hold a class discussion in which the students share their views.

Plenary

Discuss Pat's letter (see 'For your file', page 27) with the class and list the main points that they would include in their reply. End by re-emphasising that there are many reasons why parents split up, but that children are not to blame if they do.

Extension activity

Ask pairs and then groups to discuss the comments on Copymaster 6. As a class, discuss what you can say and do to help a friend who is experiencing such thoughts and feelings.

COPYMASTER

6 It's all my fault!

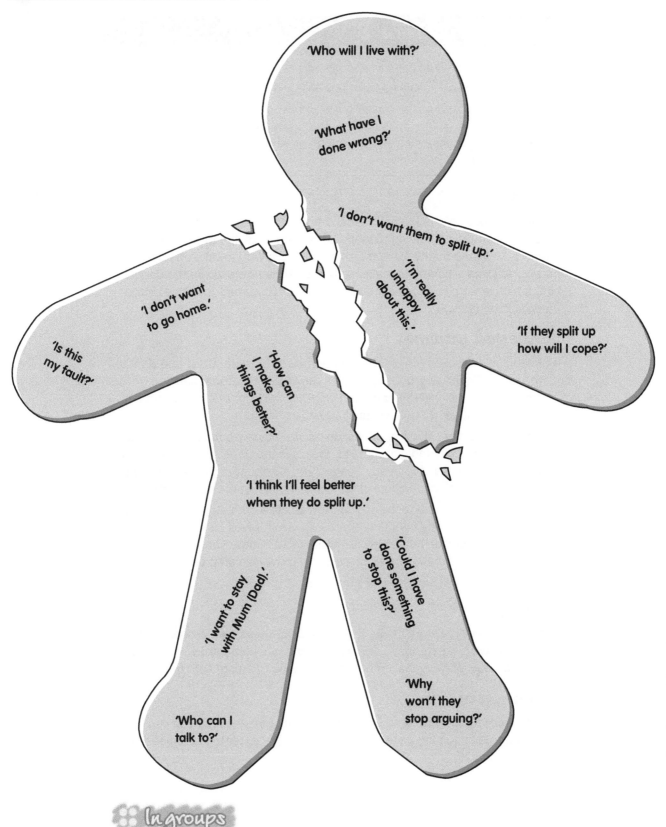

'Who will I live with?'

'What have I done wrong?'

'I don't want them to split up.'

'I'm really unhappy about this.'

'I don't want to go home.'

'Is this my fault?'

'How can I make things better?'

'If they split up how will I cope?'

'I think I'll feel better when they do split up.'

'I want to stay with Mum (Dad).'

'Could I have done something to stop this?'

'Who can I talk to?'

'Why won't they stop arguing?'

In groups

One of your friends is unhappy and having a hard time at home as their parents have decided to separate. All these thoughts have gone through their mind at some point recently. How can you help them deal with what's going on?

Discuss each of the statements and then write any helpful suggestions down on paper.

UNIT 6 You and your family – divided families

Your Life 2/Year 8

Lesson 2 *Your Life Student Book 2*, pages 28–29
Personal wellbeing – family relationships: living in step-families

> **Objective:** To explore the changes that occur when parents separate and to examine living in a step-family.

Starter

Explain the focus of the lesson. Talk about the changes that can occur when parents separate, e.g. having to move house or school, living with only one parent or in a step-family, having less money or having to take on more household chores, having to make contact arrangements to see the parent you don't live with or losing contact with them. Then read the introductory paragraph on page 28.

Suggested activities

- Read and discuss in groups the experiences of Barbara, Chris and Xanthe (page 28). Then ask groups to discuss the issues regarding keeping contact with the absent parent and whether or not to tell friends what is happening. Share their views in a class discussion.

- Ask the students: 'What problems do children face when settling into a step-family?' Read and discuss with the class the three statements in the section 'Living in a step-family' (page 29). Talk about any other problems and difficulties that members of the class suggest step-children may face.

- Ask individuals to study the article 'How to cope with step-parents' (page 29) and to make their own notes on the advice it gives on how to deal with step-parents and on how to get on with step-siblings. Then ask groups to draw up a list of their top tips on how to survive in a step-family and to share their lists in a class discussion.

Plenary

Summarise what the students have learned from these two lessons about how to deal with separation, divorce and living in a step-family by drawing up a list of 'Dos' and 'Don'ts' on how to cope when parents split up.

Extension activity

Ask students to show their understanding of the feelings a person can experience when joining a step-family by writing a letter to Leah (see 'For your file', page 29).

UNIT 7 You and your safety – at home and in the street

Your Life 2/Year 8

Lesson 1 *Your Life Student Book 2*, pages 30–31
Keeping healthy – first aid

> **Objective:** To understand how to give basic first aid for cuts, fractures, burns and scalds and what to do if a person is unconscious or suffering from shock

Starter

Explain that more people are injured in accidents at home than anywhere else. Ask the students to share experiences of accidents at home involving them, their family or friends. Discuss what happened and the causes, and whether there was anybody on hand who could give first aid. Explain that the commonest types of accidents are falls, and that among the most serious are those that cause severe bleeding. Point out how important it is to know how to give first aid and read 'First aid for fractures and breaks' (page 30).

Suggested activities

- Ask pairs to read and study 'First aid for cuts', ' First aid for burns and scalds' and 'First aid for fractures and breaks' on page 30. Then ask them to write answers to the four questions (see 'In pairs', page 30).

- Read 'Emergency first aid', 'Shock' and 'Unconsciousness' on page 31 and ask pairs to show their understanding of the information by explaining what to do with a person who is unconscious and how to treat shock. Then choose one of the pairs to demonstrate how to put someone into the recovery position.

Plenary

Explain that the priorities when giving emergency first aid are 'ABC'. First, check that the Airway isn't blocked. Then, check that the casualty is still Breathing. Thirdly, check Circulation by checking for a pulse. Then recap on how to put someone in the recovery position.

Test the students' understanding of first-aid procedures by giving them a ten-question quiz based on the information on pages 30–31.

Extension activities

Ask students to design a poster offering advice on how to give first aid after an accident in the home.

Suggest students use the resources centre and the internet to find out about first aid for other accidental injuries (e.g. suffocating or choking), and to write out sets of instructions explaining what you should do to treat them.

Ask groups to draw up plans for a short information video on first aid in the home. Then allow them to present their proposals to the rest of the class.

Invite a member of the local St John Ambulance to come and give a demonstration of first-aid procedures.

UNIT 7 You and your safety – at home and in the street

Your Life 2/Year 8

Lesson 2 *Your Life Student Book 2*, pages 32–33
Keeping healthy – child abuse

> **Objective:** To understand what child abuse is and what victims of child abuse should do.

Starter

Introduce the topic by defining what child abuse is: when adults hurt children either physically or in some other way. Explain that sexual abuse is only one form of child abuse. Ask: 'What other forms of child abuse can you think of?' List types of abuse on the board, e.g. physical punishment of children, for example hitting or spanking; neglecting children by not feeding them/changing their clothes; denying children their right to an education; forcing children to work, for example in factories; emotionally abusing children by constantly threatening them or putting them down; giving children drugs. Explain that child abuse occurs in all parts of the world, in both developed and less developed countries.

Suggested activities

- Read and discuss 'What is child abuse?' (page 32). Focus first on the kinds of abuse. Reinforce what has already been said about different types of abuse. Discuss what the article says about why child abuse happens and emphasise the points made in the final sentence (abuse is **always** wrong and **never** the young person's fault).

- Explain that people have a range of views about smacking. Invite groups to discuss their views on smacking and on the statement that 'a good hiding never did anybody any harm'. Then share their views in a class discussion.

- Read 'Facts and fictions about abuse' (page 32) and the two articles about sexual abuse on page 33. Draw attention to key points: how the offender is often someone they know rather than a stranger; how victims feel guilty and ashamed but should try to concentrate on feeling angry and the importance of speaking out.

- After discussing the information in 'What happens next?' (page 33), stress that the consequences of not speaking out can be much more harmful than those of speaking out.

Plenary

Ask the class to suggest the most important things about child abuse that they learned from the lesson and make a list on the board.

Extension activity

Talk about the dangers of internet chat-rooms, of sending your picture via the internet to a stranger whose age you may not know and how abusers may try to use the internet to make contact with young people. Suggest groups draw up a set of guidelines on how to use the internet safely, in order to protect themselves from being abused.

UNIT 7 You and your safety – at home and in the street

Your Life 2/Year 8

Lesson 3 *Your Life Student Book 2*, pages 34–35
Keeping healthy – staying safe in public places

> **Objective:** To explore how to stay safe when out and about in the street and in other public places.

Resources

Copies of Copymaster 7 'Be streetwise'

Starter

Introduce the topic by discussing how some places are safer than others (e.g. a well-lit street is safer than a dark underpass or a lonely country lane); how some times are safer than others (e.g. the rush-hour is safer than late at night); how some situations are safer than others (e.g. you're safer in a group than on your own and safer waiting for the last bus inside a café than on the pavement). Ask students to share their experiences of when they have felt unsafe and to consider what it was about the place, the time and the situation that made them feel unsafe. Explain that the aim of the lesson is to explore ways of staying safe when you are out and about.

Suggested activities

- Read 'Staying safe in the street' and 'Safety on buses' (page 34). In a class discussion talk about the reasons for each piece of advice. Can students suggest any other things to do/to avoid doing in order to stay safe in the street and on buses?

- Ask groups to discuss the eight situations (see 'In groups', page 34), to write down what they decide you should do and then to share their views in a class discussion.

- Invite pairs to read and study 'Safety in public places' (page 35) and to summarise the advice given by making a list of 'Dos' and 'Don'ts'. Then discuss the advice in a class discussion.

Plenary

Ask individuals to write down what they think are the five most important things to do/to avoid doing in order to stay safe when they are out and about. Invite some of them to read their lists to the rest of the class.

Extension activities

Ask groups either to design a leaflet or produce plans for a video advising young people on how to stay safe in the street.

Ask pairs to draw up a 'Paper-round safety code', giving advice to young people with paper rounds. Then give out copies of Copymaster 7 and ask them to compare their advice with that given in the leaflet, produced by the Metropolitan Police. Then, as a class, read and discuss the advice on looking for work.

Encourage students in groups to focus on cycling safely and to draw up a list of Do's and Don'ts for cyclists, then to compare their lists with the 'Extra Rules for Cyclists' in the Highway Code.

7 Be streetwise

A Streetwise Guide to Earning Money

Most people can do with making extra money. Here are some streetwise tips on earning money safely and without problems ...

LOOKING FOR WORK

Read the job ads in your local paper. Keep a look out for signs in your local shop windows asking for part-time help. Make sure that the ad makes it clear what you will be doing. Vague advertisements can spell danger. It may be worth calling in on shops where you know the staff and asking if they need anyone.

Be choosy. Stay away from places which make you uncomfortable or nervous. If you're visiting shops, don't go alone; take a friend or, even better, an adult you can trust.

People sometimes advertise odd jobs on cards in newsagents' windows. If you spot a possible job this way, ring the number given and find out as much as you can about the job over the phone. If the person wants to arrange an interview, take along an adult you trust – preferably the person who normally looks after you. And if the employer offers you the job over the phone, don't rush in. Say you'd like to bring this adult along to meet them and discuss the work first. Honest employers won't be put off by you involving a responsible adult. Talk to your family or the people who look after you about anything you're considering and never go to strange addresses alone.

Don't put your own card in a shop window. It's crazy to give a whole lot of strangers a way of getting in touch, when you have no idea what they're like. It's much safer – and quicker in the long run – to ask around within your own circle. Get your parents or other trusted adults to tell their friends you're looking for work.

THE PAPER ROUND CODE

Hundreds of young people have paper rounds. It's one of the most popular ways for under 16s to earn money. It can be very hard work, whether you're doing it on foot or by bike. Check out the following tricks of the trade:

- Beware of dogs! Don't pet them, even if their tails are wagging invitingly. They can turn nasty.

- In darkness or twilight, stick to well-lit roads.

- If you go by bike, check it regularly to see it's working properly, and use your lights to help drivers spot you.

- Wear bright, reflective clothing – you're on the road at a busy time. And be prepared for car drivers to be in a hurry.

- Wear a cyclist's helmet, it could make all the difference if you do have a fall.

- If you leave your bike anywhere, lock it first. It's also a good idea to mark your bike with a special property number. Your local police station will advise you how to do this. Then if your bike is stolen, the police have a better chance of finding it for you.

- Don't accept lifts from anyone, even if you are on foot, wet and tired.

- If customers ask you into their house, refuse politely. You can't afford the time and you don't want to take risks. If someone says they're ill or have had an accident and need help, tell them you'll get a neighbour.

UNIT 7 You and your safety – at home and in the street

Lesson 4 *Your Life Student Book 2*, pages 36–37
Keeping healthy – staying safe on the internet

Objective: To understand how to stay safe online

Starter

Ask the class what you can do in order to stay safe when chatting online and when shopping online. List their suggestions on the board.

Suggested activities

- Read 'Staying safe in chatrooms' (page 36). In groups, discuss the advice that is given, then plan a thirty-second safety video aimed at teenagers giving advice on how to stay safe online.

- Invite pairs to do the role play (see page 36), then discuss the arguments that were used in the role play to try to convince the person that the proposed meeting was not a good idea.

- Study 'Self Taken Images – Sexting' (page 37). Hold a class discussion about the risks of putting images of yourself online and what to do if you receive indecent images.

- In groups, ask the students to discuss the statements in 'Online Rights and Responsibilities' (page 37).

Plenary

Ask the groups to share their views on online rights and responsibilities in a class discussion.

Extension activity

In pairs, encourage the students to draft a responsible user's guide to social networking sites (see 'For your file' page 37).

UNIT 8 You and the law – the police

Objective: To understand what powers the police have to stop and search and to question people, and to explain the system of reprimands, warnings and prosecutions.

Resources

Copies of Copymaster 8 'What are your rights?'

Copies of Copymaster 8A 'Understanding your rights'

Starter

Introduce the topic by asking: 'Why do we have a police force?' 'What would happen if we did not have a police force?' 'What are the police's duties and responsibilities?' List on the board what the class think the police's duties are, then read the first paragraph on page 38.

Suggested activities

- Read the rest of 'Police duties and police powers' (page 38). Hold a class discussion in which you talk about police powers and people's rights with regard to being stopped and searched, and how to behave if you are either stopped or searched. Then debate the two views expressed in the statements (see 'In groups', page 38).

- Read 'Helping the police' (page 39). Ask: 'What are your rights if the police ask you to go to a police station and if they want to question you?' Make a list of the students' rights on the board.

- Read 'Reprimands, warnings and prosecutions' (page 39), stopping after each section to explain the information and to answer any questions. Then invite groups to carry out the discussion activity (see 'In groups', page 39) and to report their views in a class discussion.

Plenary

Recap on the system for dealing with young people who break the law, making sure that students understand the circumstances in which reprimands and warnings are given and in which prosecutions will take place. Remind students how long records are kept on young offenders and discuss what the consequences of having a record may be, e.g. when looking for a job.

Extension activity

Ask groups to discuss the rights of the three young people in the situations described on Copymaster 8.

Assessment

Use Copymaster 8A to assess understanding of their rights and the rights of the police. The answers are: 1. True, 2. False, 3. False, 4. True, 5. True, 6. True, 7. False, 8. True, 9. True, 10. False, 11. True, 12. False, 13. False, 14. True, 15. True.

8 What are your rights?

CASE 1

Jason was standing outside a greengrocer's, when some older boys came along and stole some fruit. Jason panicked and started to run off. The shopkeeper chased him, caught him and called the police. The police officer talked to Jason, then asked him to go to the police station to answer further questions.

Does Jason have to go to the police station? What will happen if he refuses to go?

CASE 2

Sally was going to stay with a friend. When she arrived, the friend was out, so Sally tried to force her way in through one of the ground-floor windows. A police officer saw her and asked to see the contents of her holdall, which she had put down in the front garden.

Does Sally have to show the police officer the contents of her holdall? Does Sally have to let the officer search her as well, if they ask to do so?

CASE 3

Trevor was arrested because he was seen leaving a block of flats about the time a burglary took place. Trevor denied being involved, but the police searched him and found a screwdriver. At the police station, the police charged him and told him they wanted to take his fingerprints.

Does Trevor have to agree to have his fingerprints taken? Must he answer the questions the police ask him about what he was doing at the flats? If the police want to take his photograph, can they do so?

In groups

Study the three cases and discuss what rights each person has in those circumstances.

8A Understanding your rights

Use this quiz to test your knowledge of what rights the police have and what your rights are. Decide which of these statements are true and which are false, and put a tick in one of the boxes.

	TRUE	**FALSE**
1. If a police officer stops you in the street, you have the right to know why.		
2. A police officer can stop you if they know you have been in trouble before.	☐	☐
3. If you are stopped in the street you must answer any questions which the police officer asks you.	☐	☐
4. If you are asked to go to a police station to help the police with their enquiries, you can refuse to go.	☐	☐
5. The police can search anyone who they think is behaving in an odd way.	☐	☐
6. If the police have a good reason for wanting to search you and you refuse to let them, you can be charged with obstruction.	☐	☐
7. Any kind of search must be carried out by a police officer who is the same sex as you.	☐	☐
8. The police can only detain you at a police station if you have been arrested.	☐	☐
9. You have the right to inform someone if you are being questioned at a police station.	☐	☐
10. The police cannot interview you without your parent's consent.	☐	☐
11. If you admit to an offence and it is your first offence, provided it is not too serious, you will get a reprimand.	☐	☐
12. If you break the law a second time, you will automatically be prosecuted, however minor the offence is.	☐	☐
13. If the police believe you have committed an offence, they can give you a reprimand or a warning, even if you do not admit the offence.	☐	☐
14. If you are reprimanded, warned or charged by the police, they will take your fingerprints and a photo of you.	☐	☐
15. Records of your offences are kept on the Police National Computer for five years.	☐	☐

UNIT 8 You and the law – the police

Your Life 2/Year 8

Lesson 2 *Your Life Student Book 2*, pages 40–41
Citizenship – the role of the police

> **Objective:** To explore the role of the police in maintaining public order, and to discuss attitudes towards the police.

Resources

Copies of a police recruitment advertisement (optional)

Starter

Explain that one of the duties of the police is to maintain public order by controlling crowds at public events such as concerts, sports events and demonstrations. Talk about how in a free society people have the right to demonstrate but they must not break certain laws by behaving violently, obstructing the highway, trespassing or causing a nuisance. Explain that the lesson will focus on how the police control large crowds, the growing use of CCTV cameras and on attitudes towards the police.

Suggested activities

- Ask students to share their experiences of being in large crowds. Ask: 'What do you think of the way the police controlled the crowd?' Then read 'Keeping the peace' (page 40). Ask: 'Do you think the police sometimes over-react and spark off trouble at demonstrations?' Discuss the senior police officer's statement on page 40, and ask: 'Are media reports of demonstrations distorted?' 'Does media presence 'egg a crowd on'?'

- Read 'Keeping you safe' (page 40). Explain what is meant by 'a surveillance society'. Then as a class students share their opinions about the growing use of CCTV cameras and whether they are concerned about living in a surveillance society.

- Ask: 'What do you think of the police?' Invite individuals to write down whether they agree/disagree/are not sure about each of the ten statements on page 41, then to share their views in a group or class discussion.

- Read 'Doing a good job?' (page 41) and discuss the results of the survey. Ask for a show of hands of those who agree with the statement (see 'In groups' page 41). Encourage them to say why they agree or disagree with it.

- Ask: 'What qualities and abilities do you think a police officer needs to have?' Get pairs to make a list of the qualities and abilities they think a police officer needs to have, then compare their lists in a class discussion.

Plenary

Ask each student to write a short statement saying what they think about the police and why.

Extension activity

Show students a copy of a police recruitment advertisement. Ask: 'Would you consider becoming a police officer?' Ask groups to list the advantages and disadvantages of a career in the police force, then hold a class discussion.

UNIT 9 You and your money – gambling

Your Life 2/Year 8

Lesson 1 *Your Life Student Book 2*, pages 42–43

Citizenship/Economic wellbeing and financial capability – gambling

> **Objective:** To examine the reasons why people gamble, to explain the laws about gambling and to explore attitudes towards gambling.

Starter

Introduce the topic by asking the students: 'Why do people gamble?' Ask pairs to write down all the reasons they can think of, then encourage them to share their ideas in a class discussion and list their ideas on the board.

Suggested activities

- Read 'Gambling – the lure and the law' (page 42). Compare the list of reasons why young people gamble with the list you made on the board. Then discuss the law on gambling. Ask: 'Is it too easy for young people to gamble?' 'Should there be tighter restrictions or should there be no restrictions on young people gambling?' Invite individuals to write a statement giving reasons why people gamble (see 'For Your File' page 42).

- Read 'Winners and losers' (page 42) and 'The National Lottery' (page 43). Then ask groups to discuss their views about the National Lottery before sharing them in a class discussion.

- Ask groups to discuss the views in 'Gambling – What do you think?' (page 43) then compare their attitudes towards gambling in a class discussion and ask them whether they would be for or against plans to build a supercasino in their town.

Plenary

Talk about how gambling is regarded as a sin in some religions. Ask: 'What are the moral and religious arguments against gambling?' Make a list on the board, e.g.:

- Gambling is a sin because you should trust in God, not chance, to provide your needs.
- Gambling is wrong because you win money by luck rather than earning it.
- Gambling causes misery because it can lead people into debt.
- People spend money on gambling which could be better spent in other ways.
- Gambling can be addictive and lead people to steal to fund their habit.
- Gambling can make people cheat and lie.

Discuss each argument in turn and get students to say why they agree or disagree with it.

Extension activities

Organise a class debate: 'This class believes that all forms of gambling should be banned'.

Encourage students to find out all they can about Fixed Odds Betting Terminals and to write a statement saying whether they think they make gambling more fun and/or more addictive.

UNIT 10 You and other people – friends and friendships

Lesson 1 *Your Life Student Book 2*, pages 46–47
Personal wellbeing – relationships with friends

> **Objective:** To explore the nature of friendship, what makes a good friend and how to make and keep friends.

Starter

Ask: 'What qualities do you value in a friend?' Ask pairs to make a list, e.g. honesty, loyalty, patience, tolerance, understanding, forgiveness, sense of humour, liveliness, sensitivity and tact. Encourage them to share their views in a class discussion and make a class list on the board.

Suggested activities

- Ask pairs to discuss the ten statements in 'What is a friend?' (page 47), then to share their opinions in a group discussion.

- Read and discuss in groups 'The secret of making friends' (page 46). Then invite them to make lists of 'Dos' and 'Don'ts', giving advice on how to behave in order to make and keep friends.

- Read and discuss the article 'Growing apart' (page 47). Discuss as a class the advice it gives. Ask: 'What other advice would you offer to someone who feels they are drifting apart from a friend?'

Plenary

Study 'The rules of friendship' (page 46). Ask the students to discuss whether they agree/disagree with the rules. Invite each student to write down which three rules they consider to be the most important, then to share their views.

Extension activities

Ask individuals to show what they have learned about friendship by writing their views on friends and friendships (see 'For your file', page 46).

Ask groups to draft a reply to this letter to a magazine's agony aunt: 'I have difficulty in making friends. What advice can you give me?' M.

UNIT 10 You and other people – friends and friendships

Lesson 2 *Your Life Student Book 2*, pages 48–49
Personal wellbeing – relationship with friends

> **Objective:** To explore how friends may influence you, how groups behave and how to resist peer pressure.

Resources

Copies of Copymaster 10 'Staying in control of your life'

Starter

Ask the students: 'How much do you think your friends influence you?' Suggest individuals use a five-point scale to rate how much influence they consider their friends have on the decisions they make (1 a lot, 2 quite a lot, 3 a fair amount, 4 not very much, 5 hardly any) and to write one or two sentences explaining the reasons for their view.

Suggested activities

- Ask individuals to complete the quiz on page 48. Then ask them to check what their answers tell them. Invite them to compare this with their rating of their friends' influence in a discussion with a partner.

- Hold a class discussion about gangs. Ask: 'Why do people go round in gangs?' Discuss the way people talk and behave in gangs, and their experiences of gangs. Ask: 'What's your opinion of gangs and how they behave?' Read 'Gangs – know the facts' (page 49) and discuss what the article says about gangs. Suggest individuals study the three statements about gangs on page 49, and then to write statements giving their own views.

- Ask pairs to act out a role play in which one friend puts pressure on another friend to do something they do not want to do. Then ask some of them to act out their role plays in front of the class and to discuss the strategies they use in order to resist pressure.

Plenary

Write the statements below on the board and encourage the students to discuss whether or not they agree with them:

Friends who pressurise you all the time are not good friends. You have to let your friends influence you sometimes or you'll lose your friends. People who won't do what their friends want them to do are spoilsports. A real friend will respect your right to choose.

Extension activities

Read Copymaster 10. Discuss the advice it gives in groups, then ask them to share their views in a class discussion.

Ask groups to develop a role play or to script a scene about someone who allows a friend to pressurise them into doing something they later regret.

10 Staying in control of your life

Stay in *control* of your life

How many times have you agreed to do something that a friend wants to do just to avoid an argument? This may be a good way to keep a friend but could lead to big problems.

If someone told us to jump from an aeroplane without a parachute, we'd tell them where to go in no uncertain terms! We would know that what they are telling us to do is dangerous to ourselves and so we would not do it. Something which seems appealing because your friends are doing it, may not seem so appealing when you are alone. If you gave the situation some thought, you would realise that your body is telling you that you shouldn't do it, but you are ignoring it. You are allowing yourself to be pressurised by your friends rather than make up your own mind.

Listen To Your Body

Your body has certain responses in situations when you do not feel safe or comfortable. These are things such as butterflies in your tummy, nausea, trembling, sweating, hairs standing up on your neck etc. In situations when you feel these responses, it may be that your body is telling you not to take part in something. Make up your own mind and don't allow friends to pressure you into something you cannot control.

Don't Do It!

We all know how difficult it is to stand up for your views – but it is vital that you do so. Criminal or dangerous behaviour benefits no one. It can only lead to trouble and injury. If friends are pressurising you into doing something that's wrong, you should exercise your own free choice. If your actions will harm another person in any way, DON'T DO IT. The victim of your actions could easily be someone close to you – maybe a relative or a friend. Would you want them to suffer?

What Can You Do?

If you are being pressured by a friend or a stranger, think about your safe choices. Could you explain to them that you will not join in with something just to please them? Could you walk away from them? Could you do anything else to stay safe? By using your judgement and common sense you can keep yourself feeling safe. Your friends will soon realise that standing up to them is by far the bravest thing to do. Once you have got away from the immediate pressure/danger, talk to someone you trust to make sure it doesn't happen again.

Once you have shown your friends that you're not the mindless copy-cat they imagined, you'll probably come to notice others who are not coping so well with pressure from their friends.

Discuss the advice given in this article and say whether or not you agree with what it says.

Do you agree or disagree with the statements below?

❝ *It is always better to risk losing friends than to do something you don't think is right.* ❞

❝ *It is braver to say 'No' than to give in and say 'Yes'.* ❞

❝ *People who always do what others want them to do are weak and will never be respected.* ❞

UNIT 11 You and the media – the power of advertising

> **Objective:** To discuss the power and influence of advertising and to understand the rules for advertisements which target children.

Resources

Copies of Copymaster 11 'Advertising issues'

Video recording of several TV commercials

Starter

Begin with a series of questions about brand names. Ask individuals to write down the name of the brand they associate with certain products, e.g. 1) crisps, 2) cola, 3) chocolate bars, 4) trainers, 5) mobile phones. Record their answers on the board and discuss which brand names occurred the most often and why. Discuss how much this is due to advertising and read the two introductory paragraphs about advertising on page 50.

Suggested activities

- Read 'Is advertising good or bad?' (page 50). Ask groups to draw up lists of the arguments in favour of advertising and against advertising. Then read 'In groups' (page 50) and invite them to share their views of the two statements in a class discussion.

- Read 'How much influence do adverts have on you?' (page 50). Then show the students the video of some recent TV commercials. In groups, ask them to talk about current TV advertisements. Which are the most popular? How effective are they? Do they just make you remember the product or do they actually influence you to buy it? In a class discussion, encourage the students to share their views on how much influence advertisements have.

- Discuss the rules about advertising aimed at children (see 'Advertising and children' (page 51). Ask: 'Do you think that all TV advertisements aimed at children under 12 should be banned in the UK as they are in Sweden?'

- Study the results of the survey and discuss the various views on advertisements (see 'In groups' page 51)

- Read 'Shock tactics' (page 51). Encourage them to talk about any adverts that they have seen which use shock tactics and discuss their views of advertisements that use shock tactics.

Plenary

Recap the arguments for and against advertising. Ask the students to write a statement saying whether they agree with the view that advertising does more good than harm. Then invite some of them to read out their statements.

Extension activities

Read Copymaster 11 and ask groups to discuss their views on the portrayal of women and men in advertisements, and on the issue of whether people from ethnic minorities are under-represented in adverts. Then invite them to cut out advertisements from magazines showing women and men, to write comments on how they are portrayed in the adverts and to make a wall display of images and stereotypes in advertising.

Ask students to research how the advertising industry is regulated by using the internet (see www. asa.org.uk) to find out what the Advertising Standards Authority is and how it deals with complaints.

11 Advertising issues

The portrayal of women

Do advertisements depict women accurately or do they promote female stereotypes? Do they sometimes use sexy images which are completely inappropriate to the product being advertised?

'Stereotype' ads face Europe ban

The days of watching scantily clad models dancing on distant beaches to promote the latest perfume could be numbered.

Any ads that promote women as sex objects should be banned, according to an EU report.

Any kind of gender stereotyping – from the Oxo mother cooking in the kitchen to the Ronseal man creosoting a fence – should also be cut out.

The report could also bolster moves to ban the use of extremely thin women, who Swedish MEP Eva-Britt Svensson said were poor role models for girls.

Although the report will not see the creation of any new laws, it calls for governments to use their existing equality laws to control advertising.

From *Metro*

Discuss the views on the right. Say whether or not you agree with them and why.

❝ *Advertising generally represents women very well these days. It's fair to use beautiful women if appropriate.* ❞

❝ *There's less stereotyping than there used to be. In the past you only got two images – either the domestic type or the beauty. Now you get more adverts showing successful career women.* ❞

❝ *Far too many adverts still use female sexuality to make their products seem attractive. Nowadays they just do it more subtly.* ❞

❝ *I find lots of adverts offensive because the message is: you're not attractive unless you're slim like the model, which is nonsense!* ❞

Discuss the way men are portrayed in advertisements. Do advertisements present a stereotyped view of young men? Are boys as much in danger of getting a complex about their appearance from comparing themselves to the models in adverts as girls are?

How many adverts do you know which feature people from ethnic minority groups? Why are people from ethnic minorities under-represented in advertisements? What can be done about it?

Lesson 2 *Your Life Student Book 2,* pages 52–53
Citizenship/Economic and financial capability – understanding advertising

Objective: To examine TV advertising, how TV and radio adverts are made and how advertisers use sponsorship and celebrity endorsements.

Resources

Video recording of several TV adverts

Copies of Copymaster 11A 'Understanding advertising'

Starter

Show the class a TV advert for a product. Ask: 'What image of the product is given?' Talk about how the image is created – by the setting, the type of people in it, the words used, and the music. Ask: 'How much actual information about the product is given in the advert?' 'How does the advert try to sell the product – by giving information and/or creating an image?'

Suggested activities

- Read 'The commercial break' (page 52). Ask groups to discuss what it says about TV adverts and to make a list of techniques used in TV adverts. Show them a further selection of TV adverts and discuss the techniques used in them.

- Read and discuss in groups 'Celebrity endorsement' (page 53). Talk about current examples of celebrity endorsement. Are some more effective than others? Can they explain why?

- Read 'Sponsorship' (page 53). Debate the view that big companies should donate their money to charities and worthy causes, rather than spend huge sums on sponsorship. Discuss whether the publicity they would generate from doing so would be as effective as the publicity they get from sponsorship.

Plenary

Summarise how advertisers get their message across by asking: 'What are the most effective adverts currently on TV?' 'What techniques do they use a) to hold your attention and b) to get their message across?'

Extension activity

Ask students to find an advertisement in a newspaper or magazine and to show their understanding of advertising by writing an analysis of it (see 'For your file', page 52).

Assessment

Use Copymaster 11A to assess understanding of advertising.

Answers: Across – 1. stereotype, 5. jingle, 6. decent, 7. sport, 9. snack, 11. logo, 12. slogan, 13. legal, 16. ITC. Down – 1. Sweden, 2. revenue, 3. prices, 4. celebrity, 8. mail, 9. sponsor, 10. honest, 12. sales, 14. eat, 15. lead.

11A Understanding advertising

Complete this word puzzle to check your knowledge about advertising.

Clues across

1. A standardised image of a particular type of person often used by advertisers. (10)

5. A catchy, little rhyme or verse used in an advert. (6)

6. All advertisements broadcast on TV and radio must be legal, _ _ _ _ _ _ _, honest and truthful. (6)

7. A _ _ _ _ _, such as football, attracts a lot of sponsorship from advertisers, because it is so popular. (5)

9. Adverts for _ _ _ _ _ foods must not suggest that such products may be substituted for balanced meals. (5)

11. A trademark or company emblem printed on a piece of clothing as a way of advertising. (4)

12. A short, snappy, easy-to-remember phrase used in an advertisement. (6)

13. All advertisements broadcast on TV must be _ _ _ _ _, decent, honest and truthful. (5)

16. The Independent Television Commission which regulates all advertisements that appear on TV. (1,1,1)

Clues down

1. TV adverts aimed at children under 12 are banned in this country. (6)

2. Most of the _ _ _ _ _ _ _ of TV companies, newspapers and magazines comes from the money that advertisers pay them. (7)

3. _ _ _ _ _ _ of products advertised to children must not be minimised by words such as 'only' or 'just'. (6).

4. What we call a famous person who uses their name to endorse a product. (9)

8. Advertisements to children must not invite them to purchase products by telephone or _ _ _ _. (4)

9. To pay money for your company's name to be promoted, e.g. by a team or an individual, or for it to be associated with a sporting event. (7)

10. All advertisements broadcast on TV and radio must be legal, decent, _ _ _ _ _ _ and truthful. (6)

12. These increase as a result of a successful advertising campaign. (5)

14. Advertisements to children must not encourage them to do this frequently throughout the day. (3)

15. Advertisements must not _ _ _ _ children to believe that unless they have or use a product they are inferior. (4)

Lesson 1 *Your Life Student Book 2*, pages 54–55
Personal wellbeing – managing your leisure time

Objective: To explore the use they make of their leisure time.

Resources

Copies of Copymaster 12 'How do you use your leisure time?'

Starter

Ask the students: 'How well do you think you use your leisure time?' 'Are you good at planning how you use your leisure time? At getting involved in school and community activities? At using your leisure time constructively?' Ask individuals to rate their use of leisure time on a five-point scale (5 = excellent to 1 = poor) and to explain the reasons for their assessment.

Suggested activities

● Ask individuals to complete the quiz (see pages 54–55), then to check what their answers tell them about their use of leisure time, and to compare this with the assessment they made before doing the quiz. Ask them to discuss, in pairs, what they have learned from the activity, then ask each student to think of at least one way in which they can make better use of their leisure time.

● Read and discuss Peta's letter (page 55). In groups, share experiences of difficulties they have had as a result of not planning their use of leisure time and brainstorm ways of overcoming the problem. How can they improve their planning skills? Then draft a reply to Peta's letter (see 'For your file' page 55).

Plenary

Read 'Four ways to make better use of your leisure time' (page 55). Ask: 'What other things can you suggest people could do to make better use of their leisure time?' Make a list on the board of their suggestions. Then invite individuals to draw up an action plan for making better use of their leisure time a) during the week, b) at weekends.

Extension activity

Ask groups to prepare a questionnaire to survey how members of the class spend their weekends. Then give the questionnaire to another group to complete. Ask them to analyse their findings and report them to the rest of the class.

12 How do you use your leisure time?

Are you making the most of your leisure time?

Do this quiz to find out about how well you spend your leisure time. Keep a record of your answers, and then discuss with a partner what you have learned from this activity about how well you use your leisure time and how good you are at:

- planning how you spend your time;
- getting involved in activities at school and in the community;
- using your leisure time to develop your knowledge and skills.

Each decide on one or more things you could do to make better use of your leisure time.

1 **At the weekend do you:**
a *always plan in advance what you are going to do;*
b *sometimes plan things in advance;*
c *never plan ahead – just wait to see what happens?*

2 **How much time do you spend each week on your hobby?**
a *4–6 hours;* **b** *1–3 hours;*
c *less than an hour a week.*

3 **What types of TV programmes do you mainly watch?**
a *'serious' programmes, such as documentaries, news and drama;* **b** *a mixture of serious programmes and light entertainment;*
c *light entertainment, such as comedies, soaps, pop music and quizzes.*

4 **How often do you stay after school for a club or a practice?**
a *2 or 3 times a week;* **b** *once a week;*
c *hardly ever.*

5 **When you go out with your friends do you usually:**
a *go somewhere to do something, for example, go to a film or a disco, or to a park to play football;*
b *go shopping or to a café;*
c *hang about hoping someone might suggest something to do?*

A test-yourself quiz

6 **How often do you read a book other than a schoolbook?**
a *most days;* **b** *every now and then;*
c *hardly ever.*

7 **How often do you take exercise (apart from in PE lessons)?**
a *5–6 days a week;* **b** *2–3 days a week;*
c *hardly ever.*

8 **When you go on a computer what do you mostly use it for?**
a *finding information from the internet;*
b *sending emails to friends and relatives;*
c *playing games.*

9 **How do you keep up with what's going on in the world?**
a *by watching the news/reading a newspaper daily;*
b *by watching the news every now and then;*
c *by relying on other people to tell you if something happens.*

10 **If you are asked to volunteer to take part in a community activity do you usually:**
a *volunteer;* **b** *wait to see if your friends do, then volunteer;* **c** *never volunteer?*

11 **How often in the holidays do you feel bored because you can't think of anything to do?**
a *very rarely;* **b** *sometimes;* **c** *most days.*

12 **How much time each day do you spend watching TV?**
a *less than 1 hour;* **b** *between 1 and 3 hours;* **c** *over 3 hours.*

Your Life 2/Year 8

Lesson 2 *Your Life Student Book 2*, pages 56–57
Personal wellbeing/Keeping healthy – managing your leisure time

Objective: To explore ways of using leisure time constructively, and to discuss the importance of exercise and to compare the benefits of different types of exercise.

Starter

Ask the students: 'Why is exercise good for you?' List the reasons on the board: Physical benefits – it strengthens the heart and keeps the circulatory system working efficiently; it keeps the lungs and respiratory system working well; it keeps muscles in good condition; it stops you getting overweight. Mental benefits – it relaxes you and helps get rid of tension; it's good for self-esteem because it keeps your body in good shape.

Suggested activities

- Read 'Choose your exercise' (page 57). Discuss with the class what the S-factors are and why each is important. Then ask pairs to study the S-factor score chart, to work out a test-yourself quiz, and to give it to another pair to complete.

- Ask: 'How would you convince someone that exercise is good for you and not a waste of time?' Suggest the students note down the arguments suggested and then to show their understanding of them by drafting a reply to Sam's letter (see 'For your file', page 57).

- Read about how to beat the boredom blues ('Getting a piece of the action', page 56). Ask students to discuss Samantha Graham's ideas in groups, then to share their views in a class discussion. Ask individuals to think about how they spent their time in the last school holidays, and to suggest one thing they might do in the next school holidays to make better use of their time.

Plenary

Ask the students to imagine that their parents have offered to give them £50 to spend over a two-week holiday period, provided that they can come up with a proposal for an activity that will be a good use of their time. Explain to a partner how they would use the money, then share some of their ideas in a class discussion.

Extension activities

Ask groups to imagine that they are members of a youth club committee and to draw up plans for a 'Summer holiday youth scheme' to run from 10.00am to 4.00pm each weekday for three weeks. Discuss the activities they would include in order to attract as many young people as possible. Then ask the groups to take turns to present the plans to the rest of the class.

UNIT 13 You and the world of work – employment and unemployment

Your Life 2/Year 8

Lesson 1 *Your Life Student Book 2*, pages 58–59
Citizenship/Economic wellbeing and financial capability – understanding the world of work

Objective: To understand how employment and unemployment affect the local community and the differences between jobs in the primary, secondary and tertiary sectors of industry.

Starter

Write the terms 'employed' and 'unemployed' on the board and ask the students to draft definitions of them. Compare their definitions with those in the book (see 'Key terms' box, page 58) and explain what the terms 'workforce' and 'full employment' mean.

Suggested activities

- Read 'How employment and unemployment affect the local community'. (page 58). Discuss with the class how full employment means more people have money to spend and how this creates more jobs and sustains full employment. Then talk about how businesses closing and rising unemployment has the reverse effect. Ask them to give examples of any local businesses that have closed in recent years and how the closures have affected the local community.

- Ask the students to read 'Different types of employment' (pages 58–59). Get them to discuss how Frank, Joe and Liz work in different sectors of industry. They should draw three columns labelled Primary, Secondary and Tertiary and list examples of jobs in each sector.

Plenary

Ask students in groups to study the pie chart on page 59 and to discuss what it tells them about changes in the UK economy. Then ask some individuals which sector of industry they see themselves working in.

Extension activity

Ask the students to look at the employment listings in the local newspaper and to write a statement saying what they learned about jobs available in the local area and the state of the local economy (see 'For your file' page 59).

UNIT 13 You and the world of work – employment and unemployment

Your Life 2/Year 8

Lesson 2 *Your Life Student Book 2*, pages 60–61

Citizenship/Economic wellbeing and financial capability – understanding the world of work

> **Objective:** To understand that you are likely to have several different types of jobs during your working life and the importance of developing transferable skills.

Resources

Copies of Copymaster 13 'Transferable skills'

Starter

Introduce the topic by asking students how many of their parents and other family members have changed their type of work at some point in their working lives. Explain that fewer people now expect to do the same job for life than was the case in the past.

Suggested activities

- Read 'Employment for life' and 'Employability for life' (page 60) and in groups ask them to discuss the differences between Alfred's, Jackie's and Mike's experiences. Then make sure in a class discussion that they understand the concept of employability for life.

- Read 'Transferable skills' (page 61). Ask the students to look at the list of jobs and to decide which are the most important skills required for each job.

- Use Copymaster 13 'Transferable skills' to get the students to think about how good they are at each skill (see 'For your file' page 61), then to write a statement saying which skills they need to work hard at developing.

Plenary

Invite a number of individuals to read out their statements and remind the class why it is so important to develop their transferable skills.

Extension activity

Ask students to write an article about how working lives have changed in the past 60 years (see 'For your file' page 60).

● **Can communicate effectively with colleagues and customers**

☐ excellent   ☐ very good   ☐ good   ☐ not very good   ☐ poor

● **Have good interpersonal skills and can work well in teams**

☐ excellent   ☐ very good   ☐ good   ☐ not very good   ☐ poor

● **Are good at solving problems**

☐ excellent   ☐ very good   ☐ good   ☐ not very good   ☐ poor

● **Are numerate and have experience of handling money**

☐ excellent   ☐ very good   ☐ good   ☐ not very good   ☐ poor

● **Have good ICT skills**

☐ excellent   ☐ very good   ☐ good   ☐ not very good   ☐ poor

● **Are willing and able to learn**

☐ excellent   ☐ very good   ☐ good   ☐ not very good   ☐ poor

● **Are flexible in their approach to work.**

☐ excellent   ☐ very good   ☐ good   ☐ not very good   ☐ poor

1 Use the 5-point scale above to rate how good you think you are at the transferable skills listed.

2 Write a statement explaining which skills you need to work hard to develop. Say why it is important to develop these skills.

Lesson 1 *Your Life Student Book 2*, pages 62–63
Personal wellbeing – drinking and alcohol

Objective: To understand the effects of drinking alcohol and to explore teenage drinking and the laws about young people and alcohol.

Resources

Copies of Copymaster 14 'How much do you know about alcohol?'

Starter

Introduce the topic with a discussion of why there is so much fuss about alcohol. Talk about how powerful a drug alcohol is and how people who get drunk often do things they later regret (e.g. get into fights, behave recklessly and cause criminal damage, have unprotected sex, drive a car and cause an accident). Talk about how alcohol can be addictive and lead to alcoholism. Stress how important it is, therefore, to know all about alcohol and what sensible drinking is.

Suggested activities

● Read about alcohol and its effects ('What's all the fuss about?', page 62) and about 'Drink strengths' (page 62). Ask the students in pairs to produce a 'True or false?' quiz based on the information in the two articles, then to give the quiz to another pair to do.

● Ask groups to discuss the statements by Kirstie and Shareen (see page 62), then to share their views in a class discussion.

● Read 'Alcohol and young people – the law' (page 63). Ask: 'Should the legal age for drinking be raised, lowered, or left as it is?' Discuss the arguments for and against changing the law and/or strengthening it by increasing the penalties for people who sell alcohol to young people.

● Read 'Shock tactics in binge-drinking ads' (page 63). Discuss how the ads try to put their message across. Ask: 'How effective do you think such adverts are?'

● Ask individuals to write a short statement saying what they think of people who get very drunk, then to share their views in a group discussion (see 'In groups', page 63).

Plenary

Ask: 'If you were designing a poster entitled 'Think Before You Drink' to make young people aware of how drinking can affect them, what messages would you want to get across? What information would you include on the poster?' Share their ideas in a class discussion.

Extension activities

Ask individuals to draw the poster based on the ideas they discussed in the Plenary session.

Test the students' knowledge of alcohol and its effects by encouraging them to do the quiz on Copymaster 13. Then ask them to join up with a partner to check their answers by referring to the articles on these pages. The correct answers are: 1c, 2b, 3b, 4c, 5b, 6b, 7b, 8d, 9b, 10a, 11c, 12 how much alcohol is drunk; how quickly it is drunk; the amount of food in your stomach; how dehydrated you are; your size; how often you drink.

14

How much do you know about alcohol?

How much do you know about ALCOHOL
Choose the right answer to each of these questions and put a circle round it.

1 How many grams of alcohol are there in one unit?
A 2
B 4
C 8
D 10

2 Which of the following contains the most alcohol?
A one glass of sherry
B one pint of normal strength beer
C one single measure of whisky
D one glass of wine

3 How many calories are there in one pint of normal strength beer?
A 120
B 180
C 240
D 300

4 Which part of the body absorbs alcohol?
A liver
B kidneys
C stomach
D skin

5 Which part of the body breaks down alcohol when we drink it?
A stomach
B liver
C pancreas
D kidneys

6 At what age can young people buy alcohol from an off-licence?
A 12
B 18
C 14
D 16

7 What is the current legal limit for the amount of alcohol in the blood when driving?
A 60 mg in 100 ml blood
B 80 mg in 100 ml blood
C 50 mg in 100 ml blood
D 90 mg in 100 ml blood

8 If a person drank six pints of normal-strength beer in fairly rapid succession, about how many hours would it take to clear all the alcohol from his or her body?
A 6
B 9
C 11
D 13

9 What is the maximum number of units recommended for an adult male to drink daily?
A 1
B 3
C 5
D 8

10 What is the maximum number of units recommended for an adult female to drink daily?
A 2
B 4
C 6
D 8

11 How many children under 15 years old are admitted to hospital each year with acute alcohol poisoning?
A 100
B 500
C 1000
D 2000

12 Name four factors which affect the amount of alcohol in a person's blood after they have been drinking:

A ....
....
B ....
....
C ....
....
D ....
....

UNIT 14 You and your body – drinking and alcohol

Your Life 2/Year 8

Lesson 2 *Your Life Student Book 2*, pages 64–65

Personal wellbeing – drinking and alcohol

Objective: To explore the problems alcohol can cause teenagers who drink too much, and to discuss how to cope with an adult in the family who has a drink problem.

Starter

Recap on how people who don't regulate their drinking can become dependent on alcohol. Talk about the effect that alcoholism can have on people's lives and discuss high-profile cases of celebrities with drinking problems. Explain that you can become an alcoholic at any age if your drinking gets out of control.

Suggested activities

- Read 'Kerry's story' (page 64). Ask: 'Is she just having fun or has she got a problem?' Ask pairs to discuss and write down what they would say to Kerry to warn her of the risks of continuing to drink as much as she does. Then share their ideas in a class discussion.

- Read 'Valerie's story' (page 65). Ask groups to list all the problems Valerie has had to face because of her mother's drinking. Ask: 'What do you think of the way Valerie has coped with the situation?' 'What advice would you give her?'

- Invite individuals to study the advice in 'Living with someone who drinks – how to cope' (page 65), then to show their understanding of it by writing a reply to Tony's letter (see 'For your file', page 65).

Plenary

Explain that the government has considered putting health warnings on alcohol containers. Discuss how effective such warnings might be and ask students to work in pairs to draft what a warning might say on: a) a can of beer, b) a bottle of wine and c) a bottle of spirits.

Extension activity

Invite students to find more information about young people and drinking by using the internet and visiting websites such as www.wreckedwd.co.uk and www.drinksmarter.org.

UNIT 15 You and the community – the school as a community

Your Life 2/Year 8

Lesson 1 *Your Life Student Book 2*, pages 66–67
Social education – the school community

> **Objective:** To understand that the school is a community of different groups, and to consider how proposals for a six-term year would affect the various members of the school community.

Starter

Talk about how the school community consists of different groups and list the various groups on the board. Discuss how any major change to the organisation or routine of the school will have an impact on each of these groups. Summarise the points you have made by reading the first two paragraphs on page 66.

Suggested activities

- Read 'A new school year?' (page 66). Ensure that students understand what the proposed pattern of a six-term year is. Ask pairs to list what they think are the advantages and disadvantages of a six-term year.

- Read the statements in 'A change for the better?' (page 67) and discuss each one in turn, encouraging the class to say whether they agree or disagree with it and why. Ask pairs to add to their list any further reasons for or against the proposal. Either organise a debate on the motion 'This house believes that a six-term year is better than a three-term year' or role play a public meeting on the issue of introducing a six-term year, in which representatives of various groups in the school community express their views.

- Ask groups to discuss how the school day is organised and to present their recommendations either for or against changing it to the rest of the class (see 'In groups', page 67).

Plenary

Explain that any changes to the school day or school year would have an impact on other groups of people, besides those in the school community, e.g. on the bus companies which supply school transport and on the catering staff who supply school meals. Discuss how they might react to the proposal for a six-term year. Stress the importance of considering every viewpoint when changes are being proposed.

Extension activity

Invite members of the different groups that make up the school community (e.g. a governor, member of the parents and teachers association, of the caretaking staff, of the administrative staff), to join a discussion of the proposal for a six-term year. Suggest the class make notes of what they say and ask them to work individually to write an article for the school newsletter reporting their views.

Your Life 2/Year 8

Lesson 2 *Your Life Student Book 2*, pages 68–69
Social education – the school community

> **Objective:** To develop skills in participation and responsible action by holding a mock election to a Year 8 council and by discussing proposals for changes to the school's dress code.

Resources

Copies of the school's uniform regulations for Year 8

Copies of Copymaster 15 'Year 8 newsletter – questionnaire'

Starter

Talk about the school council (how it is composed, how members are elected, what its function is, and how information about its meetings is communicated). Ask: 'How effective is it in dealing with the issues that concern Year 8 students?' Introduce the idea of having Year councils. Ask: 'What are the arguments for and against having Year councils?'

Suggested activities

- Read the constitution of Beach Lane School Year 8 Council (page 64). Discuss with the class what its purpose is and how it is organised. Then hold a mock election for a Year 8 council. Invite groups to help a candidate prepare a statement to read to the rest of the class. After each candidate has spoken, hold a 'question time' in which the other members of the class can ask questions. Then hold a vote by secret ballot.

- Read 'The Henry Box School – School Uniform' (page 69). Then give out copies of the school's uniform regulations for Year 8. Ask groups to compare the school's dress code with The Henry Box school's dress code and to make suggestions for changes to the school's uniform regulations.

- Ask individuals to write a letter to the school council on a Year 8 issue (see 'For your file', page 68).

Plenary

Ask the students to share their ideas for changes to the school uniform in a class discussion.

Extension activities

Draw up a class proposal for changes to the school's uniform regulations to put to the school council. Print out copies to show to parents and ask them to comment on the proposals. Then discuss parents' comments as a class and, if they think it appropriate, get them to make changes before presenting the proposals to the school council.

As a class, plan and produce a Year 8 newsletter which can be made available for downloading on the school's website. Use Copymaster 15 'Year 8 newsletter – questionnaire' to research what articles various members of the school community would find most interesting.

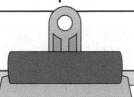

Newsletter – Questionnaire

We are planning to produce a Year 8 newsletter. Please indicate which types of information and articles you would find most interesting by ticking the appropriate box.

	Very Interesting	Quite Interesting	Not very Interesting
A calendar of forthcoming school events	☐	☐	☐
Year 8 sports results and reports	☐	☐	☐
Articles about school clubs	☐	☐	☐
Reviews of new books and videos in the resources centre	☐	☐	☐
Hints on how to study	☐	☐	☐
Articles on hobbies	☐	☐	☐
Letters from students, parents and teachers	☐	☐	☐
Interviews, e.g. with a governor, a school bus driver, the caretaker	☐	☐	☐
Jokes	☐	☐	☐
Cartoons	☐	☐	☐
Other (please specify)	☐	☐	☐

....

Please indicate which of the following you are by ticking one box:

☐ student   ☐ teacher   ☐ parent   ☐ admin. staff

☐ classroom assistant   ☐ caretaking staff   ☐ governor   ☐ other

UNIT 15 You and the community – the school as a community

Lesson 3 *Your Life Student Book 2*, pages 70–71

Social education/Economic wellbeing and financial capability – the school community

> **Objective:** To organise and plan a budget for a social event.

Resources

Copies of Copymaster 15A 'Understanding how to organise a social event'

Starter

Look at the list of types of social event on page 66. Ask students what type of social event they would like to organise for the class. Would they like it to be an evening event or a day out at the weekend? How much would they be willing to pay for the event? They share their ideas and vote to decide which type of event to organise.

Suggested activities

- Ask groups to make a list of all the jobs that need to be done in order for the event to take place. Compare their lists with the checklist given as an example on page 70 '8L ice-skating trip'.

- Appoint a planning committee (see page 70). As a class give the planning committee detailed instructions about what tasks need to be done and a timetable of dates by which each task must be done.

- Read 'Planning a budget for your trip' (page 67) and ask them in groups to work out a budget for a similar event.

Plenary

Ask students to summarise what they have learned about how to organise and plan a budget for a social event.

Extension activities

Ask them individually to draft a letter giving full details of the event and its cost, including a tear-off slip which can be signed by parents giving permission for their children to book a place on the trip. Get them to check each other's letters to ensure that they contain all the necessary information, before putting them into their files.

After the event hold a discussion in which you review it (see 'Reviewing the event' page 70).

Assessment

Use Copymaster 15A to assess understanding of how to organise a social event.

15A Understanding how to organise a social event

Draw up a checklist of things you would need to do when planning and organising a disco for your Year group. Include advice on such things as:

- choosing a date
- planning a budget
- choosing and booking the venue
- finding and booking a DJ
- printing and selling the tickets
- organising and selling refreshments
- organising adult support and supervision
- arranging clearing up after the event.

UNIT 16 You and your opinions – speaking your mind

Objective: To understand the difference between facts and opinions, to know how to form an opinion and to practise justifying an opinion in an oral discussion.

Resources

Copies of Copymaster 16 'Should sick children be filmed for TV programmes?'

Copies of Copymaster 16A 'Understanding the difference between facts and opinions'

Starter

Explain that while listening to an argument we need to be able to distinguish between a fact, which is a true statement, and an opinion, which is a judgement or belief. Read 'Facts and opinions' (page 72) and make sure everyone understands the difference between a fact and an opinion.

Suggested activities

- Ask pairs to study the list of ten statements (see 'In pairs', page 72) and decide which are facts and which are opinions.

- Talk about how, if we are going to discuss an issue, we need to research it to find out the facts and what the different opinions on it are. Read 'Forming your opinion' (page 72). Teach the students the mnemonic FIDO to help them remember how to form an opinion: Find out the facts, Identify the issues, Decide your Opinion.

- Ask individuals to study all the information and views on body-piercing ('Should body-piercing be banned?', page 73), to make notes on the facts and opinions they contain, and to form their own opinion on body-piercing. Then allow them to share their views in groups.

- Ask individuals to write a short statement expressing their opinions on body-piercing (see 'For your file', page 73).

Plenary

Ask some students to read their statements and discuss how clearly they stated their arguments and whether or not they used facts to support their opinions.

Extension activity

Ask individuals to study Copymaster 16, to form their own opinions on the issue, then to share their views in a group discussion.

Assessment

Use Copymaster 16A to assess understanding of the difference between facts and opinions.

Answers: 1. opinion, 2. fact, 3. opinion, 4. fact, 5. fact, 6. opinion, 7. opinion, 8. fact, 9. fact, 10. opinion.

16 Should sick children be filmed for TV programmes?

Some people, including a number of doctors, think it is wrong to film sick children and show them on TV in programmes such as *Children's Hospital*. What do you think? Is it ethical to film sick children?

SHOULD SICK CHILDREN BE FILMED FOR TV PROGRAMMES?

Dr Richard Barry Jones
retired paediatrician

Children shouldn't be featured in these programmes because they can't give consent, and I don't think an adult can do it for them. An adult can consent to medical treatment if it's going to improve a child's health, and you could argue that they could consent to a child being used in a research study if it's in the public interest. But when it comes to appearing in a TV programme, I don't believe it's ever in the child's interest. I don't think that you can argue that it's in the public interest either – there may be interest from the public, but that's another matter.

Verdict: **No**

Helen Scott
producer, Yorkshire TV's hospital documentary Jimmy's

In some cases it's inappropriate for a child to be in a documentary, and we fully appreciate that. But there are other children for whom it can be beneficial, and whose story can benefit the public. Obviously the parents and the children can say no, and getting them involved is a process that involves health professionals as well as the production team, the child and his parents. Some children we featured in Jimmy's gained a lot of self-esteem from being involved in the programme; it also meant that their friends could understand what they'd been through.

Verdict: **Yes**

Laura Shutt (12)
shown having liver transplant in Children's Hospital

Being on Children's Hospital was a fun way of getting through a very big trauma. I got to know the production team and I knew they were all rooting for me, and that helped. We discussed it very carefully as a family before agreeing. I was 10 at the time, which sounds young, but when you've a life-threatening condition like cystic fibrosis you've had to face up to a lot in a short time, and I feel I was able to make that decision. We could tell them to go away – and sometimes did – and were shown the video before it went out so we could object to anything we didn't like.

Verdict: **Yes**

Claire Rayner
President of the Patients' Association

I've watched the hospital documentaries, and like everyone else I find them enthralling. But good for the children? Definitely not. I'm not sure that either the children or their parents realise what they're letting themselves in for – that they're giving up their anonymity, and that everyone will find out all about them. I know everyone is asked to give their consent, but I do have worries about how far they're trading on gratitude on getting that consent. They don't mean to pressurise, but when they're saving your child's life you might not want to say no.

Verdict: **No**

Sheila Shutt
Laura's mother

Of course we thought long and hard about it before agreeing to Laura being on the programme. There was no pressure at all: initially I wasn't keen, but then I started thinking about the effect on potential donors, and on relatives of people whose organs had been used in transplants. I thought that they could be helped by seeing how Laura's life could be changed through a liver transplant – I think it had a really important educational role. Also, I feel that the film might have helped other youngsters like Laura who are facing surgery.

Verdict: **Yes**

ASSESSMENT COPYMASTER

16A Understanding the difference between facts and opinions

Study the list of statements below and decide which are FACTS and which are OPINIONS.
Put a cross in the appropriate box.

	FACT	OPINION
1. Gambling is a waste of time and money.	☐	☐
2. People can become addicted to gambling.	☐	☐
3. If you get your skin tattooed, you will regret it.	☐	☐
4. It is against the law to tattoo someone under the age of 18.	☐	☐
5. People who smoke are likely to die earlier than non-smokers.	☐	☐
6. Smoking should be banned in public places.	☐	☐
7. Foxhunting is cruel and unnecessary.	☐	☐
8. Foxhunting is a way of controlling the number of foxes.	☐	☐
9. People who are found guilty of serious crimes are often sent to prison.	☐	☐
10. Tougher prison sentences would reduce the amount of crime.	☐	☐

UNIT 16 You and your opinions – speaking your mind

Your Life 2/Year 8

Lesson 2 *Your Life Student Book 2*, pages 74–75
Social education – expressing your opinions

Objective: To understand the rules of debating, to explore techniques that can be used to make speeches effective and to participate in a debate.

Starter

Explain the difference between an informal discussion, which does not follow a set pattern dictated by rules, and a formal debate, which has a set pattern of rules. Talk about why there are rules in formal debates, and how they allow people to express their arguments without being interrupted and to hear and consider different opinions.

Suggested activities

- Read and explain 'The rules of debating' (page 74). Ask students, in groups, to compile a glossary of debating terms to put in their files.

- Plan a debate to take place in a follow-up lesson. Invite students either to suggest a motion themselves or to choose one of the three motions from page 74 (see 'Organise your own debate') and write the motion on the board.

- Explain that you are going to split the class into two groups; ask one group to prepare speeches for the motion and the other to prepare speeches against. Before they begin, read and discuss 'Tips on writing a speech' (page 75). Then allow them to start planning their speeches in pairs, by discussing where they can find out more about the issue and listing the main arguments for and against the motion.

Plenary

Hold a class discussion in which you talk about the arguments they have identified. List the arguments for and against the motion on the board and ask the students to copy them to refer to as they plan their speeches. Discuss how they can research the issue to find out more information on it.

Extension activities

Ask the students to write their speeches and hand them in. Then choose people to act as proposer and seconder and hold the debate.

Review how the debate went. Talk about whose speeches were most effective, and why.

UNIT 17 You and your body – safe sex

Your Life 2/Year 8

Lesson 1 *Your Life Student Book 2*, pages 76–77
Personal wellbeing – sex education

> **Objective:** To provide information on contraception and safer sex, and to examine the steps that can be taken to avoid unwanted pregnancies and protection against STIs.

Resources

Leaflets for teenagers, obtainable from family planning clinics, giving factual information about contraception and STIs (optional)

Starter

Explain what is meant by 'the age of consent' and why there is a legal age of consent. Talk about how it aims to protect young people and how anyone who decides to have sex before the age of consent is taking a risk. Discuss how a boy can be prosecuted for having sex with an under-age girl and how the girl is taking a risk of getting pregnant. There is also the risk of catching a sexually transmitted infection. Explain that it is important to think carefully before having sex, and to know what safer sex is and how to practise it.

Suggested activities

- Read 'Sex and contraception … your questions answered' (page 76). Hold a class discussion in which you ask whether they have any comments to make on the advice that is given or questions to ask about it.

- Read 'The rhythm method' and 'Withdrawal' (page 77). Discuss why the rhythm method is unsuitable for teenagers and why withdrawal is unreliable.

- Read 'I'm worried about protection' (page 77). Discuss the reasons Tricia Kreitman gives for advising the 13-year-old girl not to have sex with her boyfriend. Ask: 'Do you agree with Tricia Kreitman? Why?'

Plenary

In a class discussion, talk about what the students have learned from this lesson about safer sex and how to avoid an unwanted pregnancy.

Extension activities

In groups, discuss the arguments for and against either raising or lowering the age of consent (see 'In groups', page 77). Then share their views in a class discussion.

Read the leaflets on methods of contraception and how to avoid catching STIs and discuss the information and advice they give.

UNIT 17 You and your body – safe sex

Your Life 2/Year 8

Lesson 2 *Your Life Student Book 2*, pages 78–79
Personal wellbeing – sex education

Objective: To explain the rights and responsibilities that a person has in any sexual relationship and to examine common myths about having sex.

Resources

Copies of Copymaster 17 'Sex facts and fictions'

Starter

Explain that in any relationship you have rights and responsibilities. It is your *right* to be able to do only the things you want to do and to refuse to do things you do not want to do. It is your *responsibility* to respect the rights of other people and not to try to pressurise or force them to do things they do not want to do.

Suggested activities

- Read about sexual rights and responsibilities (page 78). Ask groups to discuss what they consider to be the most important points made in the article. Then encourage them to share their ideas in a class discussion.

- Ask individuals to study the list of types of behaviour (see 'What is acceptable in a sexual relationship?', page 79), and to write down which they consider to be acceptable and unacceptable or are not sure about. Then allow them to share their views in a group discussion, followed by a class discussion.

- Read 'Sex myths' (page 79). Then in groups draft a reply to this letter:

  Dear Erica,

  My boyfriend is pressurising me to have sex, but I'm not sure. He says everyone is doing it and that it will bring us closer. When I tried to talk about taking precautions, he said he'd leave me to sort them out. I'm confused. What should I do?

  Josie

Plenary

Encourage students to share their replies to Josie's letter in a class discussion, drawing attention to the points they make about Josie's rights and responsibilities. Conclude the lesson by rereading the articles on page 78.

Extension activities

Use Copymaster 17 to check students' knowledge and understanding. Read out the statements and ask them on their own to write down whether or not the statement is fact or fiction. Then hand out the sheet and ask them to check their answers, reading and discussing the explanations under each statement.

17 Sex facts and fictions

1 Britain has the largest number of teenage births in Western Europe. **FACT**

Teenage births in Britain are twice as high as in Germany and six times higher than in the Netherlands where the age of consent is much lower than in the UK.

One of the possible reasons for the high rate of teenage pregnancies is that there are a number of myths about how you can avoid getting yourself pregnant.

2 You can't get pregnant the first time you have sex. **FICTION**

Of course you can, unless you use contraception. But between one third and one half of teenagers do not use contraception the first time they have sex.

3 You can't get pregnant if your partner withdraws before he ejaculates. **FICTION**

Some sperm can and does leak out before ejaculation. So withdrawal is not a reliable method of contraception.

4 You can't get pregnant if you wash out your vagina immediately after having sex. **FICTION**

Washing out the vagina is known as douching. This doesn't work and may even increase the chances of pregnancy by helping to push any sperm further up the vagina. This may also cause infection.

5 You can't get pregnant during your period. **FICTION**

Although you are less likely to get pregnant during your period, it's not impossible. Remember, sperm can live inside a girl's body for a considerable time – five days is quite normal.

6 You can't get pregnant if you have sex standing up. **FICTION**

It doesn't matter what position you have sex in, if you don't use a reliable method of contraception you may become pregnant.

7 An unwanted pregnancy will change your life for ever. **FACT**

Getting pregnant as a teenager has many consequences. First, you may come under pressure to decide whether or not to have an abortion. This can be very traumatic. Because the pregnancy was not planned, you may miss out on the antenatal support that is available to women who plan their pregnancies.

When your baby is born, your life will change for ever. It can be very difficult for teenage mothers to continue their education. For many teenage mothers, the arrival of the baby means the end of their formal education and the beginning of a life with poor job prospects.

8 The number of sexually transmitted infections among teenagers is rising. **FACT**

This is because teenagers do not always have planned sex and therefore may not protect themselves against sexually transmitted infections by using a condom.

9 The best way to avoid an unwanted pregnancy or a sexually transmitted infection is to delay having sex until you are old enough to be in a stable relationship with a partner who you can trust. **FACT**

The longer teenagers decide to wait before having sex, the less likely they are to have unwanted pregnancies and to catch a sexually transmitted infection. This means waiting until you are old enough to have found a partner with whom you can discuss and plan your sexual relationship and how best to protect yourselves.

10 It is easy to tell if someone has a sexually transmittable infection. **FICTION**

It is almost impossible to tell whether or not someone has a sexually transmittable infection because often a person has no visible symptoms.

UNIT 18 You as a citizen – Britain's government

Your Life 2/Year 8

Lesson 1 *Your Life Student Book 2*, pages 80–81
Citizenship – understanding Britain's government

Objective: To understand what happens in the House of Commons and the House of Lords, how laws are made and to discuss proposals for the reform of the House of Lords.

Resources

A short recording of TV coverage of Parliament, e.g. Prime Minister's Question Time

Starter

Recap what they learned in Year 7 about Parliament, about the composition of the House of Commons and the House of Lords and the role of the Sovereign.

Suggested activities

- Show the recording of Parliament at work and discuss with the class what they learn from it about what happens in the House of Commons. Then ask the students to study the information on their own on page 80 and to carry out the note-making activity (see 'For your file' page 80).

- Read the information about the House of Lords on page 81. Either ask groups to discuss the views on House of Lords reform and then to report back their opinions, or hold a whole class discussion followed by a vote on whether they think the House of Lords should be replaced by an elected assembly. Students can then write an email to a newspaper explaining their opinion and the reasons for it.

Plenary

Recap what Parliament is and what it does, stressing the differences in the membership and roles of the House of Commons and the House of Lords.

Extension activities

Students can find out more about Parliament from the website 'Explore Parliament' (www.parliament.uk/education).

Your Life 2/Year 8

Lesson 2 *Your Life Student Book 2*, pages 82–83
Citizenship – understanding Britain's government

Objective: To understand what the government and the opposition are, and how the government is financed.

Starter

Discuss what a political party is and who the main political parties are. Read 'What are political parties?' (page 82) and explain that after an election the leader of the political party which has the most votes forms the government.

Suggested activities

- Read the information about the government, the cabinet and the opposition (page 82). Discuss what other ministers are members of the cabinet, e.g. Minister of Defence, Minister of Education. Start to compile a 'Who's who in Parliament'. If students are unsure who holds a particular post, ask them to check, using the internet.

- Ask individuals to study 'The finances of government' (page 83) and to make notes for their files under the headings: 'How the government raises money'; 'How the government spends money'; and 'How the government's finances are controlled'.

- Invite students to show their understanding of parliamentary terms by compiling a glossary from the information on pages 80–83.

Plenary

Recap with the class what they have learned during the lesson about how the government is organised, what the opposition is and about the government's finances.

Extension activity

Create a newsboard about the government in action by getting the students to cut out newspaper articles on current political issues and displaying them on the classroom noticeboard.

UNIT 18 You as a citizen – Britain's government

Your Life 2/Year 8

Lesson 3 *Your Life Student Book 2*, pages 84–85
Citizenship – understanding Britain's government

Objective: To understand the electoral system, who becomes an MP and what an MP does.

Resources

Copies of Copymaster 18 'Understanding Parliament and parliamentary elections'

Starter

Write the word 'democracy' on the board. Explain that it means a system of government where all the citizens share power. Talk about how it would be impossible for everyone in the UK to meet in order to make decisions, so we delegate power to elected representatives in a decision-making body – Parliament.

Suggested activities

- Read and discuss 'How MPs are elected' on page 84. Then ask pairs to compile a 'True or false?' quiz about elections. Then swap their quiz with another pair's.

- Explain that only 6 out of 10 people voted in the 2010 general election. Ask: 'Why do you think people didn't vote?' 'What can be done to encourage people to vote?' e.g. hold the vote on Sundays; introduce electronic voting and/or postal voting; put polling booths in supermarkets; make voting compulsory. Make a list of suggestions on the board.

- Read 'Who becomes an MP?' (page 85). Ask students to discuss the view that there should be more women in Parliament and to make suggestions as to how the number of women MPs and ethnic minority MPs might be increased.

- Read and discuss 'What do MPs do?' (page 85). Talk about how they divide their time between their constituency and Parliament.

Plenary

Divide the class into two teams and recap what they have learned about elections by asking them questions based on the information on these pages (e.g. How often must a general election be held? How old must you be to vote?). If one team fails to answer correctly, offer the question to the other team for a bonus point.

Assessment

Use Copymaster 18 to assess understanding of Parliament and parliamentary elections. Answers: 1) c, 2) c, 3) a, 4) b, 5) c, 6) c, 7) b, 8) b, 9) c, 10) c, 11) b, 12) a, 13) b, 14) c, 15) c.

18 Understanding Parliament and parliamentary elections

Choose the correct endings and write **a**, **b** or **c** in the box.

1. A general election has to be held at least once every
   a) 3 years
   b) 4 years
   c) 5 years

2. You cannot vote until you are
   a) 16
   b) 17
   c) 18

3. To vote, your name must appear
   a) on the electoral register
   b) in the local directory
   c) on a list of householders

4. To become a candidate for election to Parliament, you must have your name put forward by
   a) a political party
   b) ten electors
   c) a local organisation

5. You cannot stand for an MP unless
   a) you were born in the area
   b) live in the area
   c) are over 21

6. Candidates stand for election to Parliament in areas known as parliamentary
   a) commissions
   b) communities
   c) constituencies

7. You can vote in person by going to
   a) a local council office
   b) a polling station
   c) a party headquarters

8. You put your completed voting slip in
   a) a budget box
   b) a ballot box
   c) a canvassing box

9. The winning candidate is the person who
   a) gets more than 50% of the vote
   b) has more votes after first, second and third preferences are counted
   c) gets the most votes

10. The number of MPs in the House of Commons is
    a) 501
    b) 587
    c) 646

11. The leader of the party with a majority of MPs becomes
    a) the President
    b) the Prime Minister
    c) the Chancellor

12. The group of senior ministers who meet to decide the government's policies is called
    a) the Cabinet
    b) the Governing Council
    c) the Steering Committee

13. The minister in charge of the government's finances is called
    a) the Speaker
    b) the Chancellor of the Exchequer
    c) the Chief Whip

14. A law, which is made by Parliament, is called
    a) a Bill
    b) a Referendum
    c) an Act of Parliament

15. The House of Lords has
    a) more power than the House of Commons
    b) the same amount of power as the House of Commons
    c) less power than the House of Commons

UNIT 18 You as a citizen – Britain's government

Your Life 2/Year 8

Lesson 4 *Your Life Student Book 2*, pages 86–87
Citizenship – understanding Britain's government

Objective: To understand the present voting system and to discuss the arguments for and against electoral reform.

Starter

Read 'Is the present voting system fair?' and discuss what the 'first past the post' system is.

Suggested activities

- Study the arguments presented on pages 86–87. Then hold a formal debate on the motion: 'This house believes that the British electoral system is unfair and that proportional representation should be introduced.'

UNIT 19 You and the world of work – understanding business

Your Life 2/Year 8

Lesson 1 *Your Life Student Book 2*, pages 88–89
Citizenship/Economic wellbeing and financial capability – understanding business

Objective: To understand that there are different types of business and to explore the advantages and disadvantages of working in each particular type.

Starter

Explain that businesses vary in type depending on who owns them and that the smallest businesses mainly have one owner, while the largest businesses are global businesses often owned by thousands of people who have invested money in them. Share examples of small businesses owned by one or a few people (e.g. a corner shop, a firm of solicitors) and large national companies (e.g. Boots) with a chain of shops nationwide and vast international companies with interests all over the world (e.g. Shell).

Suggested activities

- Read 'Working for yourself' (page 88). Ask the students to discuss the risks involved in running your own business and to share their views in a class discussion about whether they would be prepared to take the risks themselves. Then read 'Partnerships' (page 88). Continue the class discussion by asking: What do you see as the advantages of forming a partnership? Would you prefer to work in a partnership or as a sole trader? Explain why.

- Read 'Working for a company' (page 89). Ask the students to draw up two columns and to list the advantages and disadvantages of a) working for yourself and b) working for a company (see 'In groups' page 89) then to share their views in a group discussion.

- Ask them to read 'Working in the public, private or voluntary sector' (page 89) and in groups to discuss the differences between working in the different sectors (see 'In groups' page 89).

Plenary

Recap what they have learned about working as a sole trader, in a partnership and for a large company, and about the differences between the public, private and voluntary sectors.

Extension activity

Imagine someone you know, who is in their early 20s, is considering setting up a business as a sole trader. What advice would you give them? Do you think it is a risk worth taking? Write them an email saying what you think.

UNIT 19 You and the world of work – understanding business

Your Life 2/Year 8

Lesson 2 *Your Life Student Book 2*, page 90

Citizenship/Economic wellbeing and financial capability – understanding business

---

Objective: To investigate how a firm is organised.

Starter

Explain the purpose of the lesson is to explore how a firm is organised into different departments and ask them to suggest what the different departments of a firm are. Write their suggestions on the board.

Suggested activities

- Study the organisation of a small manufacturing company (page 90). Compare its structure with the list of departments they suggested.

- Set students the task of investigating a local business to find out how it is organised (see 'In pairs' page 90). Get them to obtain any information about it that they can from the internet, to contact the firm to arrange a visit and to prepare a list of questions to ask when they do.

Plenary

After they have visited the firm, get them in turn to report their findings to the rest of the class. Draw their attention to the similarities and differences in the organisation of the firms.

UNIT 19 You and the world of work – understanding business

Your Life 2/Year 8

Lesson 3 *Your Life Student Book 2*, page 91

Citizenship/Economic wellbeing and financial capability – understanding business

> **Objective:** To understand what a social enterprise is and to suggest what kind of social enterprise would benefit the local community.

Starter

Write the terms 'social entrepreneur' and 'social enterprise' on the board and use the introductory section on page 91 to explain what they mean.

Suggested activity

● Read the article about Green Works, then ask students to share ideas for a social enterprise that would benefit their local community (see 'In groups').

Plenary

Invite them to report their ideas to the rest of the class and to vote to choose the best idea.

Extension activity

Write a statement saying why they agree or disagree with the class's decision (see 'For your file' page 91).

UNIT 19 You and the world of work – understanding business

Your Life 2/Year 8

Lesson 4 *Your Life Student Book 2*, pages 92–93
Citizenship/Economic wellbeing and financial capability – understanding business

Objective: To explore the different ways of raising money to finance a business and the choices available to someone whose business is experiencing financial difficulties.

Resources

Copies of Copymaster 19 'Business talk'

Starter

Ask the class: 'What do businesses need money for?' List their suggestions on the board. Explain that what a business spends money on are known as its 'costs'.

Suggested activities

- Read the first three paragraphs on page 92 about the reasons why businesses need money and study the diagram 'The money-go-round', then compare the reasons given with the suggestions made by the class.

- Study 'Four ways of raising money' (page 92), then ask which option they would choose if they were the owner of a small manufacturing company which required money in order to expand its production (see 'In groups').

- Read 'Risk and profit' and 'Jonathan's story' (page 93), then discuss the options available to the owners of a small factory which is facing a reduction in demand for the goods it produces (see 'In groups').

Plenary

Share their decisions about which option they would choose as a result of the falling demand for the factory's goods and discuss the reasons for their decisions.

Extension activities

Set the students the writing activity saying whether or not they agree with the view expressed by the business owner (see 'For your file' page 93).

Study Copymaster 19 'Business talk' and discuss the definitions of the business terms. Then in pairs get students to test each other on the meanings of the terms.

19 Business talk

A glossary of key terms from business

Bank loan A loan from a bank used to set up or to expand a business.

Bankrupt A business is bankrupt if it has run out of money and cannot pay its debts.

Board of directors A group of people appointed to run a company.

Business An industrial or commercial firm established to produce and sell either goods or services.

Company A business owned by shareholders who share the profits or losses made by the company.

Costs All the expenses that a business has to pay.

Entrepreneur A person who creates a new business.

Investment Money that a person or a group agree to put into a business.

Partnership A business which between two and twenty people agree jointly to own, control and finance.

Private sector The part of the economy that consists of businesses financed by private money.

Proprietor An owner of a business.

Public sector The part of the economy that provides services financed by public money.

Recession A period during which the economy shrinks and many businesses contract rather than expand.

Revenue All the money that a business makes from selling its goods or services.

Shareholder A person who invests their money in a company by buying shares.

Shares Equal parts of a company that can be either bought or sold.

Social enterprise A business set up to provide some kind of social benefit.

Sole trader A person who owns and runs their own business.

Workforce All the people employed to work in a business.

Your Life 2/Year 8

Lesson 1 *Your Life Student Book 2*, page 94
Citizenship – becoming an active citizen

> **Objective:** To investigate the condition of the school environment and to develop plans for improving it.

Starter

Ask the students: 'Whose responsibility is it to take care of the school environment?' Discuss their responses, then ask them to read and discuss the six quotations at the top of page 94. Talk about how much the school environment matters, why some people are prepared to put up with things at school which they wouldn't tolerate at home, and about how looking after the environment is the responsibility of all the different members of the school community.

Suggested activities

- Ask the students to work individually to carry out a survey of the condition of the school's buildings and grounds (see 'An environmental survey', page 94). Then ask groups to discuss their assessments of the condition of the different areas of the school and to choose three areas as priority areas for improvement. Share the groups' views in a class discussion and select one priority for the class representative to raise as an issue at the next meeting of the school council.

- Encourage groups to discuss what proposal they would put forward as a bid for £50,000 of lottery money, if it was available for a project to improve the school's environment. Make a list of different ideas, then choose one and draft a detailed proposal to put to the rest of the class. Invite the class to debate the proposals and vote to choose the proposal that has the most support.

- Ask groups to discuss what could be done to improve the appearance and atmosphere of the tutor group room and to prepare a five-point plan to improve it and keep it in good condition. Then share the students' ideas in a class discussion and agree a class five-point plan.

Plenary

Remind the students that for the school environment to be kept in a good condition then they must behave responsibly towards it. In a class discussion, draw up a list of guidelines ('Dos' and 'Don'ts') in order to respect and protect the school environment.

Extension activity

Put into action the class's five-point plan to improve the tutor group room (see point 3 of 'In groups', page 94).

Your Life 2/Year 8

Lesson 2 *Your Life Student Book 2*, page 95

Citizenship – becoming an active citizen

Objective: To understand what the Eco-Schools programme is and what sustainable development is.

Starter

Read the introductory paragraph about the environment on page 95. Ask students to work on their own to make lists of things we can all do in our daily lives to save energy, to cut down waste and reduce pollution. Hold a class discussion.

Suggested activities

- Read and discuss 'What is sustainable development' (page 95). Then ask students to produce a poster designed to get young people to lead a sustainable lifestyle, entitled 'Your Environment Needs YOU!'

- Study 'Eco-Schools'. Encourage students to use the internet to research the Eco-Schools programme and in pairs to write a statement about its achievements arguing that every school should become an eco-school (see 'For your file').

Plenary

Share their statements in a class discussion. Then draft a letter from the class to the governors of a school which is not yet an eco-school arguing that the school should become an eco-school.

UNIT 20 You and the community – taking action

Your Life 2/Year 8

Lesson 3 *Your Life Student Book 2*, pages 96–97

Citizenship – becoming an active citizen

> **Objective:** To investigate how the local environment might be improved and to participate in a project to help the local community.

Resources

Copies of Copymaster 20 'Help protect your environment'

Starter

- Read the opening two paragraphs on page 96 about how young people have become involved in activities to improve their local environment and study the article 'Derelict land transformed into a community garden' (page 96) about how one group of young people got involved in a project to improve the local environment.

- Read about the 'Tidy Towns' initiative (page 97) and how Holywell High School won an environmental award.

- Encourage groups to discuss how the local environment in the area nearby can be improved. Encourage them to share their ideas in a class discussion and to write a letter to the local newspaper saying what they think needs to be done.

- Read 'Go MADD' (page 97). Ask groups to draft a proposal for a MADD event to take place over two to three hours one evening after school or on a Saturday morning. Ask them to list activities that could help the local community.

Plenary

Encourage students to share their ideas for a MADD event in a class discussion and decide which activities to include in the event. Draw up a plan and list everything that needs to be done to organise the event.

Extension activities

Hold the MADD event. Suggest students draft a press release to send to local newspapers, either before the event saying what they plan to do or after the event reporting what they did. Students then complete Copymaster 20.

20 Help protect your environment

Launch an Anti-Litter Campaign

Litter is a major threat to our environment today. But it's a problem we could solve overnight if every single person in Britain made an effort. Why is litter a problem? Because …

✖ It can cause fires (like those at Kings Cross Station and Bradford City Football Ground).

✖ It ruins our streets, parks, rivers and countryside.

✖ It kills animals. In one recent year, 216 animals died as a result of litter such as plastic bags, tin cans and broken glass. This doesn't include wild animals.

✖ It threatens our wildlife. A whale found washed up on a beach had been suffocated by fifty plastic bags.

✖ You can be fined up to £1000 if you're caught.

Join a Youth Crime Prevention Panel

Problems like vandalism, litter, drug abuse and theft all affect your world. If you would like to help change things for the better, make new friends and have fun at the same time, why not join a Youth Crime Prevention Panel?

Youth Crime Prevention Panels are made up of young people who get together to find ways of preventing crime of all kinds.

Starting up anti-litter campaigns, making videos, planting trees and planning sponsored events are just some of the projects you can get involved in by joining a Youth Crime Prevention Panel.

'We planned a property marking day to show people how to mark things, using invisible ink that shows up under infra-red light. The day was a real success and good fun too.' – Michelle

It's up to you!

Remember, it's up to you to help to create the kind of world you want to live in. If you want to:

✓ feel safe when you go out

✓ walk in streets that are free from litter

✓ have a graffiti-free school

✓ use a public telephone that hasn't been vandalised …

It's up to you!

In groups

Prepare a proposal for an anti-litter campaign in your local area. Think up a slogan for your campaign and discuss how you would advertise it and get people involved in it.

Adapted from *Get Smart!*, Metropolitan Police

UNIT 21 You and other people – older people

Your Life 2/Year 8

Objective: To explore attitudes towards older people and what is meant by ageism, and to examine the problems some older people face.

Resources

Copies of Copymaster 21 'Attitudes to older people'

Starter

Ask students, in pairs, to brainstorm all the words and phrases they associate with old age and older people. Then ask them to decide whether, overall, they have a positive or negative view of old age and older people. Encourage students to share their views in a class discussion. Remind them of what a stereotype is and ask: 'Is your view of older people based on a stereotype?'

Suggested activities

● Read the article 'Ageism' (page 98). Ask groups to discuss what it says about attitudes to older people and how older people are presented in the media. Discuss whether society values older people. Encourage them to talk about older people they know and how they spend their time.

● Read 'Survey finds "two worlds of old age"' (page 99). Ask groups to discuss the survey's findings, talking about the factors that determine what sort of life an older person leads, and what they learn from the survey about the problems some older people face. Then focus on memory loss and read 'Old age and memory loss' (page 98). Ask pairs to identify and list the key facts about dementia that they learn from the article.

● Read 'Caring for older people' (page 99) and ask groups to discuss the issues raised in the questions in 'What role should the family play?' Encourage them to share their ideas in a class discussion.

● Ask the students individually to complete Copymaster 21 'Attitudes to older people', then to share their views in a class discussion.

Plenary

Invite the class to imagine they are working on a magazine that is going to feature an article on 'Myths about older people'. Write the headings 'Facts' and 'Fictions' on the board and make a list of the facts and fictions that the students would include in the article.

Extension activities

Ask the students to show their understanding of ageism by planning and writing an article on the causes and effects of ageism (see 'For your file', page 98).

Suggest individuals find more information about older people from the internet, such as the Age UK website www.ageuk.org.uk.

21 Attitudes to older people

Here are ten statements about older people. Put a tick in one of the boxes beside each statement to say whether you agree or disagree with it. Then, in groups or as a class, discuss your views.

	Agree	**Disagree**
1. Older people are set in their ways. You can't expect them to keep up with modern developments.	☐	☐
2. Older people can make a valuable contribution to society because of their experience.	☐	☐
3. The media often give a false picture of older people as the helpless victims of crime, poverty and neglect.	☐	☐
4. The majority of older people are quite capable of looking after themselves.	☐	☐
5. Older people have fewer needs than younger people, so they can exist on lower incomes.	☐	☐
6. Older people should be prepared to let their family make decisions for them.	☐	☐
7. It is possible for older people to enjoy life as much as younger people.	☐	☐
8. Older people should be allowed to go on working whatever their age, as long as they are fit and capable of doing the job.	☐	☐
9. It is unrealistic for older people to expect society to do more for them than it already does.	☐	☐
10. You can judge the values of a society by the provision it makes for the care of older people and by the consideration it shows towards them.	☐	☐

UNIT 21 You and other people – older people

Objective: To understand how the age profile of society is changing, and to consider the implications of an increase in the number of older people in the future.

Starter

Ask the students: 'How do you see yourself in 60 years time?' 'What sort of life will most of you have as you grow older?' 'Will you be fitter and healthier than the older people of today?' 'Will you still be able to retire and claim a pension at 65, or will you have to go on working?' 'Will you still get free healthcare or will it be rationed?' 'Will you face a comfortable or a bleak old age?' Ask them to jot down their ideas on what they think life will be like for older people in 2075 and share them in a class discussion.

Suggested activities

- Explain that the age profile of society is changing. Read and discuss 'Forecasts for the future' (page 100). Then read 'How will life be different in the 21st century?' (page 100). Ask groups to discuss the questions raised in the last three paragraphs.

- Ask groups to study the picture and caption on page 100, then discuss the questions about rationing and the provision of healthcare (see 'In groups', page 100). Challenge them to prepare a statement on their views of 'How to provide health care in the 21st century'. Encourage them to share their views in a class discussion.

- Read and discuss in groups the questions raised in the two life stories on page 101.

Plenary

Summarise what the students have been discussing by making a list of the changes that they think will result from the change in the age profile of society. Discuss which of the changes they think will have the most impact on their life.

Extension activity

Ask individuals to write about the changes that are likely to occur during their lifetimes as a result of the changing age profile of society and what, if anything, they think they need to do to prepare for them (see 'For your file' page 101).

Your Life 2/Year 8

Lesson 1 *Your Life Student Book 2*, pages 102–103
Citizenship – understanding global issues

> **Objective:** To explore concerns about how our foods are produced, and to debate the arguments for and against genetically modified foods.

Resources

Copies of Copymaster 22 'Genetically modified foods – for and against'

Starter

Talk about what we do when we're shopping for food. Ask: 'What influences your choice of one product rather than another – is it the taste, the price, the look of the products, an advertisement you've seen or someone's recommendation?' Discuss what influences us. Then ask: 'Do you ever try to find out more about food before you buy it – such as where it came from, how it was produced or what exactly is in it? Ask: 'How important do you think such questions are?' Explain that they may be more important than they think, as the article they are going to study will explain.

Suggested activities

- Read the article 'The foods you eat' (pages 102–103) discussing what it says the effects are on a) producers, b) consumers, and c) the environment, of having such a choice in our supermarkets.

- Study the section on GM foods (page 102) and the article 'Synthetic burgers – the food of the future?' (page 103). Invite students to write answers to questions 1–5 on page 103, then to share their views in a group or class discussion.

- Ask individuals to show their understanding of the issues by writing a letter to a newspaper expressing their views on one or more of the issues raised in the article (see 'For your file', page 103).

Plenary

Encourage students to share views they have expressed in their letters in a class discussion.

Extension activities

Ask groups to study Copymaster 22, listing the key points made by the writers. Challenge them to research the issue further on the internet, then to draft speeches for a debate on the motion: 'This house believes that the benefits of GM foods outweigh the risks.'

Ask students to find out about the True Feed Campaign, organised by Greenpeace to make people aware of what environmentalists regard as the true cost of food, by visiting the website www.truefood.org.

22 Genetically modified foods – for and against

FOR Prof Christopher Leaver, head of the Department of Plant Sciences, Oxford University

Society likes the benefits of technology but increasingly fears the risks, causing increasing growth in alternatives as they are perceived safer.

The row over GM foods contrasts oddly with the widespread acceptance and use of many products in health care: 25 per cent of the top 20 drugs – for example, insulin, growth hormone, hepatitis B vaccines, and antibodies to treat cancer – are produced using GM organisms.

Prof Leaver argues that the use of genomics – the study of the genetics of an organism – will transform agricultural breeding and selection techniques. This will make genetic improvements easier, and allow resistance to difficult pests to become possible.

Benefits

In addition, improved nutritional levels would be achievable, and modern biotechnologies could help provide benefits including:

* Pest and disease control;
* Weed control;
* Oil, starch and protein modification;
* Speciality crops delivering vitamin A, iron, anti-cancer properties and allergens;
* Pharmaceuticals.

He adds: 'There are major agricultural production and food challenges facing the developing world, while there are major factors reducing productivity of staple food crops. Modern biotechnologies offer the potential to accelerate improvement and provide novel solutions.

'In the next fifty years, mankind will consume twice as much food as mankind has consumed since the beginning of agriculture 10,000 years ago.

'The global food security challenge is to increase productivity of cereals at farm level by 805 million tonnes from the 1995 level of 1,776 million tonnes to 2,581 million tonnes by 2025.

'Future food security will require the development of a sustainable and environmentally friendly agriculture which combines the best of conventional plant breeding with the new biotechnologies.

'As we strive to develop more sustainable agricultural systems and protect our environment from pollution, let us not forget that the biggest pollutant in the world today is poverty, which afflicts more than 1.2 billion people.'

AGAINST Adrian Bebb, an environmental campaigner for Friends of the Earth

Genetically modified food and crops have rarely been out of the headlines. Despite assurances from the Government and the biotech industry, public confidence in this new technology has hit rock bottom.

Consumer pressure has forced supermarkets, food manufacturers and restaurants to phase out GM ingredients, and there has been opposition to the GM crop trials taking place around the country. Friends of the Earth believe the public are right to be concerned.

Concerns fall into two categories: impact on health and impact on the environment.

GM is a new way of producing foods – randomly inserting genes from other organisms. Our knowledge of what we are doing is very limited.

Fears

However, despite the fact we are already eating GM food, research into the long-term health effects is either incomplete or hasn't been undertaken. So why are we eating them?

There are also real fears about the impacts GM crops may have on the environment. Genetic pollution is a major concern.

Safety controls on trial sites are inadequate, and there are fears GM crops will cross-breed with wild plants. Indeed, GM pollen was discovered over four kilometres from a trial site in Oxfordshire.

Farmers growing non-GM and organic crops are also at risk. If their crops become contaminated, their entire livelihoods could be at risk.

The demand for organic non-GM food is soaring. Why are we risking it for something that most people don't want?

When GM foods were introduced, there was little – if any – public debate. This is exactly what the biotech industry wanted. We are now having the debate that should have taken place before these foods were placed on the market.

Along with many other organisations, Friends of the Earth is campaigning for a five-year freeze on GM food and crops. More information is needed about the potential impact.

Once we have comprehensive information about the risks, the public should be allowed to decide whether or not to proceed down this route.

At present, we clearly don't.

UNIT 22 You and global issues – food and water

Your Life 2/Year 8

Lesson 2 *Your Life Student Book 2*, pages 104–105
Citizenship – understanding global issues

Objective: To examine the causes of food shortages and famine and to explore ways of solving the problem of world hunger.

Resources

Copies of Copymaster 22A 'Understanding world hunger'

Starter

Explain what is meant by malnutrition and note that there are two main causes: 1) not getting enough food; 2) not getting enough of different foods to give all the nutrients the body needs. Explain that there are three main types of malnutrition: 1) protein energy malnutrition, due to a lack of protein and carbohydrate, which causes two illnesses in children (marasmus and kwashiorkor) both of which can be fatal; 2) vitamin deficiency caused by not having enough fruit and vegetables, which can cause beri beri and rickets; 3) mineral deficiency, e.g. lack of iron which can cause anaemia. Then read the first paragraph on page 104.

Suggested activities

● Explain what a famine is (an extreme shortage of food in one place). Read 'Why do famines happen? (page 104), stopping after each paragraph to discuss each piece of information, before asking individuals to make a list of the key points they have learned from the article.

● Read 'Unequal shares' (page 105), then invite groups to study the list of eight reasons people give for why there is hunger in Sub-Saharan Africa, and to discuss which are true. Encourage students to share their views in a class discussion.

● Ask individuals to study 'Ten ways to beat world hunger' (page 105) and to rank the ideas in order of importance.

Plenary

Invite students to share their views of the ten suggestions for beating world hunger in a class discussion. Ask: 'Which of the suggestions would be most likely to have a long-term effect?'

Extension activity

Ask individuals to write a statement expressing their thoughts about the issue of world hunger. In addition to drawing on the information from these pages, suggest they research further information on websites such as the Oxfam Cool Planet website www.oxfam.org.uk/coolplanet/.

Assessment

Use Copymaster 22A to assess understanding of the reasons for world hunger.

22A | Understanding world hunger

Below are some reasons that people give to explain why many of the people in sub-Saharan Africa do not get enough to eat. Put a tick beside those reasons that you agree with and a cross beside those reasons that you disagree with.

	Agree	**Disagree**
1. People in Africa are lazy.	☐	☐
2. The best land is used for cash crops for export.	☐	☐
3. There is not enough food produced in the world.	☐	☐
4. People have too many children.	☐	☐
5. Nothing grows in Africa because it's all desert.	☐	☐
6. Farmers are too poor to buy the seeds and tools they need.	☐	☐
7. Some people in the world get more than their fair share of food.	☐	☐
8. African farmers are not given a fair deal on the world market.	☐	☐
9. Drought and famine are natural disasters which cannot be prevented.	☐	☐
10. Governments spend money on buying arms and fighting wars, which could otherwise be spent on developing agriculture.	☐	☐

Write a paragraph explaining the real reasons for why there is hunger in sub-Saharan Africa.

Your Life 2/Year 8

Lesson 3 *Your Life Student Book 2*, pages 106–107
Citizenship – understanding global issues

Objective: To understand that there is a shortage of water in many parts of the world and to explore how this affects people's lives.

Starter

Ask the students to list all the different ways in which we use water in our homes. Then discuss how different their lives would be if their home wasn't connected to a water supply. Ask: 'What if you had to walk four to five kilometres to get your water from a well or a standpipe?' 'What if you had to spend a quarter of your income on clean water because all the rivers around you were polluted with sewage?' Explain that this is what many people in the world have to do, and read 'Millions of people still lack safe water' (page 107).

Suggested activities

● Read 'The water crisis' (page 106). Write these questions on the board and ask students to individually write answers to them: 1) Explain what people mean when they say there is a water crisis. 2) Why is there a water crisis? 3) What problems result from the lack of fresh clean water? 4) How can these problems be solved? Then invite pairs to mark each other's answers as you discuss the answers with the class.

● Ask students to individually do the quiz 'How much do you know about water?' (page 106) and discuss the answers in a class discussion.

● Read 'Water wars' (page 107). Explain how water is required not only in homes but for industry and agriculture. Ask: 'How serious a threat to world peace do you think the water crisis is: very, quite or not very?'

● Ask students to imagine they work for a charity called The Freshwater Fund which supports schemes to provide people in other parts of the world with fresh clean water. Challenge groups to plan a 30-second TV advert asking people to donate £3 a month to the charity.

Plenary

Encourage the students to share their ideas for the TV advert. Discuss the key information that each of their adverts tries to put across, and ask them to decide which group's advert would be the most effective and why.

Extension activities

Ask students to find out more information about water issues, by visiting websites of organisations such as Water Aid (www.wateraid.org.uk).

UNIT 23 You and your achievements – reviewing your progress

Your Life 2/Year 8

Lesson 1 *Your Life Student Book 2*, pages 108–109
Personal wellbeing – reviewing your progress

Objective: To review your progress and achievements in Year 8 and to draw up an action plan setting targets for Year 9.

Resources

Copies of Copymaster 23 'Action plans'

Starter

Explain that the lesson is the start of a four-step process: 1) Thinking about your progress and achievements; 2) Discussing your progress and achievements with your tutor and identifying targets for Year 9; 3) Writing a statement for your Record of Achievement; 4) Drawing up an action plan which sets targets and plans for achieving them.

Suggested activities

- Read 'Your subjects' (page 108) and ask the students to use the five-point scale to give themselves grades, before writing a statement about their progress in each subject.

- Read 'Your skills' (page 108) and invite the students to write a statement reviewing their progress in each of the skills.

- Read 'Your activities' (page 108) and challenge the students to write a statement about their most significant achievements during the year.

- Read 'Your attitude and behaviour' (page 108) and suggest they write a statement summing up their attitude and behaviour during the year.

Plenary

Allocate times for individuals to meet with you to discuss their statements and identify targets, allowing them further time (as necessary) to complete their statements.

Extension activities

Hold the discussion meetings with individuals. During the discussion, ask them to note down any points you make (see 'Discussing your progress', page 109).

Ask students to write a statement to put into their Record of Achievement (see 'Recording your achievements', page 109).

Read 'Setting targets' and 'Making an action plan' (page 109). Give the students copies of Copymaster 23 to fill in their targets for Year 9 and details of how they plan to achieve them.

23 Action plans

Use this sheet to write down what your two main targets are for next year, and to plan the steps you are going to take to achieve them.

Target No. 1

Aim: ....

....

Steps I will take to achieve my aim:

1. ....

....

2. ....

....

3. ....

....

4. ....

....

Target No. 2

Aim: ....

....

Steps I will take to achieve my aim:

1. ....

....

2. ....

....

3. ....

....

4. ....

....

UNIT 1 You and your body – adolescence

Your Life 3/Year 9

Lesson 1 *Your Life Student Book 3*, pages 6–7
Keeping healthy/Personal wellbeing – understanding who you are

> **Objective:** To develop a sense of identity by thinking about what sort of person you are, your values and ambitions and what image of yourself you want to give others.

Starter

Read the introductory paragraph and the section on 'You and your identity' (page 6). Ask the students each to think about what sort of person they are, to tell a partner and to see if the partner agrees with them.

Suggested activities

- Ask the students to study the list of characteristics (see page 6), decide which ones their ideal person would have and then rank them in order of importance. Encourage the students to share their ideas in a group discussion.

- Read 'Your goals and ambitions' (page 6) and prompt individuals to write a short statement saying how they see themselves in ten years' time, and what they hope to have achieved by then. Invite them to share what they have written, but only if they wish to do so.

- Read the introductory paragraphs and the article 'You and your image' (page 7). Ask groups to discuss each piece of advice that Jane Goldman gives (see 'In groups' page 7) and to say why they agree or disagree with it. Encourage them to share their views in a class discussion.

Plenary

Conclude the lesson with a class discussion of characteristics the students admire and ask who their role model is. Suggest they write down the name of someone whom they would choose as their role model, and then to explain why they chose that person.

Extension activities

Ask students to bring in pictures or posters of people they admire, to write comments saying why they admire them, and to make a wall display entitled 'People we admire'.

Ask students to write an article for a teen magazine's 'In my opinion' column, expressing their ideas about fashion, the pressure on teenagers to be fashionable and how to cope with such pressures.

UNIT 1 You and your body – adolescence

Lesson 2 *Your Life Student Book 3*, pages 8–9
Keeping healthy/Personal wellbeing – understanding your emotions

Objective: To develop an understanding of emotions, exploring how to cope with mood swings and how to deal with anger and frustration.

Resources

Copies of Copymaster 1 'Don't bottle it up'

Starter

Explain that an important part of being an adult is learning to recognise your feelings, what is creating them and how to deal with them. So it's useful, if you can, to identify what triggers your feelings. Ask individuals to think of three things that put them in a good mood (e.g. listening to their favourite music, being with their friends, playing sport, enjoying their hobby) and three things that put them in a bad mood (e.g. getting told off by a parent, not being allowed to do something, being made fun of by a friend). List on the board examples of the positive things that make them feel good and the negative things that make them feel bad. Explain that understanding what makes you feel bad and how you can make yourself feel good is important in learning how to handle your emotions.

Suggested activities

- Explain that identifying the causes of your feelings is not always simple. Read and discuss 'Mood swings' (page 8). Ask groups to study the list of problems and discuss who is the best person is to talk to in each case. Encourage them to share their views in a class discussion.

- Read 'Coping with your moods' (page 9). Discuss with the class the advice it gives about how to identify the cause of a bad mood and about the positive actions they can take to deal with it, and how to avoid a repetition of it. Ask willing individuals to share personal experiences of successfully coping with a bad mood.

- Read 'Difficult feelings – anger' (page 8) and 'Difficult feelings – frustration' (page 9). Invite groups to discuss the advice given, to identify what they consider to be the most useful points and to share their views in a class discussion.

Plenary

Read Aston's letter to Dave (see 'For your file', page 9) and list the main points they would make in reply. If time allows, allow pairs or groups to draft a reply.

Extension activities

Read 'I can't take any more' on Copymaster 1, and ask groups to discuss the questions in groups, before sharing their views in a class discussion.

Don't bottle it up

I can't take any more

Some teenagers feel that asking for help is a sign that they're not grown-up. But they are so wrong. A sign of being mature and responsible is knowing when to ask for help. There are times when asking for help is the only right thing to do.

"I used to love going to Scouts, but these new kids joined and they ruined it for me. When we went camping, they filled my backpack with water and knocked over my stove so that my tent almost caught fire. Even though they did lots of mean things, I stayed really cool. But then one day I went ballistic. The Scout master threw me out of the troop. If I had said something earlier, I'd be in the Scouts and they'd be out." Stefan

"When my sister died, I hid how upset I was. I thought my crying would make things harder for Mum and Dad. I was trying to be really strong, helping to run the house and doing chores and stuff. Months later, I fell to pieces and had to go into hospital." Shareema

"I got into trouble at school and had to give my Mum a note so that she would come and see my teacher. I threw the note away. I knew this was wrong, but I was embarrassed to tell anyone, even my Mum." Elaine

Here are six things to remember when you've got a problem:

- Growing up doesn't mean that you have to cope with everything alone.

- You're not to blame if there are problems at home.

- Never be silent if you are being bullied; you're only becoming the victim the bullies want you to be.

- Don't be embarrassed to show your feelings. Toughing it out won't solve anything.

- If there are problems at home, find someone you can talk to openly and honestly. It could be a teacher, a school counsellor, a religious leader, a relative, a friend or a friend's parent.

- Don't let a problem grow so that it takes over your life.

In groups

1. Discuss Stefan's, Shareema's and Elaine's experiences. How did not talking to someone make their situations worse?

2. Discuss the statements below. Which do you agree with and why? Are there certain circumstances in which it's better to keep things to yourself rather than to talk to someone?

"Sometimes you just have to put up with things. You just have to suffer in silence."

"There's no point in bottling things up. If you've got a problem, it's always best to tell someone. Talking helps."

UNIT 2 You and your responsibilities – racism, prejudice and discrimination

Your Life 3/Year 9

Lesson 1 *Your Life Student Book 3*, pages 10–11
Social education/Citizenship – racism, prejudice and discrimination

Objective: To understand what racism is and to explore why some people are racist.

Resources

Copies of Copymaster 2 'Talking about race'

Starter

Write the terms 'racism', 'prejudice' and 'discrimination' on the board. Challenge pairs to draft definitions of them and then to check the accuracy of their definitions by reading 'What is racism?' (page 10). Explain the meaning of the terms 'stereotyping' (the belief that people from one group share the same characteristics) and 'harassment' (troubling someone by persistently attacking, insulting or abusing them). Explain what 'persecution' means (unfair and cruel treatment of a person), and that racial discrimination is a form of persecution.

Suggested activities

- Read 'Racism is ...' (page 10). Ask groups to discuss what racism means to each of the five teenagers. Give them a large sheet of paper to write down what types of behaviour they regard as racist, e.g. singing chants about black players at football matches, poking fun at the way people dress, and refusing to consider someone for a job because of their race. Encourage them to share their views in a class discussion and to discuss why racist jokes are unacceptable.

- Read 'Why are some people racist?' (page 11). As a class, discuss what it tells them about the roots of racism and the human suffering that has resulted from persecution based on racist beliefs. Ask: 'How has genetic science proved that the idea of superior and inferior races is false?'

- Read 'Racists – what's their problem?' (page 11). Encourage groups to discuss the reasons it suggests for why people are racists, and to add any other reasons, e.g. ignorance (they still believe in the idea of superior and inferior races), jealousy (they are jealous when people from ethnic minorities succeed and they don't). In a class discussion, ask: 'What do you think is the main reason why some people in Britain today are racist?'

Plenary

Explain that it has been suggested that education is the key to getting rid of racism. Discuss with the students what they have learned about racism, what racist behaviour is and why some people are racist. Do they agree that education is the key to getting rid of racism?

Extension activity

Read Copymaster 2 and hold a class discussion of what it says about the terms people use. Ask whether they agree with the views it expresses about which terms are acceptable and which are unacceptable.

Talking about race

Words which people generally think are okay

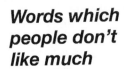

Black

People with roots in Africa or the Caribbean generally prefer this word to describe themselves. Although in the past people were often taught that 'black' was synonymous with 'bad' or 'evil', many people now want to reclaim the term to say that there is nothing bad or evil about dark skin and that they are proud of it. As long ago as the 1960s black people in the USA summed this up in the phrase 'black is beautiful'.

Afro-Caribbean

This is the term people with roots in the Caribbean tend to prefer, as an alternative to 'black'. They prefer it to what they used to be called, which was 'West Indian'.

Asian

This is the most general word for people with roots or family connections in India, Pakistan, Bangladesh and Sri Lanka. You aren't likely to annoy anyone by using it.

Pakistani, Indian, Bangladeshi, Chinese etc.

If you know someone has roots or family connections in one of these places then one of these words is fine, though people can be touchy if you suggest they are not really British when they think they are. If you had a friend with an Italian name because her Italian grandparents moved to Britain in 1950, would you call her Italian or British? Perhaps it might depend on whether she felt a bit Italian herself or spoke Italian.

Roots or family connections in ...

This is a useful expression. Taking India as an example, some people in Britain came here from India in the past few years (not many actually); some people have been here forty years, others (almost everyone under the age of 25) were born here. Some people will have Indian passports, most have British passports and a great many will know no other home than Britain. They are British, but they have roots or family connections in India.

Ethnic minorities

This is a funny phrase because it's often used in quite a vague way. Actually, you will find that people often use it when they mean black and Asian people, though ethnicity has nothing to do with colour. The Irish in Britain are a minority ethnic group. Welsh people are also thought of as an ethnic group.

Muslim, Sikh, Hindu, Christian etc.

Sometimes a person's religion is more important to them than their family's roots, so it is sometimes better to describe them as a Sikh (for example) than as Indian.

Words which people don't like much

Coloured

An old-fashioned word used in place of 'black'. This phrase implies that 'white' is the norm, or a starting point, and people can find that offensive.

Immigrant

This simply means someone who has moved their home from one country to another. This phrase is often disliked because most of Britain's black and Asian population are not immigrants, but were born here.

Paki, Chink

Sometimes people use these words as a shortened form of the full word, as an abbreviation. Asian people hate it. More often, 'Paki' is used as a general, insulting word for anyone with Pakistani, Indian or Bangladeshi roots. This generalising is a particularly insulting form of stereotyping. Simplifying or reducing anyone to a stereotype is racist.

UNIT 2 You and your responsibilities – racism, prejudice and discrimination

Lesson 2 *Your Life Student Book 3*, pages 12–13
Social education /Citizenship – racism, prejudice and discrimination

Objective: To examine racial discrimination, exploring what it feels like to be a victim, how widespread it is and what is meant by institutional racism.

Starter

Remind students of the list of types of racist behaviour that they drew up in the last lesson, referring to what they wrote on their large sheets of paper. Ask: 'What are the consequences of racist behaviour?' Talk about how racial attacks can lead to deaths, as in the cases of Stephen Lawrence and Damilola Taylor, how families can be driven from their homes by constant harassment, and how young people's lives can be made a misery by racial bullying. Explain that in the first part of the lesson you are going to be looking at what it feels like to be a victim of racism.

Suggested activities

- Read 'How great a problem is racism?' (page 12). Ask them in pairs to discuss what they learn from it about racial discrimination in the UK today, which groups are the main victims, and what the statistics show on how widespread it is. On a ten-point scale ask them to rate how serious a problem racism is today (10 being extremely serious and 1 not very serious at all) then to share their views in a class discussion.

- Read 'Racism in football' (page 12). Explain that racism in football remains despite the efforts of the *Kick It Out* campaign. Ask the students to discuss what action should be taken a) by football clubs, and b) by the football authorities against people who racially abuse players. Then invite groups to draw up a five-point plan to stamp out racism in football.

- Study 'Racism in park football' (page 12) and discuss how serious a problem it is from your experience. What action should be taken against parents or players who make racist remarks?

- Introduce students to the term 'institutional racism', discussing the quotations on page 13 to help explain its meaning.

- Read the section on Islamophobia (see 'Muslims under siege' page 13). Ask the class: 'How widespread do you think Islamophobia is?' 'Is media coverage of the Muslim community prejudiced?'

Plenary

Ask students to think about their experiences and what they have discussed in the lesson. Ask: 'Does the media exaggerate the amount of racism in society?' Share their views with the rest of the class.

Extension activities

Encourage pairs to role play a scene in which someone who has been the victim of either racial harassment or racial abuse tells a friend what happened and how they feel about it (see 'Role play', page 12).

Invite groups to research and discuss what it feels like to be a victim of racism. Then ask individuals to write a story, a poem or a playscript about a person who is a victim of racism, showing the person's feelings.

Students can use the internet to find out more about the *Kick It Out* campaign at www.kickitout.org

UNIT 2 You and your responsibilities – racism, prejudice and discrimination

Your Life 3/Year 9

Lesson 3 *Your Life Student Book 3*, pages 14–15
Social education/Citizenship – racism, prejudice and discrimination

Objective: To understand the law on racism and why it is important to take a stand against all forms of racism.

Resources

Copies of the school's anti-bullying policy

Starter

Explain that the Race Relations Act of 1976 made racial discrimination unlawful. Read 'Racial discrimination and the law' (page 14) and explain the difference between direct discrimination and indirect discrimination. Talk about how the Race Relations Act of 2000 extended the law on indirect discrimination.

Suggested activities

- Read 'Racial attacks and harassment' (page 14). Invite groups to discuss what they learn from the two stories about what it feels like to be the victim of racial harassment.

- In groups, discuss what punishment they think offenders should receive for racial crimes. Should they be sent to prison, fined or made to pay compensation, or made to do community service? Does it depend on what their offence was? Discuss the view that in all cases of racial crimes the offender should be made to write an apology and/or to meet the victims and to apologise in person. Encourage them to share their views in a class discussion.

- Read 'Take a stand against racism' (page 15). In groups, discuss the advice it gives. Then read and discuss the four statements in 'What should I do?' (page 15). Share views in a class discussion.

- Ask groups to imagine they are part of a working group that has been asked to make proposals to improve race relations in the local community and to suggest measures to eradicate racism in their area. For example, what can the local police do? What can community workers do? What can local schools do? If the students had a budget of £50,000 to spend, how would they spend it? Ask the groups to draft a proposal to discuss with the rest of the class.

Plenary

Look at the school's anti-bullying policy. Are there any special rules about racist bullying? Discuss how effective the students think the bullying policy is in dealing with racial bullying and any ways in which they think it could be improved.

Extension activities

Ask students to find out more information about how to beat racism by visiting websites such as www.childline.org.uk and www.kidscape.org.uk.

Encourage students to write an email to a newspaper giving their views on racism and explaining why they think it important to take a stand against racism.

UNIT 3 You and your decisions – how to make decisions

Your Life 3/Year 9

Lesson 1 *Your Life Student Book 3*, pages 16–17

Personal wellbeing – decision making

> **Objective:** To consider how good you are at making your own decisions, which people influence you and why.

Starter

Introduce the topic by asking: 'Do you consider yourself to be good at making decisions or poor at making decisions?' 'Do you make up your own mind or do you rely on what other people think?' Ask individuals to discuss with a partner how good they think they are at making decisions and to say why, giving examples that will support their opinion.

Suggested activities

- Ask students to do the quiz on page 16 ('Do you make your own decisions?'). Then invite them to talk with a partner about their quiz result, and to compare what it says about their decision-making ability with their own assessment.

- Ask individuals to study the list of important things to consider when making decisions (see 'In groups', page 16) and to rank them in order of importance, before sharing their views in a group and/or class discussion.

- Study the chart in 'Who influences you?' (page 17) and ask individuals to write down in order of importance five people who influence them. Then suggest they look at the list of reasons ('Why do they influence you?' page 17) and to write down why each person influences them. Then ask them to discuss in groups who influences them and why.

Plenary

Encourage the students to discuss what they have learned about who influences them and their decisions. Explain that they have been thinking about how people they come into contact with personally influence them, but that there are other influences too, most notably the media. How much do they think they are influenced by the media – by the views expressed in newspapers and magazines, in TV programmes, in songs, in books? What has the most influence on them – their family, their friends, the school, the local community, the media?

Extension activity

Ask students to reflect on a time when they had to make a difficult decision, by writing about it (see 'For your file', page 17).

UNIT 3 You and your decisions – how to make decisions

Your Life 3/Year 9

Lesson 2 *Your Life Student Book 3*, pages 18–19
Personal wellbeing – decision making

Objective: To explore ways of making decisions, to understand what peer pressure is and to discuss ways of dealing with it.

Resources

Copies of Copymaster 3 'Consequences'

Starter

Explain that all decisions have consequences. For example, if someone tells a lie, the consequence is that they lose someone else's trust if they are found out. Ask the students, in pairs, to list other examples of decisions they might take and the consequences that might follow, e.g. someone starts to smoke, truants, copies someone else's homework, shoplifts, goes joyriding, stays out all night. Then share some of the lists in a class discussion.

Suggested activities

- Read 'Consider the consequences' (page 18). Discuss with the class what it says about how we discover what is right and wrong, and the questions we need to ask ourselves when making decisions.

- Suggest groups discuss the statements in 'Right and wrong' (page 18) and to share their ideas in a class discussion.

- Read 'Stay in control of your life' (page 19). Discuss with the class what peer pressure is and the ways in which people will try to exert it. Do they agree with what the writer says about people who sink to such tactics? Talk about the difficulty of staying in control and saying 'No' when friends are putting pressure on, and encourage them to practise saying 'No' by doing the role play activity (see page 19). Ask them to rate how well a person resists the pressure on a scale of 1 to 5 (1 = very well and 5 = very badly).

Plenary

Read 'What to do when making decisions' (page 19). Discuss the five-point plan and suggest the students note down the mnemonic FACTS to help them to remember the plan.

Extension activities

Give out Copymaster 3 and ask groups to show their understanding of the consequences of different courses of action by discussing the situations, then sharing their views in a class discussion.

Ask students to develop role plays based on the three situations, or on other situations they can think of which involve difficult decisions, e.g. if they saw a friend cheating in an exam and then found out that the friend came top.

3 Consequences

We are usually able to work out the consequences of our actions. As children we often learn about consequences by quite hard experience, but as we grow up we are more able to see the possible results of our actions.

Discuss the three situations below, and consider the consequences of the various courses of action. Then share your thoughts with the rest of the class in a class discussion.

Situation 1

You have a Saturday morning job in a shop. A good friend asks if she can buy a magazine. As you get it for her, you notice her putting a bar of chocolate from the counter into her pocket.

● Do you tell her to put it back?
● Do you tell the owner of the shop?
● Do you ignore what she has done?
● Do you let her go, then talk to her about it later?
● Do you tell her parents?

What would be the consequences of each action?

Situation 2

There is a film on at the cinema that you want to see with your friends. However, you know that you are not old enough to see this particular film. Also, you have no money.

● Do you ask one of your parents for the money?
● Do you tell them what it's for?
● Do you pretend it's for something else?
● Do you tell your friends that your parents won't let you go, or tell them that you have no money?
● Do you try to borrow the money from a friend?
● Do you try to get the money another way?

What would be the consequences of each action?

Situation 3

You are with some friends when one of them, who is only 16, decides to 'borrow' his parents' car so that you can all go out for the day.

● Do you make an excuse so that you won't have to go in the car?
● Do you tell your friend's parents what he's planning to do?
● Do you try to persuade him and the others not to go?
● Do you let them go, then ask your parents what you should do?
● Do you go along with them?
● Do you watch them go and then contact the police?
● Do you go outside and let down one of the car's tyres?

What would be the consequences of each action?

UNIT 4 You and your family – becoming an adult

Your Life 3/Year 9

Lesson 1 *Your Life Student Book 3*, pages 20–21
Personal wellbeing – relationships with parents

> **Objective:** To explore the causes of tension between parents and teenagers, and to discuss ways of dealing with these difficulties.

Resources

Copies of Copymaster 4 'Parent problems'

Starter

Ask the students, in pairs, to brainstorm the things that cause tension and conflict between parents and teenagers, then make a class list on the board. Compare the class list with the 'Top ten causes of tension between parents and teenagers' on page 20. Hold a vote to decide which are the three main causes of tension.

Suggested activities

● Read 'How to deal with differences' (page 20). In pairs or in groups, students draft details of other ground rules that Dave and his parents might have drawn up. Ask the students to use a word processor to produce a contract that parents and teenagers could agree upon. Suggest they compare their contracts in a class discussion.

● Ask groups to read and discuss the two viewpoints in the section 'How to get on better' (page 20). Prompt them to note down their views on a) how much independence they think parents should give teenagers, b) what teenagers can do to win parents' trust, and c) how to improve communication between parents and teenagers. Ask them to share their views with the rest of the class.

● Read 'Arguments and how to survive them' and 'Educate your parents' (page 21). On their own, invite students to pick out what they consider to be the three most useful pieces of advice, then to share their views in a group and/or class discussion.

Plenary

Summarise the main pieces of advice about how to deal with arguments by teaching them the mnemonic BACKDOWN – Behave like an adult/Agree to listen/ Consider what they say/Keep to the point/Don't lose your temper/Offer an apology if appropriate/Work to win their trust/Negotiate a compromise. Put a copy of the mnemonic on the wall for reference.

Extension activities

Act out the role play (see page 21). Ask some students to perform their role play to the rest of the class, and discuss how the different reactions of the teenager either escalated or defused the situation. Then ask students to do the writing activity (see 'For your file', page 21).

Read Copymaster 4 and ask groups to discuss the situations and the advice, then to report their views in a class discussion.

Ask students to role play and then make a tape recording of a radio phone-in programme in which an agony aunt or uncle offers advice to teenagers on how to deal with problems with parents.

Parent problems

Parent Problem 1

THEY SAY ... You're not going out wearing that!

THEY'RE THINKING ... They're hardly wearing anything! If they go out in short skirts and skimpy tops they'll attract the wrong sort of attention!

WE SAY ...

- Don't tell your parents they don't have a clue.
- Do stay calm and ask what it is exactly that they object to and tone down your outfit.
- Don't change completely but do ask for advice.

Parent Problem 2

THEY SAY ... We don't care if your mates are allowed to, you're not!

THEY'RE THINKING ... We don't know what our kid gets up to and who they go about with, and as long as they live in our home they'll stick by our rules.

WE SAY ...

- Do learn to compromise! It's unlikely your parents are going to give in to your plans entirely – the more you moan, the more your parents will refuse to change their minds. Instead you have to meet halfway and come up with a solution that lets you do some of what you want but keeps your parents happy too!

- Don't expect your parents to change their minds overnight! Your parents need to trust you and building that trust could take time.

- Don't take advantage! If your parents do let you go to a party that they'd originally been against, then come home on time. It shows respect and maturity – two of the things that are guaranteed to win you more freedom.

Parent Problem 3

THEY SAY ... You don't talk to us any more.

THEY'RE THINKING ... they used to be so chatty! Now all they do is go out with their friends or lock themselves away in their room. Why won't they speak to us? How will we know if anything's ever bothering them?

WE SAY ...

- Don't yell that what you do is your business and ignore them completely.

- Do try to understand that they aren't being nosy – they're just worried about you and want to take an interest in your life.

- Do spend time with your parents. They'll be pleased you're showing them some attention even if it's just sitting watching TV with them for half an hour!

- Do make the effort to tell your parents about your friends and school. You'll find it much easier to discuss problems and fears that you have, and they'll find it easier to understand!

In groups

Discuss the problems and advice given on this page. Say why you agree or disagree with the advice that's given. Talk about other parent problems that teenagers have. What advice do you think the writer of the article would give you on how to deal with them?

UNIT 4 You and your family – becoming an adult

Your Life 3/Year 9

Lesson 2 *Your Life Student Book 3*, pages 22–23
Personal wellbeing – family relationships

Objective: To understand that in relationships a person has both rights and responsibilities, and to explore examples of taking responsibility within the family.

Starter

Read the introductory paragraph and 'My Bill of Rights' (page 22). Invite pairs to discuss the list of rights, ranking them in order of importance and adding any other rights they think are important. Then share their views with the rest of the class and discuss the responsibilities that they have to respect other people's rights.

Suggested activities

- Hold a class discussion of what causes tension between them and their brothers and sisters. Make a list on the board and compare the list with the 'Top ten' list on page 22. Then discuss the two statements (see 'In groups', page 22) about whether it is better to deal with problems with siblings yourself or through parents. Talk about how the advice they were discussing on how to deal with arguments with parents in the previous lesson applies to arguments with brothers and sisters. Remind them of the mnemonic 'BACKDOWN'.

- Read 'Taking responsibility' (page 23). Ask groups to discuss how the three people in the article took responsibility within their families, and to share experiences of times when they have taken responsibility for something within the family, e.g. for shopping when a parent was ill.

- Ask the students: 'How responsible are you for things in your daily life at home? Do you get your own breakfast, do your own washing or feed your own pets?' Invite them to write a statement saying whether they think they take most of the responsibility, some of the responsibility or a little responsibility for things in their daily lives at home. Then read 'Who's responsible?' (page 23) and ask them, in pairs, to discuss whether they agree or disagree with Derek Stuart's views. Ask them to look at each other's statements and suggest ways that each of them might take more responsibility in their daily lives.

Plenary

Discuss the view that the more responsibility you take for your daily lives, the more your parents are likely to let you lead an independent life and make your own decisions. Invite them to say why they agree or disagree with this view.

Extension activity

Write an article for a teen magazine about what causes arguments between brothers and sisters and how to deal with them. Give it a title, e.g. 'How to get on with your brothers and sisters'.

UNIT 5 You and your rights – civil liberties

Your Life 3/Year 9

Lesson 1 *Your Life Student Book 3*, pages 24–25
Citizenship – understanding civil liberties

Objective: To understand what civil liberties are.

Resources

Copies of Copymaster 5 'Rights and responsibilities'

Starter

Write the terms 'civil liberties' and 'human rights' on the board. Ask the students: 'What are the basic rights that every human being has?' 'What civil liberties do you have?' Hold a class discussion, listing the human rights they suggest on the board. Explain that with every right there comes the responsibility to respect other people's rights.

Suggested activities

- Read 'Your human rights' (page 24). Compare the examples of civil liberties with the list they compiled. In groups, discuss what life would be like if you lived in a dictatorship and were denied your civil liberties.

- Study 'Protecting your civil liberties' (page 24) then in groups discuss their views on identity cards.

- Read 'CCTV – A cause for concern?' (page 25). Ask groups to discuss their views on the benefits and disadvantages of CCTV, then to share their views in a class discussion.

- Read 'Mosquito alarms' (page 25) and discuss whether they think they should be banned.

Plenary

Discuss the view that the threat to society is so great from terrorism and organised crime that we must be prepared to sacrifice some of our civil liberties in order to combat it.

Extension activities

Ask the students in pairs to use the internet to find out about the Universal Declaration of Human Rights and to draw up a charter listing their top ten human rights. Invite them to share their views in a class discussion.

Test the students understanding of rights and responsibilities by asking them to study Copymaster 5, to decide which are rights and which are responsibilities, then to compare their answers with a partner and to list further examples of rights and responsibilities.

Ask students to find up-to-date information on civil liberty issues by visiting the website of the organisation Liberty (www.liberty-human-rights.org.uk).

5 Rights and responsibilities

Having rights involves having responsibilities. For example, we have the right to freedom of expression. This means that we may say what we like, but we also have the responsibility not to insult other people or say things on purpose which we know would offend them. It is our responsibility to respect the rights of others.

Study the list below, which consists of a mixture of rights and responsibilities. Think about each one carefully, decide whether it is a right or a responsibility, then put a tick in the correct column.

		Right	Responsibility
1.	A name and identity of our own	☐	☐
2.	To show respect to people of other countries	☐	☐
3.	A country to belong to	☐	☐
4.	Food, shelter, warmth	☐	☐
5.	To be educated and develop new skills	☐	☐
6.	To buy and own things	☐	☐
7.	To treat other people as individuals, not as things or just part of a group	☐	☐
8.	To have the protection of the law	☐	☐
9.	Not to steal people's things	☐	☐
10.	To share our things with needy people	☐	☐
11.	To meet together to share new ideas	☐	☐
12.	To be safe from violence and fear	☐	☐
13.	To be helped when we are old or ill	☐	☐
14.	To protect other people from unfair treatment	☐	☐
15.	To listen to others	☐	☐
16.	To always try to find out what the truth is	☐	☐
17.	To respect other people's religious beliefs	☐	☐
18.	To be able to vote	☐	☐
19.	To always be helpful and friendly to everyone	☐	☐
20.	To treat animals kindly	☐	☐

In pairs

Discuss what you have learned about rights and responsibilities from doing this activity. List three more examples of your rights and three more examples of your responsibilities.

UNIT 5 You and your rights – civil liberties

Objective: To explore issues concerned with protecting your rights and the right to freedom of expression.

Resources

Video clip of a satirical TV programme, e.g. *Have I Got News for You*

Starter

Explain that in the UK we live in a free society – that is, we are free to exercise our rights to practise whatever religion we like, and to say what we like, i.e. we have free speech and a free media. This means we can openly criticise and even make fun of the government. Explain what satire is (something, such as a programme or piece of writing, that ridicules the behaviour of people or events). Either show a video clip of a satirical programme or talk about satirical comedians who appear on TV, and satirical programmes such as *Have I Got News For You* and satirical magazines such as *Private Eye*. Explain that the right to freedom of thought and freedom of expression are two key articles in the Universal Declaration of Human Rights.

Suggested activities

- Invite students to read 'Freedom of expression' and 'Jailed for using the internet' on page 27.

- Explain what a martyr is. In a class discussion, talk about people who have been prepared to go to jail rather than give up their right to freedom of expression. Ask: 'How far would you be prepared to go if your rights were being denied you?' 'Are there any circumstances in which using force to obtain your rights can be justified?'

- Read 'Recording your every move' (page 27). Hold a class discussion and ask students to share their views on the proposal to monitor internet use and to discuss which of the two viewpoints they agree with. Then ask them whether they would vote for or against the proposed communications bill.

- Ask students to study 'Protecting your rights' and 'Can torture ever be justified?' on page 26, and in groups ask them to discuss their views, before sharing them in a class discussion.

Plenary

Ask groups to prepare a short statement saying how important they think freedom of expression is. Invite them to share their statements with the rest of the class.

Hold a class discussion on how far it is our moral duty to protect the rights of people whose human rights are being violated. Discuss how we should treat dictators who are violating the human rights of the people in their country. Ask: 'Is putting pressure on them by refusing to trade with them as far as we should go, or should we be prepared to go to war with them to remove them?' 'Do we have the right to intervene and affect how another country is governed?'

Extension activity

Write the term 'violation' on the board and explain its meaning (an act which breaks, disregards or infringes a law, agreement or right). Ask students to collect examples of human rights violations around the world from newspapers and the internet. Display them in the classroom.

Encourage the students to find out about current human rights issues by visiting websites such as www.britishcouncil.org.

Invite the students to research what Amnesty International does and to write a short statement about it and its campaigns on behalf of prisoners of conscience (www.amnesty.org.uk).

UNIT 5 You and your rights – civil liberties

Your Life 3/Year 9

Lesson 3 *Your Life Student Book 3*, pages 28–29
Citizenship – women's rights

> **Objective:** To explore women's rights and equal opportunities issues in the UK and around the world.

Resources

Copies of the school's equal opportunities policy

Copies of Copymaster 5A 'Understanding human rights'

Starter

Hold a class discussion on equal opportunities at school. Ask: 'Does your school treat girls and boys equally?' Look at the school's equal opportunities policy. How effective is it in stopping discrimination? For example, do the school uniform rules discriminate against girls? Are the lessons 'gender inclusive', i.e. do teachers stress women's achievements as much as men's? Invite groups to rate how girl-friendly the school is on a scale of 1–10 (1 = very low, 10 = very high). Share their views.

Suggested activities

- Read 'Women's rights in the UK' and 'Discrimination at work' (page 28). In pairs, ask students to discuss why they think women's pay still lags behind men's and why men still dominate the highest-paid jobs. Then hold a group discussion. Hold a class discussion of the question: 'Should all jobs in the armed forces be open to women as well as men?'

- In pairs, study 'Domestic violence' (page 29). Ask them: 'What is your reaction to the statistics?' 'Do you feel shocked, surprised, angry, indifferent?' Discuss whether hitting another person can ever be justified.

Plenary

Ask students to discuss what sort of behaviour they think are examples of sexual harassment and to compare their views with those in the statement 'What is sexual harassment?' (page 29). Talk about what action they think should be taken against anyone who sexually harasses someone either at work, in public or at school.

Extension activity

Ask groups to either draft an email to the minister for women saying what they think their priorities should be or a proposal to the school council saying what they think needs to be done to improve equal opportunities at the school.

Assessment

Use copies of Copymaster 5A to assess the students' understanding of human rights. Answers: 1. home, 2. Universal, 3. Amnesty, 4. army, 5. violence, 6. Discrimination, 7. trial, 8. thought, 9. harassment, 10. torture, 11. conscientious.

5A Understanding human rights

Check your understanding of human rights by completing this word puzzle.

		H								
		U								
		M								
		A								
		N								

1. Everyone has the right to have a _ _ _ _ to live in. (4)

2. The _ _ _ _ _ _ _ _ _ Declaration of Human Rights was drawn up in 1948. (9)

3. _ _ _ _ _ _ _ International is a group that campaigns against human rights abuses. (7)

4. Sixty-seven percent of positions in the _ _ _ _ are open to women. (4)

5. Eighty-nine countries have passed laws against domestic _ _ _ _ _ _ _ _. (8)

6. Women's rights in the UK are protected by the Sex _ _ _ _ _ _ _ _ _ _ _ _ _ acts. (14)

7. Anyone who is arrested and held in prison has the right to a fair _ _ _ _ _. (5)

8. Everyone has the right to freedom of _ _ _ _ _ _ _, conscience and religion. (7)

9. Sending lewd emails is a form of sexual _ _ _ _ _ _ _ _ _ _. (10)

10. People who use _ _ _ _ _ _ _ to extract information from a prisoner are abusing the prisoner's human rights. (7)

11. Anyone who refuses to fight in the armed forces is known as a _ _ _ _ _ _ _ _ _ _ _ _ _ objector. (13)

UNIT 6 You and your money – banking and ways of saving

Lesson 1 *Your Life Student Book 3*, pages 30–31
Citizenship/Economic wellbeing and financial capability – banks and saving

Objective: To understand what bank accounts are, and how to choose and open a bank account.

Starter

Introduce the topic of bank accounts by explaining that there are two main types – 'current accounts' and 'savings accounts'. Discuss how current accounts are designed for adults to use for their everyday needs and offer them a safe and easy way of handling their money. Explain how current account holders get a debit card to buy things and get cash from machines, and that they can use cheques or direct debits to pay bills. But you get only a small amount of interest on a current account. So savings accounts are more suitable for teenagers.

Suggested activities

- Read 'Banks – What do they offer?' and 'So you want to open a bank account? Your questions answered' (page 30). Suggest the students discuss, in groups, what the articles say about having a bank account and how to open one, then, as a class, prompt them to discuss whether or nor they think it's a good idea to have a bank account.

- Ask pairs to role play a scene in which one person explains to a friend why they think it's worth having a bank account. Then, individually, ask them to write a letter explaining the advantages of having a bank account and how to open one (see 'For your file', page 30).

- Read 'Which bank is best for you?' (page 31). Ask groups to discuss which bank account they would choose and why, then to explain their choice in a class discussion.

Plenary

Recap the advantages of having a bank account and how to go about opening it.

Extension activities

Encourage groups to conduct a survey of bank accounts which are currently available to young people in your area, either by visiting local branches, telephoning them or searching the internet to obtain information. Then ask them to report their findings in a class discussion, saying which of the accounts they would recommend and why.

Organise a visit from a local bank manager to talk about bank accounts for young people. Ask the students to prepare for the visit by drawing up a list of questions.

UNIT 6 You and your money – banking and ways of saving

Your Life 3/Year 9

Lesson 2 *Your Life Student Book 3*, pages 32–33
Citizenship/Economic wellbeing and financial capability – ways of saving

> **Objective:** To understand and to compare different forms of saving.

Resources

Copies of Copymaster 6 'An A–Z of financial terms'

Starter

Discuss how, if you want to save money, you need to ask a number of questions, e.g. How safe is my money? How accessible is my money? Is there a guarantee that I will earn a certain amount of interest? Will I have to pay tax on the money I invest? Make a list on the board of all the questions students need to think about when deciding where to put their savings.

Suggested activities

- Read the explanations of the various ways of saving on pages 32 and 33, and answer any questions students have about each method. Then ask groups to list the advantages and disadvantages of each type of saving and to decide which they would recommend to a young person and which they would recommend to an adult. Ask: 'Would it make a difference according to how much money the person was saving?'

- Invite pairs to discuss whether they would put £100 into a National Savings and Investments fixed interest savings certificate or premium bonds (see 'In pairs' page 32).

- Give out copies of Copymaster 6 and test students' understanding by challenging pairs to compile a glossary of financial terms for their files.

Plenary

Recap the information given on these pages by giving the class a quick quiz consisting of true and false statements, e.g. 'You get interest on the money you invest in premium bonds'; 'The interest you earn from ISAs is tax-free'.

Extension activity

Ask pairs of students to pick a company that is listed on the stock market and to follow the progress of its shares over a month by looking at the share values in a daily newspaper or on the internet. Then ask them to report how much their money would have increased or decreased in value if they had bought £1000 worth of shares in that company at the beginning of the month. You could explain what the FTSE 100 is and allow them to compare the movement in their shares' values with the movement of the FTSE 100.

An A–Z of financial terms

Work with a partner and write down a definition next to each of these terms. You will end up with a useful glossary of financial terms.

balance _____

bank account _____

cash card _____

deposit _____

dividend _____

inflation _____

insurance premium _____

interest _____

ISA _____

NS&I _____

PIN number _____

premium bond _____

share _____

statement _____

UNIT 7 You and your feelings – dealing with loss

Your Life 3/Year 9

Lesson 1 *Your Life Student Book 3*, pages 34–36
Personal wellbeing – dealing with bereavement

> **Objective:** To explore how you may feel when someone close to you dies, to discuss how to cope with those feelings and how you can help someone who has been bereaved.

Resources

Copies of Copymaster 7 'Helping someone who has been bereaved'

Starter

Explain that when someone close to you dies there is always a feeling of shock – especially if it's sudden and unexpected. You're bound to be sad too. Write 'shock' and 'sadness' on the board and explain that you may also feel other emotions. Write 'AARG!' on the board and explain that it stands for Anger Anxiety Resentment and Guilt. Explain that these are other feelings you may experience when grieving after a death.

Suggested activities

- Read 'How you may feel after a death' (page 34). Discuss with the class what they learn from this article about the different feelings that people who are bereaved may experience and why they have them.

- Read 'Showing emotions' (page 35). In groups, discuss what the writer says about expressing grief, about how long grief lasts and why she suggests that talking helps. Ask individuals to draw up a list of 'Dos' and 'Don'ts' about how to cope with grief, then invite them to share their ideas in a class discussion.

- Read 'Funerals' (page 35). Ask pairs to discuss the arguments for and against children (whatever age they are) attending the funeral of a close relative or friend. Then share your views in a class discussion.

- Ask individuals to do the quiz 'Can you help a friend in need?' (page 36), then to join up with a partner to compare their answers and to read the answers together.

Plenary

Ask the students to write down what they think were the most important things they learned from this lesson about grief, how to cope with it and how to help someone who is experiencing it. Then encourage some students to read their ideas to the class.

Extension activities

Ask groups to read Copymaster 7 and to discuss the advice it gives on what to do when someone they know has been bereaved. Then ask them to draft a letter to Gera who has asked for advice on what to do because she has a friend, Howard, whose teenage sister has died in a road accident.

Ask students to investigate what the charities Cruse (www.cruse.org.uk) and Winston's Wish (www.winstonswish.org.uk) do to help people who have been bereaved.

Helping someone who has been bereaved

What are you supposed to do when someone you know suffers a bereavement?

If the bereaved person is someone you see a lot, you should definitely talk to them about the death, but you can write to them too. If you're not likely to run into the bereaved person soon, it's usual to write a special letter to them, called a letter of condolence. Whether you write or talk, here are some handy hints.

✦ You usually start a letter of condolence by saying 'I'm so sorry to hear about your sad loss.' If you're speaking to the person, it's usual to start by saying 'I'm so sorry …'. I know this sounds like it was your fault that the person died, and you're apologising, but it's a well-known phrase and it's fine.

✦ Most people go on to write or say things like 'I'm thinking of you', and 'Please let me know if there's anything I can do.'

✦ After that, write or say whatever you feel. If you can't imagine what it's like to lose someone you love, say that. If you don't know what to say, you can say that too.

✦ If you're close to the person you're writing or talking to, it's nice to mention something personal, like a happy memory you have of the person who died. You can do this even if you never met them, e.g. 'I know I never met your granny, but I always smile when I think of that funny story you told me about her dancing on the table at your cousin's wedding. She sounded brilliant.'

✦ Always stick to the subject – it's not the time to write or talk about yourself and your news, however important.

✦ Never make wild statements that the bereaved person may not agree with (e.g. 'He was so ill, I'm sure he's quite glad to be dead').

✦ If you're face-to-face, it's thoughtful to ask a bereaved person if they feel like talking about their loss. Most people find that far from making them sadder, talking helps them to cope better. If they don't want to talk, at least you'll know.

At the funeral: what are you supposed to say to the dead person's family?

Basically, the same as the 'I'm so sorry' bit above. If you knew the person who has died well you can also say something about how much you'll miss them and how lovely they were. Funerals can be very emotional events, though, and it's often hard to say anything. If you're stuck for words, everyone will understand. Remember that sometimes, giving a hug or putting your arm gently around someone's shoulder can say everything you want to say just as well as any amount of words.

Discuss what you learn from the advice on this page about what to do when someone you know has been bereaved.

Your Life 3/Year 9

Lesson 2 *Your Life Student Book 3*, page 37

Personal wellbeing – coping with rejection

> **Objective:** To examine the feelings you may experience when a close relationship ends and to explore how to cope with rejection.

Starter

Write the word 'recrimination' on the board and explain that it means making accusations about someone's behaviour. Talk about how, when a relationship comes to an end, we may feel rejection and that the feelings we experience may be similar to those of the grief we feel when a person close to us dies. Explain that we may be tempted to indulge in recriminations, either self-recrimination or accusing a former friend of doing things that caused you to drift apart, but that recrimination is not productive.

Suggested activities

- Read the article by Erica Stewart on page 37. Ask groups to discuss the advice she gives, then to make a list of 'Dos' and 'Don'ts' on how to cope with rejection and to share their views in a class discussion.

- Ask students to read the advice Louisa Fairbanks gives about how to end a relationship in 'Announcing it's over' (page 37), to discuss in groups whether they agree with it and to decide on the best way to end a relationship.

- Invite the students to write letters in reply to a pen pal on how to cope with the ending of a relationship (see 'For your file', page 37).

Plenary

Ask some of the students to read out their letters. Discuss which of their letters gives the best advice and why.

Extension activity

Ask students to imagine they work for a teen magazine. Their task is to write an article entitled 'Pat's story' in which they tell the story of how a teenager coped with the break-up of a relationship which had lasted for 18 months.

UNIT 8 You and your body – drugs and drugtaking

Your Life 3/Year 9

Lesson 1 *Your Life Student Book 3*, pages 38–39
Keeping healthy – drugs and drugtaking

Objective: To explore the factors which affect the risk involved in drugtaking and to explore the arguments for and against legalising drugs.

Starter

Introduce the topic by explaining that while all drugtaking involves risks, the risks involved vary. Ask the students on their own to write down what they consider to be the risks of **a)** taking ecstasy, **b)** smoking cannabis and **c)** injecting heroin. Hold a class discussion in which they share some of their ideas. Explain that how dangerous drugtaking is depends on the drug that is taken, the person taking it and how and where it is taken.

Suggested activities

- Ask individuals to read the article 'How dangerous is drugtaking?' (page 38) and to make notes under the headings: 'The drug and its effects', 'The person', 'The environment'. Then invite groups to discuss the main points they have learned from the article about the factors that influence how dangerous drugtaking is.

- Ask individuals to write an article explaining 'Why drugtaking is a risky business' (see 'For your file', page 38).

- Read the articles about drug legalisation on page 39, then ask groups to discuss the questions (see 'In groups' activity). They share their views in a class discussion.

Plenary

Ask the students to imagine they are designing a poster to make young people aware of the risks involved in taking drugs, and to decide what main points they would try to put across.

Extension activities

Invite groups to draw up plans for a two-minute public information video designed to warn young people of the risks of drugtaking. Ask someone from each group to present their ideas to the rest of the class for the class to rate how good the proposal is on a five-point scale (1 = excellent to 5 = poor).

Organise a debate on a motion such as 'Illegal drugs are too dangerous to be made legal' or 'The laws about taking drugs should be abolished because they are ineffective.'

UNIT 8 You and your body – drugs and drugtaking

Lesson 2 *Your Life Student Book 3*, pages 40–41
Keeping healthy – drugs and drugtaking

Objective: To examine the problems drugs can cause, to explain how to help a friend with a drug problem and what to do in an emergency caused by drugtaking.

Resources

Copies of Copymaster 8 'Drugs problems'

Starter

Ask: 'What problems can a person have if they take drugs?' Invite pairs to brainstorm their ideas and then share them in a brief class discussion. Point out that: health problems can be mental as well as physical; drugtaking can affect relationships with family and friends; it can cause a person to steal in order to pay for drugs; it can affect their work.

Suggested activities

- Read 'My life's a mess' (page 40), then invite the class to discuss how drugtaking has affected Sarah's life. Then read 'How to help a friend who has a problem with drugs' (page 40). Prompt pairs to imagine they are Sarah's friends, to decide what they would say to try to help her and to role play a scene in which they talk to Sarah.

- Ask individuals to write Melanie's reply to Shania, offering advice on how she can help a friend with a drugs problem (see 'For your file', page 40).

- Read 'What to do in an emergency' (page 41). Ask pairs to draw up a ten-question test based on the information given in the article, e.g. 'Question 1: Name two drugs which may cause someone to become tense and panicky'. Then ask them to join up with another pair, to swap tests and to answer each other's questions. Ask individuals to draw a cartoon strip showing how to give first aid to a teenager who becomes ill after taking drugs (see 'For your file' page 41).

Plenary

Recap how to give emergency first aid, focusing on overheating and dehydration. Remind them of steps to prevent it occurring, what the warning signs are and what to do if someone overheats.

Extension activities

Study the letters about drugs problems on Copymaster 8 and ask groups to discuss the advice that the drugs counsellor gives. Ask them to decide which they think are the most useful pieces of advice and why, and hold a class discussion.

Ask students to use the internet to research information and advice on drugs problems.

Invite a member of the local St John Ambulance branch to talk about how to give emergency first aid to someone who has become ill after taking drugs.

8 Drugs problems

CHECK IT!

Got a problem? Our drugs counsellor, Gwyn Byrne, is here to help...

QUESTION

I started sniffing glue and aerosols when I was in care. For the last two years, I've lived with a foster family but now my foster parents and I argue all the time and I've started sniffing aerosols again. My foster mother found out and is threatening to send me back into care. I'm unhappy all the time and sniffing aerosols doesn't help anymore. What can I do?

ANSWER

Sniffing glue and other solvents can be very dangerous and, as you realise, it's not the answer. Both you and your foster mother are feeling very worried and you both need specialist help. Get in touch with the FRANK, the National Drugs Helpline on 0800 776600 where a trained counsellor will advise you. Your foster mother could also ring Young Minds parent helpline on 0808 802 5544, which gives help and support to families of drug users.

QUESTION

My older sister is much prettier and more popular than I am. Last Saturday, before she went out, I saw her and her friend giggling and rubbing what looked like white powder onto their gums. Was this a drug? Would doing the same help me to make more friends?

ANSWER

They were probably using a stimulant like speed or cocaine and yes, they do make people feel more confident, energetic and outgoing – but not for long. Afterwards, your sister is likely to feel panicky or depressed, and if she keeps using cocaine, she is also risking serious damage to her heart. Don't be tempted to follow her example; you don't have to follow the crowd to attract friends. Being caring, loyal and thoughtful are more important qualities that people look for in friends. If you are worried about your sister, call Families Anonymous on 020 7498 4680.

QUESTION

I'm 14 and hang out with an older crowd. We go clubbing all night and take ecstasy. Although I only take half a tablet, I'm so shattered during the week that I often miss school and my work is suffering. Now my parents are giving me grief, so I'm thinking of going to live with my friend. Can my parents make me come back?

ANSWER

Your older friends are doing you no favours. Ecstasy is a Class A drug and even half a tablet can be very dangerous as you never know what you are getting, or how your body will react to it. If you leave home, your parents can make you come back and constantly playing truant may even lead to you ending up in care. So try to find other ways of having fun, like listening to music, playing sport, making friends of your own age and going to the local youth club.

QUESTION

I'm 15 and my older brother is into hard drugs. Sometimes I smoke a couple of joints with my mates, but now my mum has found out. She's very upset and says I'll end up like my brother. Can drug addiction run in the family? I want to join the army when I leave school – will smoking cannabis affect my chances?

ANSWER

Predilection to addictive behaviour isn't hereditary, so there's no reason why you should become addicted like your brother. Having said that, some young people who smoke cannabis do move on to heavier drugs, so it is understandable that your mum is worried. A police record would be a drawback in starting any career. Tell your mum you have no intention of following in your brother's footsteps and instead of smoking cannabis with your friends, why not sign up to be an army cadet so you can make a flying start to your career?

Discuss the problems that these people are having and the advice that the drugs counsellor gives on how to deal with them. Talk about what he says and what you have learned from it about how to deal with drugs problems.

UNIT 9 You and the law – crimes and punishments

Your Life 3/Year 9

Lesson 1 *Your Life Student Book 3*, pages 42–43
Citizenship – young people and crime

Objective: To explore why so many young people commit crimes and to discuss shoplifting.

Starter

Explain that young people commit one in three crimes of burglary, theft and criminal damage. Ask: 'Why do so many young people get involved in crime?' Write students' suggestions on the board, e.g. to show off, to rebel, to take revenge on society because they're unhappy, to get a thrill, to get money for things they can't afford, because they get drunk or high, to be 'one of the gang'.

Suggested activities

- Read 'Why do so many young people commit crimes?' (page 42). Invite groups to discuss the reasons given in the article and to compare them with their own suggestions. What do they think are the main reasons?

- Read 'Girls and crime' (page 42). Ask pairs to discuss the reasons given in the article, to suggest any other reasons and to share their views in a class discussion.

- Study the information on shoplifting and 'Rebecca's story' (page 43). Ask students to write answers to the four questions (see 'In groups', page 43) and then to share their views in a group and/or class discussion.

- Ask individuals to write a story about a young person who is caught shoplifting (see 'For your file', page 43).

Plenary

End with a general discussion on stealing. What are the students' attitudes to different forms of stealing, e.g. fare dodging, fraud, robbery, burglary, shoplifting? Are some forms of stealing more serious than others or are all forms of stealing equally wrong? Should anyone caught stealing always be taken to the police?

Extension activity

Develop a role play of a TV studio discussion on the issues raised in the lesson by suggesting that some of the students act as a panel of people with differing views on why there is so much youth crime. The other members of the class can act as the studio audience, and the person chairing the discussion can invite them to give their views.

UNIT 9 You and the law – crimes and punishments

Your Life 3/Year 9

Lesson 2 *Your Life Student Book 3*, pages 44–45

Citizenship – crimes and punishments

Objective: To explore the aims of punishment, to discuss the effectiveness of imprisonment and to consider what different types of punishment should be given for particular crimes.

Resources

Copies of Copymaster 9 'A punishment to fit the crime'

Copies of Copymaster 9A 'Understanding crimes and punishment'

Starter

Ask the students: 'What should the aims of punishment be?' and list their ideas on the board. Explain that there are five main theories about punishment. Write the words 'deterrence', 'protection', 'reform', 'retribution' and 'reparation' on the board, explain their meanings and ask the students to study the chart at the top of page 44.

Suggested activities

- Read 'Imprisonment – does it work?' (page 44). Then invite groups to discuss the four statements about prisons, to decide whether they agree with them and to share their views in a class discussion.

- Talk about the different types of punishment that can be given and read 'A glossary of punishments' (page 45). Ask individuals to write down what punishments they would give the seven people a) if they were first-time offenders and b) if they were repeat offenders (see 'In groups', page 45), then to share their views in a group discussion.

- Read 'What about the victim?' (page 45). Ask groups to discuss how far the effect on the victim should be taken into consideration when deciding a punishment, then to share their views in a class discussion.

Plenary

Discuss all the things that magistrates need to take into account when deciding what punishment to give someone, e.g. the type of crime, the severity of the crime, how much the victim has suffered, the age of the offender, whether or not they have offended before, the purpose of the punishment, the effect it is likely to have on the offender. Ask: 'What should the magistrate's main consideration be?'

Extension activities

Ask groups to do the activity on Copymaster 9 (to draw up lists of crimes in categories according to how serious they consider them to be and to decide on maximum and minimum punishments for each offence).

Ask pairs to discuss their views on prisons (see 'In pairs' on Copymaster 9), then each to write their views on how prison should be used as a punishment.

Invite individuals to use the internet to research information about prisons and alternatives to prisons, e.g. by visiting websites such as www.nacro.org.uk (the website of the National Association for the Care and Resettlement of Offenders).

Assessment

Use copies of Copymaster 9A to assess the students' understanding of crimes and punishments.

9 A punishment to fit the crime

 **In groups**

1 How serious do you think the following crimes are:

@ Driving without a licence

@ Selling cigarettes to someone under the age of 16

@ Carrying a knife with a lockable blade

@ Physically abusing a child

@ Handling stolen goods

@ Spraying graffiti on a bus shelter

@ Travelling on a train without paying

@ Punching someone in a brawl

@ Setting fire to a building?

2 List all the different crimes you can think of, ranging from murder to riding a bicycle on the pavement. Then put them into categories according to how serious you think they are:

Category 1 – very minor offences

Category 2 – minor offences

Category 3 – serious offences

Category 4 – very serious offences

Category 5 – extremely serious offences

Which punishment?

In law, there are maximum and minimum punishments that can be given to a person who is convicted of a particular offence. Go through your lists of crimes and decide what type of punishment you think would be appropriate for each offence, and what you think the maximum and minimum punishments should be for that offence.

In considering which punishments should be given, bear in mind the different purposes that punishments can have:

@ **Deterrence** – To stop the offender from doing it again and to discourage others from committing a similar offence.

@ **Protection** – To protect society by making it impossible for the offender to commit further offences.

@ **Reform** – To help the offender change their behaviour, so that they will stop committing crimes.

@ **Retribution** – To make the offender suffer for the crime.

@ **Reparation** – To repay or compensate the victim.

In pairs

In your view, what are the main reasons for sending a person to prison? Which crimes do you think should carry a custodial sentence? Should persistent offenders be given custodial sentences whatever the nature of their crimes?

Write a short statement explaining your views on how prison should be used as a form of punishment.

9A Understanding crimes and punishments

On a separate sheet, answer these questions as fully as you can, giving reasons for your views.

1. What do you think are the main reasons why so many young people commit crimes?

2. Why do you think girls today are more likely to commit crimes than girls of 50 years ago?

3. How serious an offence do you think shoplifting is?

4. Should shopkeepers always call the police if they catch someone shoplifting?

5. What do you think should be the main aims of a punishment given to someone found guilty of a criminal offence?

6. For which criminal offences do you think a person should always receive a custodial sentence?

7. What alternative punishments are there to prison sentences? Give examples of cases in which you think these punishments should be given rather than prison sentences.

8. Do you think monitoring young offenders is a good way of reducing crime? Give reasons for your answer and say what measures you think would be most effective in cutting down crime.

UNIT 9 You and the law – crimes and punishments

Your Life 3/Year 9

Lesson 3 *Your Life Student Book 3*, pages 46–47
Citizenship – gangs and knife crime

Objective: To explore the issues of gang crime and knife crime.

Starter

Introduce the topic of gang crime by getting students to share their views on why people join gangs, then compare their ideas with those given in 'Why do people join street gangs?' (page 46).

Suggested activities

- Read 'I'm being pressured into joining a gang, what can I do?' (page 46). Discuss the advice that is given, then encourage the students to do the role play (page 46).
- Study the statements 'Have your say about carrying knives' (page 47) and ask groups to discuss which ones they agree with and why.

Plenary

Hold a class discussion of the suggestions made in 'Cutting down on knife crime' (page 47). Ask: 'If you were the Home Secretary what measures would you introduce?'

Extension activities

Ask the students to write down their own views on knives and knife crime. Encourage students to visit the Crimestoppers website www.crimestoppers-uk.org.

UNIT 10 You and other people – being assertive

Your Life 3/Year 9

Lesson 1 *Your Life Student Book 3*, pages 48–49
Personal wellbeing – developing assertiveness skills

> **Objective:** To understand the difference between assertive, aggressive and passive behaviour.

Resources

Copies of Copymaster 10 'How assertive are you?'

Starter

Write the words 'assertive', 'aggressive' and 'passive' on the board. Explain that these describe, in broad terms, how people behave in their dealings with other people. Give an example: 'Your sister has an irritating habit which is getting on your nerves.' Explain that getting angry and shouting at her about it would be aggressive, saying nothing would be passive, but talking to her calmly about it and why it irritates you would be assertive. Then read the introductory text on page 48.

Suggested activities

- Ask the students, in pairs, to study the chart at the top of page 49. They then discuss the eight situations and write down what would be assertive, aggressive and passive behaviour in each situation. Ask them to compare their answers with other pairs in a group discussion. Then, as a class, discuss why in each case the best way to handle the situation is to be assertive.

- Invite pairs to choose one of the situations and to role play it in three different ways (see 'Role play' page 49). Alternatively, ask them to write contrasting scripts showing a person behaving assertively in one script and either passively or aggressively in another.

- Read 'It doesn't pay to be passive' (page 48). Discuss, as a class, what the article says about why people sometimes behave passively, and what the consequences of behaving passively are.

Plenary

Without referring to the chart on page 49, ask pairs to make a list of the various ways an assertive person behaves. Check their lists against the chart and discuss with them why it is preferable for someone to behave assertively rather than aggressively or passively.

Extension activity

Give out copies of Copymaster 10 and ask students to complete the quiz individually. Then discuss, in pairs, what they learned about how assertive they are.

How assertive are you?

Do this quiz to find out how assertive you are. Keep a record of your answers and then check what your answers tell you about how assertive you are.

1 One of your friends starts expressing opinions which you find offensive. What do you do?
- **a)** Tell them you find their views offensive.
- **b)** Wait till someone else says something, then join in.
- **c)** Stay quiet in order to keep the peace.

2 Your parents tell you off for getting in an hour later than you said. What do you do?
- **a)** Accept you were in the wrong and that they're right to be cross.
- **b)** Let them go on at you but say nothing.
- **c)** Get angry and say it's time they stopped treating you like a child.

3 You've been out with a friend, who asks you to go back with them to watch some YouTube videos, but you're tired and have some homework to do. What do you do?
- **a)** Thank them for inviting you, but say why you want to go home.
- **b)** Drop a hint that you don't want to and hope they'll get the message.
- **c)** Go in anyway, because that's what they want.

4 You see someone you fancy in a queue that you're about to join. What do you do?
- **a)** Go straight up to them and start a conversation.
- **b)** Try to attract their attention in some way and hope they'll speak to you.
- **c)** Do nothing, except hope that they'll do something.

5 You and some friends are making a lot of noise. A neighbour comes out and complains. What do you do?
- **a)** Listen to what they say and agree that perhaps you were being a bit noisy.
- **b)** Wait to see what the others do, then follow their lead.
- **c)** Shout back at them and say it's none of their business what you do.

6 You feel that a teacher keeps on picking on you in class. What do you do?
- **a)** Ask to see the teacher in private and tell them how you feel.
- **b)** Get a friend to tell another teacher what's going on.
- **c)** Keep your head down in the teacher's lessons and hope it stops.

7 There's a trip being organised to see a show in London, but you're short of cash. What do you do?
- **a)** Work out how you can raise the cash by doing some odd jobs.
- **b)** Tell your parents and try to persuade them to come up with the cash.
- **c)** Pretend you don't really want to go.

8 A group of friends try to pressurise you into climbing into an old building to have a look around. What do you do?
- **a)** Tell them it's dangerous and you don't want to.
- **b)** Make an excuse that you've got to go and hope they'll accept it.
- **c)** Go with them, because you're frightened of being called a chicken.

9 People in your class start teasing you because you made a fool of yourself in a lesson. What do you do?
- **a)** Make a joke about what you did and laugh at yourself.
- **b)** Put up with it, because you know they'll soon get tired of it.
- **c)** Lose your temper and say you'll hit them if they keep on teasing you.

10 You keep arranging to go out with a friend, but they keep on phoning at the last minute to cancel. What do you do?
- **a)** Calmly tell them you're annoyed because they keep letting you down.
- **b)** Ask another friend to speak to them about it.
- **c)** Say nothing even though you're very cross.

How did you score?

Mostly 'a's You've plenty of self-confidence and know how to be assertive.

Mostly 'b's You don't always express your feelings directly and openly and you're inclined to sit on the fence too often. You need to become more assertive.

Mostly 'c's You need to think carefully about your behaviour and to learn not to react passively or aggressively when faced with difficult situations.

UNIT 10 You and other people – being assertive

Your Life 3/Year 9

Lesson 2 *Your Life Student Book 3*, pages 50–51
Personal wellbeing – developing assertiveness skills

Objective: To understand assertiveness techniques and how to use them.

Starter

Remind the students of the differences between assertive, aggressive and passive behaviour explained in Lesson 1, of the consequences of behaving aggressively or passively, and of the benefits of behaving assertively.

Suggested activities

- Read the article 'How to be assertive' (page 50). Ask individuals to take notes on the key points, then, as a class, discuss the advice it gives.

- Read 'Saying what you want – confidence tips' (page 51). Ask groups to discuss each of the six steps and to decide which two pieces of advice are the most useful. Then share their views in a class discussion.

- Ask pairs to practise being assertive by performing the role plays (page 51). Alternatively, if the lesson is taking place in a classroom where it is impossible to do role plays, invite pairs to script rather than to act out the scenes, then to take it in turns to read them aloud.

Plenary

Hold a class discussion. Ask: 'Is it easier to talk about being assertive than to be assertive in practice?' 'Is it harder to be assertive with your family and friends than it is to be assertive with people you don't know well?' 'How important do you think it is to develop assertiveness skills?' 'What are the key things you have learned from the lesson about how to be assertive?'

Extension activity

Ask individuals to write a story describing a situation – either real or imaginary – in which a person behaves assertively, and consequently brings about an important change in their life (by altering the situation, changing a relationship or developing their self-esteem).

UNIT 11 You and the world of work – investigating careers

Your Life 3/Year 9

Lesson 1 *Your Life Student Book 3*, pages 52–53

Citizenship/Economic wellbeing and financial capability – investigating careers

Objective: To review your strengths, interests and personal qualities and to understand the qualities and abilities required for different types of work.

Starter

Explain that when you are thinking about careers you need to consider your interests and personal qualities. Ask students to think about their out-of-school hobbies and activities and to write down any activities that particularly interest them. Then read 'Your interests' (page 52). Ask pairs to discuss any skills or strengths that they may have developed as a result of their interests and to suggest jobs in which they might be able to use these skills.

Suggested activities

- Study the list of personal qualities and invite the students to make a list of their own strengths and to discuss them with a partner (see 'In pairs', page 52).
- Read 'Different types of work' (page 53). Ask pairs to discuss the qualities and abilities required in each area, to refer to their list of personal qualities and to decide which area of work they would prefer, if they had to choose between them (see 'In pairs' page 53).
- Ask students to list the qualities and abilities required for other areas of work (see 'In pairs' page 53).

Plenary

Recap what they have learned from the lesson about the importance of matching their qualities and abilities to those required for a particular job, when considering possible careers.

Extension activity

Write a statement about your qualities similar to Orla's statement (see 'For your file' page 53).

UNIT 11 You and the world of work – investigating careers

Your Life 3/Year 9

Lesson 2 *Your Life Student Book 3*, pages 54–55
Citizenship/Economic wellbeing and financial capability – investigating careers

Objective: To understand the various ways of finding information about careers.

Resources

Copies of Copymaster 11 'Job factsheet'

Starter

Ask the students to suggest different ways of finding information about jobs, and make a list of their suggestions on the board.

Suggested activities

- Encourage the students to go online to find out about jobs in which they may be interested. Get them to share details of websites that they find useful, in addition to the 'National Careers Service' website (page 54).

- Read 'Talk to someone who is doing the job' and 'Arrange to visit a workplace' (page 54). Encourage the students to use their initiative to find someone to talk to or a workplace to visit.

- Read 'Work shadowing' (page 54). Discuss Jamie's story. Ask: 'What did Jamie learn about working as a plumber?' Encourage the students to arrange a day's work shadowing.

Plenary

Stress that it is important to plan for any conversation about a job or a visit to a workplace by making a list of what information they need to find. Read and discuss the 'Job factsheet' (page 55). Then give them each a copy of the Copymaster 11 for them to refer to during their conversations and visits.

Extension activities

In a class discussion ask individuals to share the information they found out about particular jobs and why they would or would not consider doing the job.

Suggest that they put their completed copies of the job factsheets into a file on the computer to make them available to the rest of the class.

11 Job factsheet

Name of job _____

Researched by _____ Date _____

1. What particular activities does the job require you to do? (For example, answering the telephone, using a computer, handling money etc.)

2. What sort of place would you be working in? (For example, would you be working indoors or outdoors, in an office, out on a site, in a factory, in a shop or somewhere else?)

3. Would you be working on your own or with others?

4. What are the particular qualities and skills you require for this job?

5. What qualifications do you require in order to do this job?

6. Where can you get the necessary training, education or experience for this job?

7. Are there any particular restrictions about this job? (For example, do you have to be over a certain age? Are there any medical restrictions, such as not being colour blind?)

8. What are the rewards of this job? (For example, high salary, flexible working hours, challenges, excitement, job satisfaction.)

9. What are the drawbacks of this job? (For example, shift work including night shifts, years of training, repetitive work, unchallenging.)

10. What is the career structure in this type of work? Are there plenty of opportunities for promotion?

11. What is the competition like for this type of job? Are there plenty of these jobs available or are there a lot of people competing for a few jobs?

12. Where are there opportunities for this type of job? (For example, only in large cities or in particular areas of the country where companies are located.)

Conclusion

Now that you have researched this job, what conclusion have you reached? Give the reasons why you think you would or would not consider doing this job as a career.

UNIT 12 You and the media – the power of the press

Lesson 1 *Your Life Student Book 3*, pages 56–57
Social education – understanding the media

> **Objective:** To examine the press in Britain, exploring the issues of press ownership, news management and what controls the content of newspapers.

Resources

Copies of two or three newspapers from the same day

Copies of Copymaster 12 'Telling it straight?'

Copies of Copymaster 12A 'Understanding the press'

Starter

Explain what is meant by 'a free press' and how it is free from government controls. Discuss how in undemocratic states there is state control of the press through censorship. Read 'Case study – North Korea' (page 56) and discuss how the North Korean government uses the press to control information and to suppress opposition.

Suggested activities

- Read 'The press in Britain' (page 56). Talk about how even in a democracy there are some curbs on the power of the press. Then ask groups to discuss their views on newspaper ownership by companies run by people who are not British citizens and on the ownership of several papers by one company.

- Explain what spin doctoring is. Talk about what a press release is and how big businesses and political parties time press releases so they appear to coincide with the issuing of reports. Then read and discuss with the class 'News management' (page 57).

- Read 'What controls the content of newspapers?' (page 57). Then invite groups to study copies of two or three different newspapers, to compare the different space given to different kinds of reports and to discuss what this tells us about the news values of the different newspapers.

Plenary

Sum up in a class discussion what the students have learned about the different influences on the content of newspapers in Britain.

Extension activity

Ask groups to study the article 'Telling it straight?' on Copymaster 12, to discuss the issues it raises, then to share their views in a class discussion.

Assessment

Use copies of Copymaster 12A to assess students' understanding of press issues.

Telling it straight?

In the age of the communications satellite, there are more sources of information about events and issues at home and abroad than ever before. How does the media treat the information they receive? Are we well-informed or misinformed?

Only the biggest and most prestigious organisations can afford to keep many reporters 'in the field'. Most rely heavily on news agencies, press releases and briefings from government sources, political parties, campaigning organisations and businesses to provide them with information.

The source of the information perhaps does not matter very much, as long as it is properly identified and treated in a balanced way. Most broadcasting organisations are legally required to do this, at least in their news coverage.

Leading newspapers in the USA also pride themselves on their impartial reporting.

> 66 A reporter's opinion should not figure in the story at all. What a reporter contributes to a story is expertise and analysis. 99
> Leonard Dowie, former executive editor, *Washington Post* newspaper

However, it can be very hard to report issues totally impartially. The prominence that is given to one story over another, and tiny differences in the use of language can imply support or criticism, so that even the BBC and US newspapers are attacked for biased reporting.

The British press does not even set out to offer an impartial view. The way in which news is reported can be influenced by various factors: the need to please the owner, to attract advertisers, or a wish to promote a particular political or social agenda.

Newspaper owners see nothing sinister in this – they are reflecting their readers' interests rather than influencing them.

Many people would argue, however, that if a newspaper is tailored to the interests of its readers it can sometimes be difficult for the readers to gain an impression of what is really important. All the facts need to be known – and the facts need to be clearly separated out from opinion – to discover the whole truth behind any media story.

> 66 Much of the content of the national press is inspired by companies wishing to plug some product, some service or some personality, and is therefore little more than covert advertising. 99
> Henry Porter, *Lies, Damned Lies and Some Exclusives*

> 66 The notion of impartiality lies at the heart of the BBC ... We must not recycle received opinion as though it were unassailable truth. We must be alert to the dangers of stereotypes and preconceptions. 99
> BBC guidelines for producers

> 66 The Daily Telegraph is Tory; we advance a strongly conservative (and generally Conservative) political line in the paper. 99
> Charles Moore, former editor, *The Daily Telegraph*

> 66 The public certainly has no duty to support newspapers. It is the duty of the publisher to provide the type of newspaper the public wants to read. 99
> Rupert Murdoch, newspaper owner

 In groups

Discuss the issues raised in this article. Is there any harm in British newspapers promoting particular political agendas? Would the public be better informed if British newspapers were to report events impartially in the way that the BBC and US newspapers do? Do you think we are well-informed by the press or are we in danger of being misinformed?

12A Understanding the press

On a separate sheet, answer these questions as fully as you can, giving reasons for any views you express.

1. What is a free press? How important do you think it is to have a free press?
   (See 'Case Study' on page 56.)

2. What is a newspaper proprietor? Is it right that a proprietor should have so much control over the political message of a newspaper?
   (See 'What controls the content of newspapers?' on page 57.)

3. Explain what the term 'spin-doctoring' means. How do political parties try to manage the news?
   (See 'News management' on page 57.)

4. How is the content of newspapers influenced by a) consumer demand and b) advertisers?
   (See 'What controls the content of newspapers?' on page 57.)

5. Explain what the term 'news value' means. Who decides how much space a story should be given in a newspaper?
   (See 'Who controls the content of newspapers?' on page 57.)

6. Do people have the right to know about the private lives of public figures? Or do public figures have a right to privacy in their private lives? When does media interest become an invasion of privacy?
   (See 'Public interest versus private rights' on page 58.)

7. Should investigative journalists be able to use whatever means are available to uncover information? (See 'Press regulation' on page 58).

8. Should the press be self-regulated? (See 'Press regulation' on page 58.)

UNIT 12 You and the media – the power of the press

Your Life 3/Year 9

Lesson 2 *Your Life Student Book 3*, page 58
Social education – understanding the media

> **Objective:** To explore the issues of public interest and private rights and of press regulation.

Starter

Discuss how people are interested in the private lives of celebrities and how magazines such as *Hello!* will pay huge sums of money to have the exclusive rights to report a celebrity wedding. Ask: 'When does media interest become an intrusion of privacy?' Talk about how journalists doorstep famous people who are involved in scandals and even in the past have used phone hacking in order to get a story.

Suggested activities

- Read 'Public interest versus private rights' (page 58). As a class, discuss the issues it raises, focusing in particular on the two statements (see 'In groups'). Ask: 'Who has the right to decide what the public should know or not know?' 'Who should decide what is in the public interest?'

- Study 'Press regulation' (page 58). Then in groups ask the students to discuss whether phone hacking can ever be justified and whether the press should be self-regulated.

Plenary

Ask groups to report their views on phone hacking and regulation of the press in a class discussion.

Extension activity

Encourage individuals to use the internet to research the Leveson inquiry. Ask them to find out what its recommendations were and whether they have been implemented and to report their findings to the rest of the class.

UNIT 12 You and the media – the power of the press

Your Life 3/Year 9

Lesson 3 *Your Life Student Book 3*, page 59
Social education – understanding the media – the press

Objective: To explore teen magazines.

Resources

Copies of teen magazines

Starter

Ask the students: 'What do you think of teen magazines?' 'Are they useful sources of information on serious topics?' 'Are they simply fun to read – full of gossip about celebrities and fashion?' 'Do the editors and writers patronise young people?' Invite them to share their views in a class discussion.

Suggested activities

- Read 'What do you think of teen magazines?' (page 59). Ask groups to discuss the views expressed in the article, then to share their own views in a class discussion.
- Ask groups to draft proposals for a new teen magazine, and to present their ideas in a class discussion.

Plenary

Discuss how the students' ideas for new teen magazines differ from existing magazines. How does their view of what teenagers want to read differ from adults' views?

Extension activities

Ask pairs or groups of students to carry out a detailed study of a teen magazine (see 'For your file', page 59).

Prompt groups to imagine they have been asked to edit a page for young people to appear weekly in a national newspaper. Ask them to draw up proposals for its contents, and to discuss them with the rest of the class. They could then work together as a class to prepare articles, to design and produce a specimen page.

UNIT 13 You and your body – eating disorders

Your Life 3/Year 9

Lesson 1 *Your Life Student Book 3*, pages 60–61
Keeping healthy – eating disorders

Objective: To explain what anorexia nervosa is, to explore what triggers it
and to discuss how it affects people.

Resources

Copies of Copymaster 13 'The diet trap'

Starter

Remind the students that in order to stay healthy we need to eat a balanced diet (that is,
the right amount of the right foods). A balanced diet consisting of a range of foods gives
us enough proteins for our bodies to grow, enough energy for our physical needs, enough
vitamins to keep us healthy, and enough fibre to help us get rid of waste. Remind them that
if we eat too much we may get obese, and if we eat too little we may become ill through lack
of nutrition.

Suggested activities

● Read 'Anorexia nervosa' (page 60) and 'The red flags of an eating disorder' (page 61).
Discuss, as a class, what the articles say about anorexia and what the signs of an eating
disorder are.

● Read 'Portia's story' (page 60) and 'Mark's story' (page 61). Discuss, as a class, what they
learn from them about what triggers anorexia and how anorexia affects people's lives.

● Study 'What causes an eating disorder?' (page 61) and discuss with the class what the
factors are that may cause an eating disorder. Talk about how helping a person with
anorexia involves trying to sort out the underlying cause of the illness, in addition to
getting them to eat more.

Plenary

Sum up the key facts the students have learned in the lesson by holding a class discussion
and listing on the board 'Ten things you should know about anorexia'.

Extension activity

Give out copies of Copymaster 13. Ask groups to study it and discuss what it says about
why people diet, what bad reasons are for dieting, what the only good reason is and what
dieting can do to you in adolescence. Then invite them individually to write a letter to a
friend who is planning to go on a diet, explaining why they don't think it's a good idea.

13 The diet trap

Why do you want to lose weight?

Before we even look at why diets are bad news, the first question you have to ask yourself is, why do you want to diet? Is it for health reasons? Has your doctor told you that you need to lose weight? Is it because you feel you are too fat? If so, are you sure you are actually overweight? (It sounds a silly question, but many people have such a distorted view of their body that they assume they are overweight when they're not.)

Or are you planning to go on a diet because you think it will improve your life, get you a boyfriend/girlfriend or make you feel happy? If it's for one of these reasons, then sadly, losing weight is not the answer. Dieting is not a magical cure for all the things you're unhappy about. Weight gain or loss is just that and nothing else. It doesn't have the power to make your life perfect or happy. So why put yourself through a diet regime if what you're looking for has nothing to do with weight?

⚡ Bad reasons to go on a diet ⚡

◎ You want to wear a particular size of clothes

◎ You feel fatter than your friends

◎ You think people will fancy you more

◎ Someone else is making you diet

◎ Someone else says you're fat

◎ You feel it's something you should do

⚡ What dieting does to you in adolescence ⚡

'How can dieting be so bad for you? Everyone I know does it. It's not like being anorexic or anything.' Annie 14

⚡ One good reason to go on a diet ⚡
You have been told to lose weight for your health.

Go on a diet and it will make you feel:

◎ tired;

◎ depressed;

◎ anxious;

◎ food obsessed;

◎ cranky;

◎ lacking in confidence;

◎ tearful;

◎ irritable;

◎ unhappy.

Diet frequently and this is what will happen to your body ... you'll:

◎ increase your risk of brittle bones thanks to a lack of calcium;

◎ increase your chances of being shorter, thanks to lack of bone growth;

◎ increase your chances of having an eating disorder;

◎ mess up your metabolism;

◎ affect your menstrual cycle (girls);

◎ affect your fertility;

◎ affect the growth rate of your hair and nails;

◎ diminish your energy levels;

◎ sleep badly;

◎ be constipated.

As you can see, dieting is bad news, but it's particularly bad for you when you're going through puberty. Food is fuel and the teenage body needs fuel to grow to an adult size. If you diet during puberty you'll not only deprive yourself of energy but also of vital nutrients and minerals the body needs in order to activate your growth spurt.

The sad truth is that dieting leads to food and weight preoccupation, feelings of failure about yourself, a poor body image, lack of self-esteem and depression.

Study the information on this page, then write a letter to a friend who has written to say that he's planning to go on a diet, explaining to him why you don't think it's a good idea.

UNIT 13 You and your body – eating disorders

Your Life 3/Year 9

Lesson 2 *Your Life Student Book 3*, pages 62–63
Keeping healthy – eating disorders

Objective: To examine bulimia and to discuss media pressure on young people to be a particular size and shape.

Starter

Recap on what the students learned about anorexia in the previous lesson. Explain that there are other eating disorders which involve eating too much rather than eating too little (compulsive overeating which causes obesity, and bulimia which involves binge-eating and purging).

Suggested activities

- Read 'What is bulimia?' and 'What to do if a friend has bulimia …' (page 62). Invite individuals to make notes on what bulimics do, what causes bulimia and what to do if a friend has bulimia. Then allow them to discuss what they have learned about bulimia in groups.

- Read 'Is there too much pressure to be thin?' (page 63). Ask students, in groups, to discuss whether they agree with the views expressed by the two teenagers, then to share their views in a class discussion.

- Ask groups to discuss Adele Lovell's statement (see 'In groups', page 63), before writing their own statement about what they think matters most – personality or looks – and giving their views on the effects of media pressure.

Plenary

Conclude the lesson by allowing some of the students to read out their statements and discussing how far there is general agreement on the issues that have been raised about the importance of personality and looks, and the influence of media pressure.

Extension activity

Ask students to find out more about eating disorders using the internet. Useful websites to visit include Mirror Mirror (www.mirror-mirror.org/eatdis.htm) and the Eating Disorders Association (www.b-eat.co.uk).

UNIT 14 You and your choices – for Years 10 and 11

Your Life 3/Year 9

Lesson 1 *Your Life Student Book 3*, pages 64–65
Personal wellbeing/Economic wellbeing and financial capability – understanding courses and pathways

> **Objective:** To understand the courses that are available for students in Years 10 and 11 and the qualifications that they will give you.

Resources

Copymaster 14 'Understanding qualification levels'

Starter

Ask: 'What do you know about the courses available to you in Years 10 and 11?' Share what knowledge they have in a class discussion, then stress the importance of knowing as much as you can, because the choices you make now may influence what courses or job you decide to do after Year 11.

Suggested activities

- Read the information about what courses are available (pages 64–65). Discuss with the class what they have learned about the options and encourage them to ask questions about the different courses and the forms of assessment they have. Then ask them in pairs to draw up a quiz consisting of true and false statements about the options and to give the quiz to another pair to do.

- Read Copymaster 14 'Understanding qualification levels'. Explain that the courses they take at Years 10 and 11 will lead to qualifications at entry level, level 1 or level 2. Encourage them to ask you questions about the different qualification levels. Draw their attention to the fact that, if they are hoping to achieve qualifications at level 3 by the end of Year 13, then they need to choose options that will lead to level 2 qualifications at the end of Year 11.

Plenary

Recap what they have learned about the main options and draw up a list of the advantages of each one. Then discuss any disadvantages there are in each one.

Extension activity

Encourage individuals to research what options the school offers, then to write a short statement about which option attracts them and why.

14 Understanding qualification levels

All qualifications fit into a national framework. The framework has nine levels that people often use as shorthand to describe the qualifications needed for a particular job or course.

Entry Level qualifications

These qualifications, called Entry Level Certificates, develop basic knowledge, skills and understanding in a particular subject or area. You can use Entry Level Certificate courses as a stepping stone to further learning, training, employment and independent living.

Level 1 qualifications

These qualifications include NVQs at Level 1, GCSEs at grades D–G and the Foundation Diploma. They improve basic knowledge, understanding and skills in a subject, a specific work area or a broad economic sector. You can use Level 1 qualifications as a stepping stone to further learning, training and employment.

Level 2 qualifications

These qualifications include NVQs at Level 2, GCSEs at grades A*–C and the Higher Diploma. They build knowledge, understanding and skills in a subject, a specific work area or a broad economic sector. You can use Level 2 qualifications to prepare for qualifications at Level 3. Most employers use this level as their minimum entry requirement.

Level 3 qualifications

These qualifications include NVQs at Level 3, AS and A Levels, the Advanced and Progression Diplomas and the International Baccalaureate. They develop detailed knowledge, understanding and skills in a subject, a specific work area or a broad economic sector. You can use Level 3 qualifications to prepare for qualifications at Level 4. Universities require most applicants to be qualified to this level. Employers will increasingly look for applicants who are qualified to at least this level.

Levels 4–8 qualifications

These qualifications include NVQs at Levels 4 and 5, Foundation degrees and honours degrees and Higher National Certificates and Diplomas. They involve in-depth learning about a specific occupational role or area of study. They help people to become specialists in their area of learning or work.

UNIT 14 You and your choices – for Years 10 and 11

Lesson 2 *Your Life Student Book 3*, pages 66–67

Personal wellbeing/Economic wellbeing and financial capability – understanding courses and pathways

Objective: To understand the range of GCSE courses available, what each GCSE involves and the career opportunities to which each is linked.

Starter

Remind students what GCSE courses are and that they can lead to either level 1 qualifications (grades D–G) or level 2 qualifications (A*–C). Explain that there are three GCSE subjects that everyone must take – English, Mathematics and Science – because they are required for so many careers, and that each of the other non-compulsory GCSE subjects can be linked to certain careers.

Suggested activities

- Study the list of 'Compulsory subjects' (page 66) and discuss whether in your school any of the subjects, other than English, Mathematics and Science, leads to a qualification.

- Read the details of 'Optional subjects' (page 67), then in pairs students discuss their interests and choose up to three subjects that they might enjoy studying because they match their interests.

- Ask the students to write down one or two careers in which they are currently interested, then to match them to any GCSE subjects which are linked to them.

Plenary

Talk about which GCSE subjects are available at your school. Explain any links your school has with local colleges to make it possible for them to study GCSE courses that are not offered at school at a local college.

Extension activity

Students look again at the details of the different GCSE courses. They make notes of the GCSE subjects that interest them and the reasons why they are interested in them. They put the notes in their file for reference.

UNIT 14 You and your choices – for Years 10 and 11

Your Life 3/Year 9

Lesson 3 *Your Life Student Book 3*, pages 68–69
Personal wellbeing/Economic wellbeing and financial capability –
understanding courses and pathways

> **Objective:** To advise students on how to make decisions about which options to choose.

Starter

Explain that there can be good reasons and bad reasons for choosing options. Ask students to suggest what these are. Draw two columns on the board and make lists of their suggestions. Read 'Choosing GCSE courses' (page 68). Compare your list with the lists of Dos and Don'ts and add to the appropriate column any extra reasons mentioned in the article that are not on the class list.

Suggested activities

- Ask students in groups to study the two case studies on pages 68–69 and to discuss what they learn from them about how Chris and Sarah-Jane made their decisions and how the options they chose related to their skills and interests.

- Read 'Getting help and support' (page 69). Encourage students to select their options, using the form provided by their school, then to show the completed form to an adult they know and trust and discuss it with them.

Plenary

Refer back to the class list of good and bad reasons for choosing options. Stress that the decisions they are making are too important for them to make their choices for the wrong reasons.

Extension activities

Encourage students to seek expert advice, as necessary, within the school or by contacting a Connexions Direct adviser online or by phone. (see details on page 69).

Ask the students to write a statement about the options they plan to choose, explaining the reasons for their choices.

UNIT 15 You and the law – youth justice

Lesson 1 *Your Life Student Book 3*, pages 70–71
Citizenship – youth justice

Objective: To understand youth courts and to explore what sentences a youth court can give.

Resources

Copies of Copymaster 15 – 'Why do young people commit crimes?'

Starter

Give out copies of Copymaster 15. Invite groups to discuss the reasons and to list them in order of importance, before sharing their views in a class discussion.

Suggested activities

- Explain that young people charged with committing an offence are tried in a youth court. Read and discuss what a youth court is like (page 70). Explain that any young person in trouble with the law will be contacted by a member of a youth offending team and read 'Youth Offending Teams' (page 70).

- Ask groups to study the sentences a youth court can impose (page 71). Which of the sentences do they think are most likely to act as a deterrent? Share their views in a class discussion. Ask: 'Should all young offenders be made to meet the victims of their crimes and to apologise to them?'

- Read 'Criminal records' (page 71). Ask: 'What is the main disadvantage of having a criminal record?' 'Do you think the time it takes for a criminal record to be spent is too long?'

Plenary

Explain that youth courts are less formal than adult courts, for example the language used is different – you promise rather than swear to tell the truth. There are restrictions on reporting and the naming of defendants. Point out that some people think these restrictions should not apply and that young offenders who are found guilty should be 'named and shamed'. Share their views on whether or not reporters should be able to name young offenders. Ask: 'Should the media be able to name young offenders aged 14 and over, but not those who are under the age of 14?'

YOUR LIFE 3 UNIT 15 You and the law – youth justice

Why do young people commit crimes?

- Under 18s are responsible for a quarter of all crimes. Why do so many young people commit crimes?

- 'TV and the media are to blame. Kids and teenagers mimic the violence they see on TV and in films. Violent video and computer games are responsible for making them violent and aggressive.'

- 'Greed. Young people are materialistic. They see the adverts for designer trainers, mobile phones and tablets and they want to have the luxurious lifestyle that they portray.'

- 'Boredom. There's nothing for young people to do. Doing something criminal relieves the boredom.'

- 'Young people are naturally rebellious. They commit crimes in order to take revenge on society.'

- 'Peer pressure. They don't want to be left out, so they join in when their mates suggest something that's illegal.'

- 'A lot of it is because of drink or drugs. Many crimes are committed because the person is either drunk or high on drugs, or needs money to feed their addiction.'

- 'It's due to a lack of morality. They commit crimes because they think it's alright to damage property or take other people's things.'

- 'The main causes are poverty and unemployment. They have nothing to look forward to, so they turn to crime.'

- 'It's because of the breakdown of so many relationships. This affects boys especially who don't have a father figure to look up to.'

Discuss these views. List what you think are the reasons why young people commit crimes starting with the most important. Then compare your lists in a class discussion.

Morality is more important than environment

Children commit crime because they lack morals rather than because of the environment.

A study of around 700 people in Peterborough for over a decade found that most adolescent crime is not just youthful opportunism.

While it is agreed that urban environments trigger some young people to commit crime, it is their morality which is the biggest factor.

Daily Mail 24 June 2012

Do you think morality is more important than environment? Write a short statement saying which you think is more important.

UNIT 15 You and the law – youth justice

Your Life 3/Year 9

Lesson 2 *Your Life Student Book 3*, pages 72–73
Citizenship – youth justice

> **Objective:** To explain what it is like to be in youth custody and to explore ways of reducing crime.

Starter

Ask the students: 'What effect would it have on your life if you were sentenced to a period in youth custody?' Encourage them to think about how it would affect you not only by taking away your freedom, but also the effect it would have on your relationships with your family and friends, your career and job prospects and the effect on you mentally.

Suggested activities

● Read and discuss what Matt and Ryan said about their experiences in youth custody (page 72). Ask: 'What do you learn about what it is like to be in youth custody from their experiences?'

● Ask: 'What's the best way to treat young offenders in order to reduce crime?' Invite the students to imagine that a Home Office minister has asked them to suggest one action that the government should take, which would reduce the amount of youth crime. Ask them to brainstorm their ideas in groups, then hold a class discussion.

● Read 'How can crime be reduced?' (page 73). Ask groups to discuss the four ways of dealing with young offenders, then discuss with the class their views on what is most likely to reduce crime. Ask individuals to write a short statement expressing their views on what measures they think would be the most effective in cutting down youth crime.

Plenary

Ask some of the students to read out their statements. Invite them to imagine the class is a government 'think tank' who have been asked to advise on what measures the government should take to reduce youth crime. What advice would they give the government?

Extension activities

Find out what is done to help to stop young people from reoffending on their release from youth custody. Then, in groups, discuss how you would spend the £20 million legacy (see 'In groups' page 72).

UNIT 16 You and your opinions – which political party do you support?

Your Life 3/Year 9

Lesson 1 *Your Life Student Book 3*, pages 74–76
Citizenship – understanding politics

> **Objective:** To explain what political parties are, which political parties there are in the UK and what they stand for.

Resources

Copies of Copymaster 16A 'Voting intentions'

Starter

Explain what a political party is (a group of people who share common ideas about how a country should be governed). Introduce the terms 'left-wing' and 'right-wing' and explain how, in broad terms, left-wing parties are radical parties which favour change, while right-wing parties are conservative parties wanting to uphold traditional ideas.

Suggested activities

- Reinforce what you said during the Starter activity by reading the first three paragraphs of the article 'Political parties and the political spectrum' (page 74). Write the terms 'ideology' and 'political spectrum' on the board and explain what they mean.

- Read the remainder of the article, and invite groups to study the article and to discuss the four questions on it (see 'In groups', page 74). Then ask them individually to write answers to the questions.

- Read the descriptions of British political parties on pages 75 and 76. Ask groups to study the key policies of the three main parties and discuss which policies they agree with.

- Ask groups to work out policies for a new political party, following the guidelines in the section 'Forming a political party' (page 76).

Plenary

Encourage representatives from each group to explain the policies of their new parties to the rest of the class.

Extension activities

Encourage individuals to use the internet to visit the websites of the British political parties to research what their current policies are on key issues.

Ask students to contact the constituency organisations of the main political parties to invite them to send a member to talk to the class. Before the visit, allow them to prepare some questions.

Assessment

Use Copymaster 16A to assess understanding of political parties and their policies.

ASSESSMENT COPYMASTER

16A Voting intentions

1. Would you vote in the next general election, if you were old enough to do so?   Yes/No
   Explain why you would or would not vote.

2. If voting was compulsory, and you were old enough to vote, which party would you vote for?
   Explain why. (Remember – you could vote for one of the fringe parties rather than one of the
   three main parties.)

UNIT 16 You and your opinions – which political party do you support?

Your Life 3/Year 9

Lesson 2 *Your Life Student Book 3*, page 77
Citizenship – understanding politics

> **Objective:** To examine what influences whether or not people vote and what decides who they vote for.

Resources

Copymaster 16 'Contemporary issues – where do you stand?'

Starter

Recap what the students found out about political parties in the previous lesson and talk about how, at general elections, political parties try to get people to vote for them by producing a manifesto (a statement of the policies they would follow if they were to form the government). Explain that in order to be able to choose between political parties, voters need to have thought through where they personally stand on the main issues of the day.

Suggested activities

● Ask students either to study the six statements on page 77 or the 15 statements on Copymaster 16, to decide their opinion on each issue and to share their views in a group discussion, being prepared to change their minds if they find other people's arguments convincing.

● Ask: 'What other issues are key issues that would determine how you would vote, if you were old enough to do so?' Invite the students to look again at the key policies of the three main parties (page 75) and to discuss in groups which party they would vote for, before individually writing about which party they would support and why.

● Read 'To vote or not to vote' (page 77). Ask groups to discuss the reasons why people may choose not to vote, then to debate which of the two statements they agree with and why (see 'In groups', page 77).

Plenary

Explain that in some countries voting at general elections is compulsory. Discuss with the class whether or not they think voting in UK general elections should be compulsory and hold a vote to decide what the class's view is.

Extension activity

Hold a mock election. Candidates could stand for either real political parties or the new political parties formed in the previous lesson. Ask groups to help candidates draft their manifestoes. Encourage the candidates to give speeches explaining their policies and to answer questions about their policies, then organise a secret ballot.

COPYMASTER

16 Contemporary issues – where do you stand?

Where you stand on contemporary issues will help you to decide which political party you want to support. On your own, decide where you stand on each of these issues by putting a tick if you agree with the statement or a cross if you disagree with the statement. Then share your views in a group discussion.

1. The possession of drugs for personal use should be decriminalised. .... ☐

2. All forms of hunting should be legal. .... ☐

3. Proportional representation should be introduced for parliamentary elections. .... ☐

4. University students should not have to pay fees for their degree courses. .... ☐

5. Vivisection should be banned. .... ☐

6. Abortion should be freely available on demand. .... ☐

7. The monarchy should be abolished. .... ☐

8. The age of sexual consent should be lowered to 14. .... ☐

9. All forms of cloning should be illegal. .... ☐

10. There should be stricter controls on asylum seekers and the granting of refugee status. .... ☐

11. Homosexual couples should not be allowed to adopt children. .... ☐

12. Capital punishment should be reintroduced for certain crimes. .... ☐

13. All eye tests and dental examinations should be free. .... ☐

14. Britain should stop manufacturing arms for export. .... ☐

15. The retirement age for both men and women should be raised to 70. .... ☐

UNIT 17 You and your body – safe sex, STIs and AIDS

Your Life 3/Year 9

Lesson 1 *Your Life Student Book 3*, pages 78–79
Keeping healthy – Safer sex

Objective: To explain what safer sex means and to provide information about sexually transmitted infections.

Resources

Copies of Copymaster 17 'Sexually transmitted infections'

Starter

Explain that some young people have their first experience of sex without realising the risks involved and wish afterwards that they had waited longer. Read the first two introductory paragraphs and 'What is safer sex' (page 78). Explain that there is no such thing as totally safe sex; there's always some risk of infection or pregnancy involved involved, which is why health experts use the term 'safer sex' rather than 'safe sex'.

Suggested activities

- Read 'What is safer sex?' (page 78) and discuss with the class the 'Four rules for safer sex'.
- Read Anna's statement (page 78). Discuss why adolescents run a greater risk of catching an STI. Ask: 'What do you think of Anna's boyfriend's attitude?' 'Do you think the situation is unusual?' 'What would you say to to either of them?'
- Read 'Sexually transmitted infections' and 'Chlamydia' (page 79). Reinforce what the article says by drawing up a list on the board of ten things young people should know about STIs and how to avoid them.
- Invite pairs to read 'What to do if you think you have an STI' (page 79), then to draft Lucy's reply to Sam (see 'For your file', page 79).

Plenary

Recap what the students have learned about STIs and what they should do if they think they have caught an STI by sharing some of their replies to Sam's letter.

Extension activities

Give out copies of Copymaster 17 and discuss with the class the detailed information it gives on the symptoms of STIs. Emphasise that while thrush and cystitis produce symptoms similar to some STIs, neither of them is sexually transmitted and both can be easily treated.

Sexually transmitted infections

The table below gives details of the most common STIs and their symptoms.

STI	Symptoms
Chlamydia	Caused by bacteria and very easy to catch, because there are often no symptoms, so people often don't know they have it. May cause a slight discharge, pain when urinating and some soreness. Can be cured by antibiotics if caught early, but if left untreated can lead to pelvic inflammatory disease and infertility.
Gardnerella	A heavy, greyish fishy-smelling discharge or there may be no symptoms at all. Often confused with thrush (see below) but requires different treatment. Can be cured by antibiotics.
Genital herpes	Painful blisters in the genital area which burst leaving little red ulcers, often accompanied by flu-like symptoms. Caused by a virus which can be treated but not completely cured. Half the people who have one attack go on to have another in the future. Very contagious while the sores are there, but only a slight risk of passing on the virus once the sores have gone.
Genital warts	Reddish-pink, painless warts around the genital area. Caused by a virus. Can be burnt off chemically.
Gonorrhoea	Males and females have slightly different symptoms. Women suffer an unusual vaginal discharge, a burning feeling when urinating and a sore throat. Men suffer a yellow discharge from the penis, pain when urinating and a sore throat. Can easily be treated with antibiotics.
HIV/AIDS	AIDS stands for Acquired Immune Deficiency Syndrome. It is a condition caused by the HIV virus. The virus damages the immune system which normally protects the body from infections. There is no known cure.
Pubic lice	Little brown 'nits', usually found at the base of hairs, which cause fierce itching. Can be treated with a lotion to kill the lice.
Syphilis	A painless sore around the genital area, followed by a body rash, mouth sores and flu-like symptoms. Can be easily treated at this stage, but even though the symptoms disappear without treatment, the disease remains and can eventually lead to death. Not common in the UK these days.
Trichomoniasis	A parasite that causes a nasty smelling grey discharge. Can be treated with cream and tablets.
There are two other infections, which are not sexually transmitted, but which result in symptoms similar to those caused by some STIs and which require medical treatment – thrush and cystitis:	
Cystitis	An infection and/or inflammation of the bladder. Causes a burning sensation when urinating and a constant urge to go to the toilet. Affects around 50% of women at some stage. Easy to treat.
Thrush	A vaginal discharge and soreness when urinating, caused by a yeast-like fungus that normally lives quite harmlessly on the skin, in the mouth and in the vagina. Can easily be treated by cream and pessaries. Can be diagnosed by a GP and you do not need to go to a GUM (genito-urinary medicine) clinic to get treatment.

UNIT 17 You and your body – safe sex, STIs and AIDS

Your Life 3/Year 9

Lesson 2 *Your Life Student Book 3*, pages 80–81
Keeping healthy – Safer sex

Objective: To provide information about HIV and AIDS, and to explore attitudes to sex and AIDS.

Starter

Ask groups to do a brainstorm and list what they know about HIV and AIDS. Then explain that while some of the things they have written down may be true, others may be false because there are a lot of myths about HIV and AIDS.

Suggested activities

● Invite the students in groups to study 'AIDS – the facts' (page 80) and to check whether the lists they made in the Starter activity were accurate. Then ask them to draw up a test-yourself quiz (see 'In groups', page 81) and to give the test to another group to do.

● Ask pairs to design a page for an internet website giving teenagers essential information on AIDS.

● Read the statements in the section 'Attitudes to sex' and 'Teenagers think HIV is 'irrelevant'' (page 81). In groups, invite students to discuss the comments and the attitudes reported in the article and then to share their views in a class discussion.

Plenary

Ask the students to imagine they have to design an AIDS awareness poster to make young people realise that AIDS is a health issue they need to be concerned about. Discuss ideas on how they can get the message across, then ask them to design the posters.

Extension activity

Encourage them to use the internet to find out further information about AIDS.

UNIT 18 You and your money – you as a consumer

Your Life 3/Year 9

Lesson 1 *Your Life Student Book 3*, pages 82–83
Citizenship/Economic wellbeing and financial capability – consumer affairs

Objective: To understand how prices are set and what haggling and bartering are.

Starter

Ask: 'Who do you think decides the price of goods in shops – the manufacturer? the retailer? The customer? The government?' Write RRP on the board and ask them what it stands for. Explain that the manufacturer sets a recommended retail price, but that it's up to the seller to decide the price to charge the consumer, and that this decision is influenced by what price consumers will be prepared to pay. Explain that the government is also involved in determining the final price. Write VAT on the board. Explain that Value Added Tax is a tax on most goods, which the retailer has to include in the price. Then study the glossary box on page 82 and ensure that the students understand what the different terms mean.

Suggested activities

- Read 'Is the price right? Your questions about prices' (page 82). Invite students to share experiences of getting a bargain and being ripped off (see 'In groups').
- Study the information about 'Haggling' and 'Bartering' on page 83, then ask groups to discuss the different views expressed and to make a list of the advantages and disadvantages of haggling and bartering compared to having fixed prices.

Plenary

Ask students to write down the three most important things that they have learned in the lesson. Then share what they have written in a class discussion.

Extension activity

Students could investigate websites where you can swap things, then write a short report on the pros and cons of each website (see 'For your file' page 82).

UNIT 18 You and your money – you as a consumer

Your Life 3/Year 9

Lesson 2 *Your Life Student Book 3*, pages 84–85
Citizenship/Economic wellbeing and financial capability – consumer affairs

Objective: To understand your rights as a consumer and to explore the things you need to consider when buying a mobile phone.

Resources

Copies of Copymaster 18 'Buying a mobile phone'

Starter

Ask students to share any experiences they have had of taking back goods. Ask them to explain why they took them back, how the seller reacted and whether they received a refund or were able to change the goods. Do they think they were treated fairly? Explain that there are certain laws which protect them as consumers.

Suggested activities

- Read 'Know your consumer rights' (page 84). Ask pairs to draw up a quiz consisting of true and false statements about consumer rights, then to give their quiz to another pair to do.

- Invite pairs to act out the role play in which one of them asks for a refund because an item broke the first time they used it (page 84).

- Ask students in pairs to make a list of all the things you need to consider when buying a mobile phone. Read 'Buying the right mobile phone' (page 85) and encourage them to add to their lists any other points made in the article that they had not thought of and then to compare their lists.

- In pairs, ask students to role play a scene in which two friends discuss how to get the best deal when buying a mobile phone (page 85).

Plenary

Ask the class to draw up a list of facts they need to know about their rights as a consumer, without referring to the book, and write the list on the board.

Extension activity

Ask individuals to fill in Copymaster 18 'Buying a mobile phone', then to use the completed copymaster for reference when writing an article for a teen magazine 'Top tips – How to get the best deal out of your mobile phone'.

18 Buying a mobile phone

On your own complete this checklist of things you need to consider when you are buying a mobile phone.

1 How many minutes do you think you will use up calling people each month?

2 When will you make most of these phone calls?

   a Morning

   b Evening

   c Weekends

3 How many texts do you think you will use texting people each month?

4 When will you send these texts?

   a Morning

   b Evening

   c Weekends

5 Are you looking for a pay as you go phone, or a contract?

   a Pay as you go

   b Contract

6 If it's a contract phone, how long do you want the contract to last for?

7 Are your friends on any particular network? List the number of friends on each of the main networks:

   a Vodafone

   b T-Mobile

   c Orange

   d O2

   e Other

8 What special features do you want your phone to have?

   a Camera phone

   b Video messaging

   c Good internet browser

   d Bluetooth

   e File sharing

   f Other (please specify)

9 Are you willing to pay for your new phone, and if so, how much?

10 Is there anything else you think is important when getting a mobile phone?

UNIT 18 You and your money – you as a consumer

Your Life 3/Year 9

Lesson 3 *Your Life Student Book 3*, pages 86–87
Citizenship/Economic wellbeing and financial capability – consumer affairs

Objective: To explore ways of being a green consumer.

Starter

Brainstorm ideas of things students can think of that people can do to be green consumers. Write 'Green consumer' in the centre of the board and build up a spidergram of their suggestions. Prompt them, as necessary, to suggest things we can do at home, when shopping and when we travel.

Suggested activities

- Write 'carbon footprint' on the board and invite pairs to write a definition of the term. Then read the explanation of it in the introductory paragraphs on page 86.
- Read 'Going green at home' (page 86), then ask each of the students to write a note to their parents or carers suggesting what they could do in order to make their home greener.
- Read and discuss 'Green shopping' (page 87). Then ask them to design a poster to encourage shoppers to 'go green'.
- Study 'Being a green tourist' (page 87) and discuss how Sam and her family took a 'green holiday'. Invite pairs to plan and perform a role play in which one person tries to persuade another, who is planning to take a holiday abroad, not to take a flight, because of the effect it will have on their carbon footprint.

Plenary

Look again at the spidergram you drew in the Starter activity. Add any further suggestions that they have as a result of what they have been considering during the lesson.

Extension activities

Encourage students to use the website (see 'For your file' page 86) to calculate their individual carbon footprint, then ask them to write about how they could reduce it.

Suggest that they visit the Eden Project website and write a paragraph about it for their files (www.edenproject.com).

UNIT 19 You as a citizen – of the world

Starter

Write the term 'globalisation' on the board. Explain what it means and read the two introductory paragraphs on page 88.

Suggested activities

- Read 'What are the causes of globalisation?' and 'Multinational corporations' (page 88). Discuss, as a class, the causes and effects of globalisation, then prompt the students, in groups, to discuss the three statements on page 88 (see 'In groups') before sharing their views with the rest of the class.

- Read 'Supermarkets and sweatshops' and 'The real price of trainers' (page 89) and in groups discuss how the goods that we buy in our supermarkets are often produced in sweatshops. Then read 'Stamping out sweatshops' (page 89) and talk about what people in the UK can do to bring an end to sweatshop labour (see 'In groups' page 89).

Plenary

Recap what the students have learned about the causes and effects of globalisation by drawing two columns on the board labelled 'Causes' and 'Effects', and eliciting points from them in a class discussion. Ask the students to make copies for their files of the chart you draw up on the board.

Extension activities

Explain what a boycott is and discuss with the class whether they would be prepared to support a boycott of goods produced in sweatshops, before getting them to write their views (see 'For your file' page 89).

Encourage students to use the internet to find out about campaigns to stamp out sweatshop labour, e.g. No Sweat (www.nosweat.org.uk).

UNIT 19 You as a citizen – of the world

Your Life 3/Year 9

Lesson 2 *Your Life Student Book 3*, pages 90–91
Citizenship – globalisation

Objective: To explore problems connected to the development and spread of the internet.

Resources

Copies of Copymaster 19 'Cyberbullying quiz'

Starter

Introduce the topic by talking about how the internet has spread.

Suggested activities

- Study 'The internet – Positive and Negative Effects' (page 90). Ask groups to debate whether the positive effects outweigh the negative effects.

- Read and discuss 'Problems of the internet' and 'Cybercrime' (page 91). In groups, discuss the view that some censorship of the internet is essential.

- Discuss 'Lara's story' (page 91). In pairs, make a list of all the things you should do in order to stay safe online. Then compare their lists in a class discussion.

Plenary

Read 'Policing the internet' (page 91) and discuss the suggestions (see 'In groups').

Extension activity

Ask individuals to answer the quiz on cyberbullying (Copymaster 19) and share their views in a class discussion.

19 Cyberbullying quiz

Test yourself to see what you think about cyberbullying, then share your answers in a group or class discussion.

 What do you think of when you hear the term 'cyberbullying'?

a I don't – it doesn't affect me

b It's when someone is excluded from an online group on purpose

c It's when rude, angry or gossipy messages are sent on the text or online

d It's bullying that can be tracked because it leaves cyber footprints

e B, C and D

 Someone sends you a mean text on your phone. Do you:

a Decide to delete

b Text back and tell them to leave you alone

c Feel confused and then save it. You'll think about it later

d Send them a mean text back

e Immediately tell your parents or teacher

3 Someone sends you a spiteful message on instant messenger. How do you react?

a Ignore it and start chatting to someone else

b Reply back to them and find out what their problem is

c Shut down the computer and hope they'll leave you alone in future

d Report them to the Internet Service Provider

e Go to an older person, and let them know you feel uncomfortable

 If you feel like someone is cyberbullying you, who would you go to for help?

a No one, you can deal with it

b Get a friend to join in against them

c If it gets really bad you might tell a parent or teacher

d The Internet Provider or the social networking site

e Parent, teacher or police officer

 Sometimes people encourage cyberbullying without even being aware of it. Which of these would you say could make a situation worse?

a You hear about a friend being cyberbullied but you tell them to ignore it, because it's not that serious

b Passing on someone's pictures or details without them knowing, or even if they'd asked you not to

c Voting for someone in an insulting online poll

d Joining in with the insults even in a small way

e B, C and D

 What are the laws about cyberbullying?

a There aren't any, we don't need them

b There aren't any, but if it gets really bad then it might be an idea to say that you'll tell the police

c The government are thinking about putting some laws in place

d There aren't any, but internet service providers and social networking sites have rules and acceptable use policies that can result in bans for cyberbullying

e It can be classified as 'harassment', is illegal and can be reported to the police

 Is cyberbullying more invisible than face-to-face bullying?

a Yes, you often can't tell who the cyberbullies are

b Even if everyone knows who they are, you feel more detached because you can't see each other's reactions

c It isn't really, but it can feel more scary because you don't immediately know who is contacting you

d If you report the incidents to your internet service and social network providers they can locate the address the emails have been sent from

e Cyberbullying always leaves cyber footprints, both of the person who generated the bullying messages and anyone else who has joined in

UNIT 19 You as a citizen – of the world

Your Life 3/Year 9

Lesson 3 *Your Life Student Book 3*, pages 92–93
Citizenship – understanding global warming

Objective: To understand the causes and effects of global warming and the measures that can be taken to reduce it.

Resources

Copies of Copymaster 19A 'Understanding global issues'

Starter

Ask the students: 'What do the terms 'global warming' and 'the greenhouse effect' mean?' Encourage them to help you draft definitions on the board. Then read the introductory paragraph on global warming and the two paragraphs on the greenhouse effect on page 92.

Suggested activities

- Ask individuals to read and make notes on 'Greenhouse gases' and 'The effects of global warming' (page 92), before discussing, in groups, what causes global warming and what its effects are.

- Allow pairs to read and discuss the three extracts on page 93, then to draft an email to a newspaper expressing their concern about global warming and saying what they think the government should be doing about it.

- Ask the students, in groups, to read each other's emails, then to discuss what businesses and institutions, such as schools, can do to use energy more efficiently. Invite them to draft a series of questions about energy efficiency for the class representative to raise at the next school council meeting.

- Ask the class how energy conscious they are as individuals. What can individuals do to change their energy habits and reduce energy use? Then, on their own, ask them to design posters encouraging people to conserve energy.

Plenary

Ask: 'If you were invited to put your views on global warming to an international conference on the issue, what would you say?' Make a list on the board of the points the students would want to make.

Extension activity

Ask the students to use the internet to research global warming and the greenhouse effect by visiting websites such as the Friends of the Earth (www.foe.org.uk).

Assessment

Use Copymaster 19A to assess understanding of globalisation and global warming.

ASSESSMENT COPYMASTER

19A Understanding global issues

Answer these questions as fully as you can. If necessary, continue on a separate sheet.

Globalisation (see pages 88–91)

1. What do you understand by the term 'globalisation'?

2. What are the main causes of globalisation?

3. What do you think are the main effects of globalisation?

Global warming (see pages 92–93)

4. What is global warming?

5. What has caused global warming?

6. What are the effects of global warming?

7. How can global warming be reduced?

UNIT 19 You as a citizen – of the world

Your Life 3/Year 9

Lesson 4 *Your Life Student Book 3*, pages 94–95

Citizenship – keeping peace

> **Objective:** To explore the role of the United Nations in keeping peace and to examine the arms trade.

Starter

Ask the students: 'What do you know about the United Nations?' Explain that it was set up after the Second World War to try to keep peace in the world and to defend human rights, and that one of its key bodies is the UN Security Council. Read the introductory paragraph and the paragraph on the UN Security Council (page 94). Explain what a veto is.

Suggested activities

- Read the articles on page 94. Discuss with the class why the UN's attempts to bring peace to the world have largely failed.
- Study the information about 'The arms trade' on page 95. Ask individuals to draw up a list of the main points entitled 'Five things you should know about the arms trade', then to compare their lists in groups.
- Ask groups to discuss the two statements about the arms trade (see 'In groups' page 95), then to share their views in a class discussion.
- Invite students to write their views on the arms trade and Britain's involvement in it.

Plenary

Ask pairs to say why they would or would not ever take part in a demonstration against Britain's involvement in the arms trade. Encourage them to share their views in a class discussion.

Extension activities

Ask students to find out more about the arms trade by visiting the website of the Campaign Against the Arms Trade (CAAT) at www.caat.org.uk.

Organise a debate on the motion: 'This house believes that Britain should stop manufacturing and selling arms to anyone except our partners in the European Union'.

UNIT 20 You and the community – pressure groups and campaigning

Your Life 3/Year 9

Lesson 1 *Your Life Student Book 3*, pages 96–97
Citizenship – pressure groups and campaigning

Objective: To explore what pressure groups are and the techniques they use, and to examine how Living Streets campaigns to make walking safer.

Starter

Explain what a pressure group is. Give any examples of local pressure groups, together with examples of national pressure groups (e.g. League Against Cruel Sports, The Countryside Alliance) and international pressure groups (e.g. Amnesty International, Greenpeace). Then read the paragraphs explaining what pressure groups are (page 96).

Suggested activities

- Read 'Pressure group techniques' (page 96). Discuss with the class the different techniques that pressure groups use. Ask them to share their views on whether non-violent civil disobedience can ever be justified.

- Ask: 'What do they think of pressure groups that are prepared to use violence?' Encourage them to write a statement saying why they agree or disagree with this opinion: 'Pressure groups should never resort to violence.' Then allow them to share their views in a class discussion.

- Invite groups to discuss issues about which they feel so strongly they would be prepared to campaign for them. Ask them to choose an issue from 'In groups' (page 96), and to explain the reasons for their choice in a class discussion.

- Read the article 'It's time to put your foot down' (page 97). Invite students to discuss in groups the hazards that the pressure group Living Streets campaigns against and what particular hazards there are for pedestrians locally.

Plenary

Ask groups to report on the hazards for pedestrians which they have identified in your area.

Extension activity

Ask students to find out more about Living Streets by visiting their website (www.livingstreets.org.uk).

Your Life 3/Year 9

Lesson 2 *Your Life Student Book 3*, pages 98–99
Citizenship – pressure groups and campaigning

Objective: To organise a campaign to make roads safer in your local area.

Resources

Copies of Copymaster 20 'Making residential roads safer'

Copies of Copymaster 20A 'Understanding how to organise an action group and run a campaign'

Starter

Remind the students of what a pressure group is and the techniques they use. Draw a flowchart on the board, explaining the steps they will need to take to form a pressure group and mount a campaign. Step 1: Identify the problem and name the group; Step 2: Survey opinions; Step 3: Plan the campaign; Step 4: Produce materials, organise events and get media coverage; Step 5: Review strategy.

Suggested activities

- Ask groups to identify a problem with traffic in your area. Use Copymaster 20 to help groups choose an area in which there is a problem. Then invite them to present their ideas to the rest of the class. Discuss the ideas, agree on what the class is going to campaign for and choose a name for the group. Read 'Surveying opinions and collecting information' (page 98) and, in groups, ask students to draft a leaflet or questionnaire to survey other people's views.

- Hold a planning meeting and discuss what they would do as part of their campaign (see list in 'Planning your campaign', page 98). Read 'Hitting the headlines' (page 99). Discuss with the class the various ways of attracting media attention. Then study the press release and the helpful hints on page 99.

Plenary

Discuss what the students have learned about how to plan a campaign. If appropriate, appoint an organising committee to put their campaign into action.

Extension activities

Ask students to develop their campaign by first researching opinions to see if there is sufficient support for their point of view to make the campaign worthwhile. Then ask them to design and distribute a newsletter to get their message across. If appropriate, allow students to develop the campaign further by organising a petition and/or getting media coverage by sending out a press release. Discuss with the class how successful their campaign was and get them to write a statement reviewing how the campaign went (see 'For your file', page 99).

Assessment

Use Copymaster 20A to assess understanding of how to organise an action group and how to run a campaign.

What can be done to make roads safer?

Is there a problem with traffic in the streets in your neighbourhood? Perhaps there is too much traffic or it is travelling too fast. Vehicles will use residential roads as short cuts if it is quicker and they can avoid traffic jams by doing so. If your street is being used as a 'rat run' and has become dangerous for pedestrians and cyclists, you can contact the local council and campaign for them to introduce measures that will make it safer.

What can be done to make roads safer?

Reduce the amount of through traffic

Ways of doing this include:

- altering the priority of local roads and junctions, e.g by preventing traffic from making a right or left turn into a street;
- closing off roads in one direction;
- barring through traffic by blocking the road halfway down;
- restricting the flow of traffic by the use of 'street-furniture'.

Reduce the speed of vehicles

This can be done by:

- building speed humps;
- lowering speed limits and introducing 20 mph zones;
- narrowing the road by making 'chicanes' where at selected places the pavement is built out to create artificial bends in the road;
- altering the road surface by putting in 'rumble strips' – stretches of granite or brick cobbles in the road.

Provide special facilities for cyclists

If roads are closed, cycles can be made exempt. One-way streets can be provided with contra-flow cycle lanes. On larger and busier roads, cycle lanes and special junctions for cyclists can be provided.

Other measures to make cycling safer and to encourage people to cycle rather than go by car include providing cycle-only paths, e.g. across parks or through cul-de-sacs, and building links across railway lines, canals and other obstacles to provide cyclists with short cuts and more direct routes.

Provide special facilities for pedestrians

Pavements can be widened to increase pedestrian space (especially near schools, shops and play areas) and reduce road space – hopefully causing vehicles to travel more slowly. These pavements can be protected from pavement parking by using bollards and street furniture.

Particularly dangerous junctions can be made safer by measures such as installing traffic lights and widening pavements so that there is less roadway to cross.

Discuss these suggestions of ways to improve residential streets.

If any of these measures have been introduced in your area, how successful have they been?

Write an email to your local council stating your views about how the streets in your area could be made safer.

20A Understanding how to organise an action group and run a campaign

Explain how to organise an action group on a local issue and how to run a campaign by either writing a step-by-step guide or drawing up a list of tips. Include advice on:

- how to find out if there is enough support to form an action group;
- how to set up the action group;
- how to plan the campaign;
- how to communicate information about what the action group is doing;
- how to draw the attention of local politicians to the action group and its purpose;
- how to use the media to gain publicity for the campaign.

UNIT 21 You and other people – people with mental illnesses

Lesson 1 *Your Life Student Book 3*, pages 100–101
Social education – understanding mental illness

Objective: To explain what mental illness is, to discuss attitudes towards it and learn how to cope with a mental illness in the family.

Resources

Copies of Copymaster 21 'Types of mental illness'

Starter

Write the terms 'mental illness' and 'mental handicap' on the board and explain that whereas mental illnesses can often be successfully treated, mental handicaps are disabilities, which affect a person permanently. People who are mentally handicapped may be born with a damaged brain or suffer brain damage in an accident. There are many sorts of mental illnesses which, like physical illnesses, can develop at any time during a person's life.

Suggested activities

- Read 'Mental illness – some questions and answers' (page 100). Label two columns on the board, 'Facts' and 'Myths', and use the information from the article to make lists of statements about mental illness that are true and false.

- Ask: 'Why is it socially acceptable to be physically ill but less acceptable to be mentally ill?' Encourage the students, in groups, to discuss attitudes towards mental illness, then to share their views on the two questions on page 100 (see 'In groups') in a class discussion.

- Read 'Mental health problems' (page 101). Discuss with the class what they learn from it about how a person with mental illness may behave, how other family members can help them and how a young person might feel if a family member develops a mental illness.

Plenary

Invite the students, in pairs, to list the points they would make to try to reassure a friend who confides in them that she is feeling ashamed, upset and worried, because her mum has developed a mental illness. Encourage them to share their ideas in a class discussion.

Extension activity

Give out copies of Copymaster 21 and discuss with the class the information it contains, before asking the students, in pairs, to test each other's knowledge of the different types. Ask them to read out the definitions one by one, while their partner names the illness.

Ask students to use the internet to find out more about mental illnesses. A useful site is the website of the Mental Health charity MIND (www.mind.org.uk).

21 Types of mental illness

This sheet gives information about some of the most common mental illnesses.

Agoraphobia See PHOBIA.

Anorexia See EATING DISORDER.

Anxiety disorder Any form of NEUROSIS characterised by an intense state of anxiety which occurs at times of acute stress. People suffering from anxiety disorders become over-whelmed by their fears and thoughts. They may have PHOBIAS, OBSESSIVE COMPULSIVE DISORDERS or EATING DISORDERS.

Bi-polar affective disorder A PSYCHOSIS characterised by extreme changes of mood. People who have this disorder switch from being 'manic' (or high, when they feel very happy and powerful) to being very DEPRESSED. Also called 'manic depression'.

Bulimia See EATING DISORDER.

Claustrophobia See PHOBIA.

Depression An emotional state characterised by feelings of gloom, unhappiness and inadequacy. People who are clinically depressed don't just feel low – they may feel utterly miserable or hopeless, often for long periods. They may feel they want to kill themselves.

Eating disorder An extreme concern about your body shape, so that you eat too little (ANOREXIA) or repeatedly binge and vomit (BULIMIA). People with eating disorders are often obsessed with food in order to avoid huge emotional problems in their life.

Neurosis Any form of mild mental disorder in which the person does not lose touch with reality. Common forms of neurosis are ANXIETY DISORDERS and DEPRESSION.

Obsessive compulsive disorder An inner urge causing a person to repeat an action over and over again. This may be repeatedly washing your hands, or checking obsessively that you have turned the oven off.

Phobia An acute and unreasonable fear, especially of a particular object or situation. CLAUSTROPHOBIA, for example, is an extreme fear of being in confined spaces. AGORAPHOBIA is an extreme fear of being in open spaces.

Psychosis Any form of severe mental disorder in which the person's contact with reality becomes highly distorted. People who suffer from a psychosis (described as 'psychotic') cannot tell the difference between what is real and unreal. Two of the most common psychoses are SCHIZOPHRENIA and BI-POLAR AFFECTIVE DISORDER

Schizophrenia A PSYCHOSIS in which sufferers lose touch with reality. People with schizophrenia may think that they are famous or have special powers. They may see, hear or feel things that don't exist. Sufferers may also believe that people are controlling their thoughts or wanting to harm them. Their thoughts can become very muddled, and they may lose interest in everyday life.

UNIT 21 You and other people – people with mental illnesses

Your Life 3/Year 9

Lesson 2 *Your Life Student Book 3*, pages 102–103
Social education – understanding mental illness

Objective: To understand what depression is and to discuss ways of dealing with depression.

Starter

Read the two introductory paragraphs on page 102 and discuss the difference between a mild form of depression and severe depression.

Suggested activities

- Read 'Symptoms of depression among teenagers' (page 102). Ask the students in groups to discuss why teenagers get depressed and then to share their views in a class discussion.

- In pairs, ask students to draft the answer to a letter from Ria who has written to a magazine's agony aunt saying: 'I think my friend may be severely depressed. How can I tell?'

- Study 'How to defeat depression' and 'I'm feeling so depressed' (page 103). Invite groups to discuss the advice given in these articles about how to deal with depression. Ask: 'What do you think are the three most useful pieces of advice?' Invite them to share their views in a class discussion.

- Ask the students to write an article for a teen magazine about depression, its causes and how to deal with it.

Plenary

Re-emphasise the importance of getting help if you are severely depressed. Read 'Don't do it!' (page 102) and discuss with the class how they can get confidential help by contacting either the Samaritans or ChildLine if they are feeling desperate.

UNIT 22 You and global issues – poverty

Your Life 3/Year 9

Lesson 1 *Your Life Student Book 3*, pages 104–105
Citizenship – global issues – poverty

Objective: To understand what poverty is and to explore poverty and homelessness in the United Kingdom.

Starter

Explain that people who are regarded as very poor in a developed country may not be considered to be very poor in a developing country. Introduce the terms 'absolute poverty' and 'relative poverty', and explain them by reading 'What is poverty?' (page 104).

Suggested activities

- Read 'What causes poverty?' and 'Who are the poor?' (page 104). Discuss with the class what they learn from these articles about what causes poverty and who is poor in Britain today. Then discuss the view that the rich should pay more taxes to provide increased benefits for the poor (see 'In groups', page 104).

- Study 'Street life' (page 105). Ask the students, in pairs, to make notes on homelessness in Britain (the extent of the problem, its causes and ways of reducing the problem), before discussing, in groups, the view that homeless people have only got themselves to blame.

- Ask groups to discuss what can be done to reduce the problem of homelessness, before individually drafting an email to their MP suggesting what the government should be doing to reduce it.

- Challenge students to write about living on the street from the point of view of a homeless teenager (see 'For your file', page 105). The writing could take the form of either a story, a letter, a poem or a song.

Plenary

Recap on which groups of people are the poorest in the UK today. Discuss the view that it's everyone's responsibility to help the poor and we shouldn't just leave it to the government. Ask: 'Should people who can afford to do so give regular sums to charities which help the poor?' 'What's your attitude towards beggars?' 'Should you give money to beggars?'

Extension activity

Ask students to use the internet to find out more about homelessness in the UK. They can visit the websites of Shelter (www.shelter.org.uk) Crisis (www.crisis.org.uk) and Centrepoint (www.centrepoint.org.uk).

UNIT 22 You and global issues – poverty

Your Life 3/Year 9

Lesson 2 *Your Life Student Book 3*, pages 106–107
Citizenship – global issues – understanding world poverty

> **Objective:** To examine world poverty, exploring how the world is divided into rich and poor countries, and the effects of excessive consumption of resources by rich countries.

Resources

Copies of Copymaster 22 'Fairtrade – your questions answered'

Copies of Copymaster 22A 'Understanding the global issues of poverty and inequality'

Starter

Read the two introductory paragraphs on page 106 and explain how the world can be broadly divided into richer and poorer countries.

Suggested activities

- Read 'Differences between the rich and the poor' and 'Worlds apart from birth' (page 106). Ask the students, in pairs, to discuss the main differences between developed countries and developing countries and to make a copy of the chart for their files.

- Read 'Education and poverty' (page 107). Discuss with the class the link between education and poverty. Prompt them to imagine what their life might be like if they were living in poverty in a shanty town on the edge of a city in the developing world. Ask: 'What would be the main differences from the life you lead as a teenager in Britain?'

Plenary

Recap what they have learned about the main differences between the richer countries of the world and the poorer countries and the links between education and poverty.

Extension activities

Ask the students to write a statement explaining why education for all should be top of the agenda for governments in Less Economically Developed Countries.

Develop the students' understanding of fair trade by asking groups to study and discuss the information on Copymaster 22. They could use the internet to find out more about fair trade by contacting the Fairtrade Foundation website (www.fairtrade.org.uk).

Assessment

Use Copymaster 22A to assess understanding of global poverty and inequality.

22 Fairtrade – your questions answered

What is Fairtrade?

Fairtrade is about fair terms of trade, local sustainability, better prices, and decent working conditions, enabling producers to improve their lot and have more control over their lives. By requiring companies to pay above market prices, Fairtrade addresses the injustices of world trade, which traditionally discriminates against the poorest, weakest producers. Fairtrade is not about charity. It is about a better deal for producers in developing countries, because when they are paid a fair price they don't need charity.

What is the Fairtrade Mark?

The Fairtrade Mark is an independent consumer label which guarantees a better deal for third world workers and producers. The Mark is awarded by the Fairtrade Foundation, a registered charity set up by CAFOD, Christian Aid, New Consumer, Oxfam, Traidcraft Exchange and the World Development Movement.

What does this mean for producers in developing countries?

For over 100,000 third world workers and farmers in developing countries, the Fairtrade Mark means:
- fair wages;
- decent working conditions;
- health and safety standards;
- fair terms of trade;
- guaranteed better prices;
- the security of long-term contracts.

The Fairtrade Foundation maintains these standards by regularly inspecting third world suppliers, and checking contracts and trade terms.

Where can I find Fairtrade products?

They are available in most major supermarkets, wholefood and one world shops. Look for the Fairtrade Mark on the product, and if your store doesn't have the product you want – ask the manager to stock it! If there is a demand, most stores will be happy to supply them.

Why do some products claim to be fair trade but not carry the Mark?

Some organisations like Oxfam and Traidcraft have been trading fairly for many years, and sell a wide range of fair trade products. Consumers can trust these organisations, because challenging poverty is their main purpose. However, some other companies make 'fair trade' claims without having the interests of the producers at their heart, and without the independent scrutiny of the Fairtrade Mark. Tea, coffee and cocoa products that you find in the supermarket without the Fairtrade Mark are just not Fairtrade.

What is the difference between fair and ethical trading?

Some supermarkets have joined the Ethical Trading Initiative (ETI), beginning a process of discussing how to ensure safe and decent basic standards for the employees of all suppliers. The Fairtrade Mark goes beyond this. It addresses the injustice of low prices of commodities by guaranteeing that producers receive fair terms of trade and fair prices – whatever the conventional market does. It means small and disadvantaged producers can improve their position and take more control over their own lives.

Study the information above and discuss what you learn about Fairtrade, how it operates, what the Fairtrade Mark is and what it means for the producers.

What is the Ethical Trading Initiative? Why is Fairtrade of more benefit to the producers?

ASSESSMENT COPYMASTER

22A Understanding the global issues of poverty and inequality

Answer these questions as fully as you can. If necessary, continue on a separate sheet.

1. What are the main differences between the rich countries of the developed world and the less economically developed countries? (See 'Differences between the rich and the poor' on page 106.)

2. How are education and poverty linked? (See 'Education and poverty' on page 107.)

UNIT 23 You and your achievements – reviewing your progress

Your Life 3/Year 9

Lesson 1 *Your Life Student Book 3*, pages 108–109

Personal wellbeing – reviewing your progress

Objective: To review your progress and achievements in Year 9, to set targets for Year 10 and to assess your study habits.

Resources

Copies of Copymaster 23 'How good are your study habits?'

Starter

Explain that the lesson is the start of a four-step process: 1) Preparing your self-assessment; 2) Discussing your progress and achievements with your tutor; 3) Identifying and setting targets for Year 10; 4) Writing a statement for your Record of Achievement.

Suggested activities

- Read 'Preparing your self-assessment' (page 108). Then ask the students to follow the four steps and to draft statements commenting on their progress in their subjects and on their key skills, reviewing their achievements in their activities, and reflecting on their attitude and behaviour during the year.

- Use the quiz on Copymaster 23 to encourage the students to think about their study habits. Then ask pairs to read and discuss 'Assessing your study habits' (page 109), before writing a statement reflecting on their study habits and saying what they could do to improve them in Year 10.

Plenary

Allocate times for individuals to meet with you to discuss their statements and identify targets, allowing them further time (as necessary) to complete their statements.

Extension activities

Hold the discussion meetings with individuals. During the discussion, encourage them to note down any points you make (see 'Discussing your progress', page 108).

Ask students to draw up an action plan, setting targets for Year 10. (See 'Setting targets', page 108.)

Ask students to write a statement to put into their Record of Achievement (see 'Recording your achievements', page 108).

23 How good are your study habits?

Do this quiz to assess how good your study habits are. Then discuss with a partner what your answers tell you about your study habits and what you could do to improve them.

1 Do you usually get your work in on time?

A) Yes **B)** No

2 Do you keep a diary/workbook in which you write details of the work that has been set and when it is due?

A) Yes **B)** No

3 Do you set aside regular times for doing your schoolwork on weekdays?

A) Yes **B)** No

....at weekends?

A) Yes **B)** No

4 Do you always put your books/files in the same place so that you can find them easily?

A) Yes **B)** No

5 Do you spend some time each week sorting out your files and putting the papers in order?

A) Yes **B)** No

6 Do you have an index and use dividers in a file to keep work on different topics separate?

A) Yes **B)** No

7 Before settling down to work, do you prioritise so that you get the most urgent pieces of work done first?

A) Yes **B)** No

8 Do you set yourself short-term targets to achieve during each particular period of study?

A) Yes **B)** No

9 Do you take regular breaks when you are studying to make sure your concentration level does not drop?

A) Yes **B)** No

10 Do you allow people to interrupt you when you are studying?

A) Yes **B)** No

11 Before examinations, do you draw up a revision timetable?

A) Yes **B)** No

12 When you are revising do you use strategies like highlighting or making revision cards to identify the key facts you need to learn?

A) Yes **B)** No

Acknowledgements

The publishers gratefully acknowledge the following for permission to reproduce copyright material. Every effort has been made to trace copyright holders and to obtain their permission for the use of copyright materials. The publishers will gladly receive any information enabling them to rectify any error or omission at the first opportunity.

Extract from *Wise Guides: Sex* by Anita Naik, published by Hodder & Stoughton Limited, reprinted by permission of Hodder & Stoughton Limited (p.19); 'The Visitors' by Barrie Wade, used with the kind permission of the author (p.23); extract from *Shout*, issue 107, copyright © D.C.Thomson & Co Ltd, reprinted with kind permission of D.C.Thomson & Co Ltd on behalf of *Shout* magazine (p.34) extract from *Shout*, issue 124, copyright © D.C.Thomson & Co Ltd, reprinted with kind permission of D.C.Thomson & Co Ltd on behalf of *Shout* magazine (p.45); extract adapted from 'When the hitting has to stop', published in *Right Angle*, Winter 1999, by Save the Children, used with permission (p.54); definitions from *Wise Guides: Drugs* by Anita Naik, published by Hodder & Stoughton Limited, reprinted by permission of Hodder & Stoughton Limited (p.63); 'Why do people start taking drugs?' from Wise Guides: Drugs by Anita Naik, published by Hodder & Stoughton ©Anita Naik, 1997 (p.64); extracts taken from *The Use and Abuse of Animals* by Zoe Richmond-Watson, published by Wayland Publishers, reprinted by permission of Hodder & Stoughton Limited (p.74); extract from *Shout*, issue 103, copyright © D.C.Thomson & Co Ltd, reprinted with kind permission of D.C.Thomson & Co Ltd on behalf of *Shout* magazine (p.80); extract from *What Do You Know About People With Disabilities?* by Pete Sanders and Steve Myers, © Aladdin Books Limited, used with permission (p.93); extract from *Shout*, issue 133, copyright © D.C.Thomson & Co Ltd, reprinted with permission (p.103); extract from *Gambling Trigger Pack*, produced by National Association for Gambling Care Educational Resources and Training, Suite 1, Catherine House, 25-27 Catherine Place, London SW1E 6DU, Helpline 0845 6000 133, used with permission (p.132); extract from *Tell Me About It! Living and Growing Study Guide*, by Ruth Hilton, published by Channel 4 Learning, reprinted with permission (p.119); extract from *A Streetwise Guide to Earning Money*, produced by the Metropolitan Police Service, reprinted by permission of the Metropolitan Police Service (p.124); extract from *Respect: Your Life Your Choice*, published by National Children's Safety Books, reprinted with permission (p.133); extract from *Metro*, 4 September 2008 (p.135); extract adapted from the teacher's notes to *Finding Out ... About Drinking Alcohol* by Derek Garwood and Christine Richards, reprinted with permission of CRL Education, Cambridge (p.145); extract from 'The panel: this month's Journal of Medical Ethics attacks shows such as Children's Hospital and the parents who allow their offspring to take part. Is it ethical to film sick children?', interviews by Joanna Moorhead in *The Guardian*, 27 October 1999, © Joanna Moorhead, first published in *The Guardian*, used with permission (p.153); extract adapted from *Get Smart*, produced by the Metropolitan Police Service, reprinted by permission of the Metropolitan Police Service (p.172); extract from 'Frankenstein's food or the way ahead?', from the *Oxford Mail*, 3 February 2000, used with permission (p.177); extract adapted from *Young Citizen...Growing Up* by Kate Brookes, published by Wayland, reprinted with permission of Hodder and Stoughton Limited (p.185); extract from www. britkid.org, reprinted with permission (p.187); extract adapted from *Contemporary Moral Issues* by Joe Jenkins, published by Heinemann Educational, reprinted with permission of REPP (p.192); extract from *Shout*, issue 147, copyright © D.C.Thomson & Co Ltd, reprinted with permission (p.194); extract from *For Weddings, a Funeral and When You Can't Flush the Loo* by Jane Goldman, published by Piccadilly Press, reprinted with permission (p.205); extract from *Check It* produced by the Metropolitan Police Service, reprinted with permission (p.209); extract from *Viewpoints: Media Power*, first published in the UK by Franklin Watts in 1997, a division of the Watts Publishing Group Limited, 96 Leonard Street, London EC2A 4XD, used with permission (p.222); extract from *Wise Guides: Eating* by Anita Naik, published by Hodder and Stoughton, reprinted with permission of Hodder and Stoughton Limited (p.227); extract from 'Which Way Now?', Connexions, DCSF Publications, Nottingham (p.230); extract from www.need2know.co.uk (p.249); extract from Fairtrade Action Pack 6, reprinted with permission of the Fairtrade Foundation (p.262).

Notes

Notes